ENCOUNTERS FROM A KAYAK

Native People, Sacred Places, and Hungry Polar Bears

NIGEL FOSTER

FALCONGUIDES

GUILFORD, CONNECTICUT
HELENA, MONTANA
AN IMPRINT OF GLOBE PEQUOT PRESS

FALCONGUIDES®

FalconGuides is an imprint of Globe Pequot Press.

Falcon, FalconGuides, and Outfit Your Mind are registered trademarks of Morris Book Publishing, LLC.

All photos by Nigel Foster unless otherwise noted.

Map created by Melissa Baker © Morris Book Publishing LLC

Library of Congress Cataloging-in-Publication data is available on file.

ISBN 978-0-7627-8106-5

Printed in the United States of America

10 9 8 7 6 5 4 3 2 1

CONTENTS

Flotsam and Jetsam

FOREWORD

Kayaking offers ample time to observe one's surroundings, and also plenty of time for idle speculation. So it's not surprising that all manner of ideas get airtime during a kayaking excursion. For me this airtime for ideas has turned variously into a better harmony with wind and waves, into new paddle and kayak designs, into how to better teach kayaking technique, into stories for winter evenings.

On a deeper level I've had time enough to ponder what I am and how I fit into my surroundings, or how best to try. Seldom otherwise is my mind for long periods almost entirely open for deep thought. Such periods of thought are punctuated by encounters, during which the focus is entirely outward.

Taking time to explore new places delights me, but small events often fascinate me most. These may only last a few moments or might not even be significant without the benefit of hindsight after multiple visits to the same place.

Such is the eye-to-eye connection with a fulmar gliding past just a few feet away. It's something I've seen so many times, yet with each sighting extra detail is added to my mental collage. A story can develop slowly like this, aggregating over the years until, with the positioning of a pivotal fragment, it becomes complete.

Different is the experience of first being scared and then emboldened by curiosity to approach a large creature wallowing in the swell, only to discover with relief that it was just a wooden cable reel. Such an encounter is probably a one-off, never to be repeated.

Sometimes the most noteworthy moment of a kayaking trip comes not from being on the water at all but from talking with someone on the beach.

Many of my experiences, like these examples, could be grouped into the four general categories I've chosen for this book: creatures, people, places, and flotsam and jetsam.

So I collect stories. If each story were a bead, then my kayaking would be the thread that strings them together, and like that thread it remains mostly invisible. As with a string of beads, the magic of a stray bead is accentuated by the threading; these beads belong together.

I like to think of stories as works in progress that shift their position and their emphasis, rounding and polishing themselves like pebbles on a beach to expose previously hidden facets or sometimes to reveal a gem. Such is the way of waves produced by a storm. In time and with distance, the irregular and chaotic wild lop becomes filtered out to reveal the balanced rhythm of ocean swell. So too is the way of stories in the oral tradition of epic and song, where the irrelevant and superfluous are filtered out until only the best words remain to tell the tale—and only the best story remains to be told.

Each story here is complete, yet as with the multiple images of fulmars, the collaboration of each story with all the others weaves a more complex pattern. Revelations early in the *Encounters* collection add substance to later stories, and facets from later stories recall earlier ones. I hope this will bring a sense of completeness and familiarity. My wish is to reveal the essence of who I am through what I enjoy about kayaking.

—Nigel Foster, 2012

CREATURES

Amusing, scary, repulsive, puzzling, curious; creatures can make me stop what I'm doing to watch or make me anxious to escape.

1

MONKEY BUSINESS IN THE FLORIDA KEYS

In the shallow water of the Florida Keys, transparent needlefish skate the wavelets to evade the jaws of predatory fish that feed on them from below. A gleaming bright streak of silver erupts from the water beside me: A barracuda has launched itself from the water along my paddle blade and come to rest across my arms, whacking its silvery body against my face, spreading me with the pungent smell of oily fish. A moment later it flicks itself into the water, leaving me with a distinct aftertaste and badly smeared sunglasses. Bill's mouth is agape, having seen the sharp end of the fish.

A rhesus monkey watches from the mangroves at Raccoon Key, Florida.

Yes, today the fish are jumping as if water's gone out of fashion. I watch the many splashes on the brightly glaring water now with a wary eye, the sun burning with an intensity that makes me squint behind my sunglasses.

My friends Bill and Ellen and I reach Tarpon Belly Keys. Everywhere are No TRESPASSING signs. These keys were mutilated by developers before the plan to build a road out across the bay was dropped. Now the narrow canals and the white sandy platforms for waterfront houses are gradually vanishing beneath new growth. We pause to eat lunch in the shallow water tucked close beside the mangroves. The coolness of the water is refreshing against my legs. Around us is a horizon of low mangrove trees. The sky appears to push the horizon back to make the sea slope down in every direction. We know one of the mangrove strips must be Raccoon Key. We study the map, study the horizon, figure out which bits of horizon are closer than other bits, and identify our target. The compass makes it easy. It's not so far away, across the shallow water, so we cut straight toward it.

As we approach we see massive white boards with bold red writing in English and Spanish that say No LANDING. Bill explains a little about the place: "There's a colony of monkeys here. People tell stories about how big and fierce they are. They're said to pull passing fishermen from their boats and drag them into the mangroves!"

Rhesus monkeys on Raccoon Key and on the not-too-distant Lois Key were bred to supply the laboratories of the US Food and Drug Administration. Monkeys were imported in large numbers from India until an export ban was implemented in 1977. A primate in many ways similar to man, the rhesus has long been used in drug and vaccine research, has been launched into space, and was instrumental in the discovery of the blood factor known as Rh (for rhesus) positive and negative. And just recently I read in the *New York Times* that scientists have managed to "successfully" transplant the head of one rhesus monkey onto another in a full body transplant—or would it be a head transplant?

We pause at the edge of the mangrove. We have no intention of landing, but we do decide to creep, just a little way, into a waterway that weaves between the mangrove trees. Mangroves grow from the water with their spider-leg prop roots branching and reaching ever outward across the shallow water. There's a gap in the mangroves wide enough for our kayaks, and we paddle through. We discover a tall, straight mesh fence blocking the channel. We are about to turn around here but discover a gap in the fence. We consider for a moment, and then we paddle through the gap. We still haven't technically landed on the island, but I'm feeling we are now somewhere we shouldn't be.

Leaving the fence behind us, we paddle gently onward between clumps of mangrove. There's no land, just trees sticking out of the water, copper-red prop roots looping in every direction creating a chaotic tangle with just a few narrow channels. Sometimes I have to limbo beneath low branches or maneuver around a root spike. I try to memorize the route so we can get back.

We reach a bigger pool. Suddenly there's a crash above us. Bill shouts out "Monkey!" and points, but all I see is the branch settling. "It was a monkey! A big one!" he stammers. Personally I think it might have been a heron, but I keep quiet. I think Bill might be setting Ellen up. Indeed, Ellen does look a little uncomfortable. Soon she announces that she's going to return to open water to wait. Bill says nothing to encourage her to stay with us, so I begin to wonder whether perhaps he had really seen a monkey. We all turn back now. Secretly I feel a little relief, but by the time we reach the fence, Bill and I admit to each other that we're still curious. We just have to have another look.

Now it's just the two of us. This time we follow the line of the inside of the perimeter fence so that we have some point of reference in this watery forest. I'm very aware that we are on the inside of the fence with the animals, not on the outside looking in. Now, ahead, we see a straight canal—straight and narrow. It's too straight to be natural and too narrow to turn around in. We consider stopping here but decide to continue. My heart is beating a little faster, and I'm feeling a little anxious. The crowd of birds in that bush seems to be singing louder than usual. As we glide farther the mangroves seem shorter. It looks like new growth. But why is there so much new growth just here? Was this area cleared and allowed to grow back? I jump as a heron takes off nearby. Ahead of me Bill is paddling so silently that I hear each individual gleaming drop of water that falls to the surface from his blade. A whisper would startle us.

We see a wall. Perhaps it is part of a building, or maybe it's a barrier. Suddenly there's a monkey on top of it. It's not a little monkey but a great big rhesus monkey the size of a small adult human, only looking more powerful. It clambers along the edge on all fours. Then it's joined by two more monkeys. Not wishing to attract their attention, we both freeze and slowly drift to a stop. I'm anxious about our position in this narrow waterway. I would feel better if there was enough space to turn around, but the low mangroves are within arm's reach on either side. I can see a wider area just ahead of Bill. The reflections of the vegetation and the bright inverted image of Bill, motionless in his kayak, gleam up from the water. Then there's a slight movement in the vegetation just behind Bill. Slowly a large, ginger-colored head rises up! It has a big doglike snout and a great flat forehead. Its eyes are set toward Bill. Beneath its snout I can see huge teeth in the jaws. Bill still doesn't know it's there. I don't want to draw attention to myself by warning him. Very quietly and with great caution, I slowly turn my head to see if there are any near me. But my stealth is to no avail. There's a sudden commotion at the top of the wall. The monkeys there have spotted us.

They posture and shriek, then quickly and noisily clamber down toward us. My heart immediately races. In a split second, Bill launches into action and sprints forward to the wider area ahead to turn his kayak. His paddle pushes the water into ridges with each powerful sweep stroke. I'm on his heels, and in my eagerness to turn around, I block his exit. Bill tries to squeeze past. I can imagine being swamped by just one of these big beasts. They look as if they could tear us apart.

We sprint along the narrow channel. Then we slalom through the mangroves and out through the gap in the fence. As we speed through the last section of big old mangroves toward open water, I can still feel the heat of adrenalin in my blood. We cruise out onto open water, and there's no sign of Ellen. I feel a rush of anxiety. Could the monkeys have found her? Surely we would have heard her even from that distance if she had run into trouble. A moment later we spot her waiting patiently outside the fringe of trees.

Now at ease, we circle the island to try to see the monkeys from the outside. Even though the fence is mostly invisible, crowded by overgrown vegetation, just knowing it is there, and having some open water between the monkeys and us, makes me feel more comfortable.

At the only place where the fence is visible, near a small dock, monkeys cluster in the trees, watching us as we watch them. Bill and Ellen raft, arms around each other, and drift past. We continue our circuit of the island, reaching the end that's sheltered from the wind.

I drift into shallows close to the mangroves and see flat rock beneath me. It's coral rock that glows yellow-orange through the water. The water's much warmer here where it's trapped in the shallows in the sun. I'm delighted by the clarity, but as I watch I spot a dark shape cruising slowly. It's a nurse shark. I can identify it by its squat shape and the double set of dorsal fins. And then I realize that it's not alone. There are barracuda too, lots of them. They're only small ones but impressive in their stiff motion and their stillness when they hang above their shadows. Then a young black-tipped shark cruises past, the black tip on its tail fin almost breaking the surface. I keep my fingers from dipping into the water as we paddle away from Raccoon Key.

2

1666 AND THE SEA HARE

The year 1666 was a memorable one for Britain. After a particularly deadly year of plague, London suddenly went up in smoke in the Great Fire of London. It's one of the few dates in history I can remember from schooldays. Also in 1666, in then-enemy France under "Sun King" Louis XIV, work began to create a "new Mediterranean port" for the king's trade. This was intended as not only a new gateway east to Mediterranean trade but also west via a new "Canal du Midi," which was to begin construction the same year. This canal would pass through the productive Languedoc region to the Garonne River, which passes through Bordeaux on its way to the Atlantic. The new route would be a safe alternative to ships that otherwise had to closely follow the coast of enemy Spain to avoid the watchful eyes of Barbary corsairs to the south.

Sète was built on the limestone Mont St. Clair—an island joined by a long sand beach to the neighboring towns of Agde to the west and Montpellier to the east. Construction began with a stone breakwater more than a third of a mile long and the Royal Canal, cutting through from the Mediterranean to the saltwater lagoon inland.

If Mont St. Clair was once an island, it is technically not quite an island today. To make a circumnavigation by kayak we had to climb a concrete dock to portage a single new road. But that was a small if challenging detail. We spent a morning of blissful freedom wandering from the Ètang de Thau, a saltwater lagoon known for its cultured oyster production and its seahorses, past fishing docks dedicated to catching the tasty sea bream, *dorade royale*, that swarm past in annual migration from the Ètang de Thau to the sea.

Sea hare, Sète, France.

But the Royal Canal in the morning sparked my curiosity more than some of the other places. I'll elaborate: Here stands the great pale modern statue of a man armed with a lance and carrying a protective shield on his arm. Jousting has been an annual event here since 1666. But unlike the jousting fields with knights in heavy armor hurtling toward one another on their chargers trying to unseat their opponents—a form of competition that declined in Europe in the seventeenth century with the rising use of firearms—here the "field" is a section of the Royal Canal. Rowing boats take the place of chargers. From the stern of each boat a wooden ramp slopes upward over the water to a small platform where the jouster stands. Each boat, rapidly propelled by its rowing team, hurtles toward and past its opponent until up above the water, with bone-shaking impact, two heavy men engage with lance and shield in an attempt to dislodge each other. Hairy stuff! And of course there's an ignominious descent into the canal for at least the loser.

Today the water is quiet. It is late season, and the tourist crowds have gone. We have the harbor and the canal to ourselves, so a tiny movement in the water is enough to catch our eye. It's a piece of swimming seaweed! That's odd! Looking more closely I see the dark shape of a bat swimming just below the surface . . . or something similar. But what is it? It's about eight inches long, and it's "flying," apparently in reverse, by rippling its dark seaweed wings. It's taking absolutely no notice of us as we cluster close to get a better look, and I've never seen anything like it!

Patrick says, "It's called a sea . . . what is that big kind of rabbit called?" "A jackrabbit?" Kristin ventures. "Okay!" continues Patrick. "It's a sea jackrabbit."

I look down and try to imagine why it might be called that. It looks more like a backward-swimming bat to me. I turn my camera to video mode and shoot for a few seconds. Nobody will believe me otherwise. Then I snap a few stills of what will look like a piece of seaweed. I'll have to find out more when I get home.

Martine, meanwhile, has ventured closer and stretches out her hand. She's going to touch it! I imagine it either fleeing or snapping at her fingers with needle-sharp bat teeth, but neither happens. It gently continues on its way just below the surface unfazed. Weird! I'm reassured to touch it myself, and I maneuver close. Reaching down I feel something somewhat earlike, with a smooth funguslike surface caressing past my palm. It feels a bit like those Chinese black fungi that grow on stakes, the ones you get in soups, but animated. The fungi are firm to bite into and a bit slippery, although I'm not tempted to bite this.

Patrick explains a little more. It's a kind of sea snail, but it doesn't have a shell. Does that make it a sea slug, I wonder?

We drift and watch the slow but tireless movement of this strange creature as it wanders down the canal. Eventually we must take up our paddles and continue on our way; otherwise we'll never reach our lunchtime spot on the little beach beside the stone breakwater that protects the harbor.

We pass more of the jousting boats, colorfully painted in team colors, and reach a line of large fishing boats against the quay. "Tuna fishing boats," Patrick explains. These boats can cost four million euros each. Initially subsidized by European grant, all they catch is yellowfin tuna, purse-seining the swarms that venture into the Mediterranean. In a successful sweep they net whole schools at a time, towing them

Jousting boats rest peacefully on the Royal Canal, Sète, France.

offshore for fattening. A single good-size specimen can fetch eighty thousand euros on the Japanese market, where the tuna's red meat is highly prized for sushi. It tastes good, but there are fears that the fish will be persecuted to extinction.

Industrial-style fishing of the yellowfin has already made some Sète fishermen millionaires and provided them resources to purchase the most up-to-date military sonar available to civilians to locate schools of fish. Just twenty-eight of these high-tech boats now account for 90 percent of all the French catch, most of which is destined for Japan. There has been quite a lot of protest against what is seen as overfishing of this species, and the threat of European quotas has led some boat owners to reregister their craft in Libya, which is not bound by such legislation. Meanwhile the boats still operate from Sète.

We pause beneath the cursive Arabic name on one boat we pass, although we have no idea how to read it. A little to our east are the timber docks. These too have been controversial this decade, apparently importing illegal hardwoods from Africa, but Patrick says little about this. He shrugs his shoulders and suggests they are probably making changes.

That evening Patrick and Martine's daughter brings us her fish book. She has found a picture of the "sea jackrabbit"! It's a gastropod with the scientific name *Aplysia fasciata*. When I look it up later, I find its common name is actually sea hare. That makes sense, as it was named long ago in Europe for its pair of long earlike protuberances, and Europe doesn't have jackrabbits.

Despite the fact that sea hares are found around Britain in small numbers, and varieties exist all over the world, I had never encountered one of these strange creatures before. I wanted to know more about them. Every encounter with something strange is an opportunity to research and learn. *Aplysia fasciata* is a kind of sea slug with an internal shell. The mantle over it extends symmetrically to either side and enables it to "fly" in the water. It's pretty well camouflaged in the seaweed where it is typically found because it is shaped like a seaweed frond and absorbs the pigment of its seaweed food to appear the same color, so maybe there are plenty around to be seen if you know what to look for. Like the squid and octopus, sea hares can release ink from ink glands. The ink acts like a smokescreen and may also affect the scent sensors of predators. The ink varies in color depending on what the sea hare feeds on and can be white, red, or purple. According to some sources it may have been used in ancient Jerusalem for writing sacred texts. Apparently it is of no use as a dye, as it washes out.

"What about sex?" I hear you ask. Well, these weird creatures do have weird sex. The sea hare has a penis on its head, just behind its rear anterior tentacle. And that's not all. Being a hermaphrodite, it also has a female organ, so groups form mating chains with each individual mating simultaneously as a male with the sea hare in front and as a female with the one behind.

I wondered what people thought of them in the past. The genus was first allocated by Linnaeus in 1767, a century after Sète was founded. What about before then? I haven't been able to find out much. The ancient Greeks in their debates decided they were poisonous to touch, which is untrue, although recent accounts of people "tasting" them have reported the flavor disgusting!

Nowadays there are a couple of promising lines of research under way. The first is in the neurology field. The nerve cells in the sea hare's ganglia are ten to fifty times larger than in mammals, which makes the sea hare, with its ten thousand easily identified neurons, an interesting animal on which to study reactions to stimuli. Another discovery is an antibacterial protein, escapin, found in the ink. Escapin might offer an environmentally friendly alternative to heavy metals like copper for antifouling ships and nets.

So if you run into a funny batlike creature when you're kayaking off the coast of Devon or down in the Mediterranean, it is possibly a sea hare—harmless, perhaps useful to science, and, although a gastropod, not worth serving up with garlic as escargot.

Ironically, when it comes to the race between the tortoise and the hare, or in this case the sea turtle and the sea hare, the tortoise wins yet again. Sea turtles eat sea hares and apparently enjoy them.

3

TUBENOSES

The sun rolled slowly along the horizon, gradually melding with the bright edge and leaving the sky glowing pink and purple. With the clear sky it would not get completely dark tonight. We waited quietly and patiently, our voices little more than murmurs, until the sunrise began to intensify the colors of the sky. A thick mist rolled in from the sea, darkening our surroundings and bringing with it strange cries and cackles. Through the darkness and mist hordes of winged shapes streamed past, blundering into us, darting between our legs, and flicking against our faces.

We were standing at the edge of a cliff on the islet of Mykineshólmur in the Faeroe Islands, waiting for the nocturnal appearance of three species of oceanic birds: the Manx shearwater, the Leach's petrel, and the storm petrel. All three are members of the tubenose family, distinguished by the tubelike nostrils resembling hollow worm casts along the tops of their beaks. It was the loud cries of shearwaters and the unearthly laughter of the Leach's petrels that made such a din. From within a dry stone wall immediately behind us we heard the quiet, almost continuous *churring* sound of storm petrels punctuated by sudden hiccups. The petrels' gentle calls were directing their mates, flitting back and forth along the length of the wall in the gloom, to the correct nests. Nesting time for all three species is hazardous. They are slow to take off and are easily caught, so parents change watch over the hidden nests in darkness, lest they fall prey to the ever-vigilant gulls.

I remember the first time I saw a storm petrel. It was huddled underneath a car in a parking lot near a quay in St. John's Harbor,

Fulmar chick.

Newfoundland. I cradled it in my palm, it was so small. It had a dis-tinctly musky odor, which later found I could recognize when trying to locate the well-hidden nests as part of a nest survey. After phoning around to friends for advice, a seabird specialist at the local university told me that storm petrels have difficulty taking off from land. This one, he said, probably mistook the dark flat tarmac for water, landed, and then couldn't take off again.

I returned to the quay and dropped the bird onto the water as the specialist had recommended. Sure enough, it skipped across the water surface, flew up, caught the breeze, and was easily away. For a brief moment I felt good about what I had done. But a large herring gull swooped down from the sky. I winced at the impact that sent the storm petrel spiraling down onto the water. The gull chased close behind it and moments later lifted away again with the petrel held firmly in its beak.

The storm petrel is the smallest European seabird. It is brown and black with a white rump. Such small birds are easily overlooked by the sea kayaker or mistaken for house martins or swallows. Sailors of old often referred to them as "Mother Carey's chickens," believing that such small birds must have the protection of Mother Carey, the Virgin Mary, in order to survive in the open ocean. Because they were often seen speeding along at the forefront of heavy weather, they became known as "storm" petrels. The "petrel" part is in reference to Saint Peter walking on the water; the storm petrel, like other petrels, patters quickly along the surface during takeoff.

The Leach's petrel is a bit larger than the storm petrel and has a slightly forked tail, in contrast to the square tail of the storm petrel. In Britain Leach's petrels nest mainly on the remote islands off northwest Scotland, tempting destinations for experienced paddlers.

The Manx shearwater is a much larger bird, about the size of a rock dove, with a black back and a pale underside. The name Manx, as in "from the Isle of Man," refers to the huge colonies once found there. As it sweeps across the water with its narrow wings held stiffly, it flashes from black to white or white to black each time it changes direction. Shearwaters gather in huge rafts on the sea near their breeding sites, awaiting the cover of darkness before approaching their nests, typically at the ends of long burrows. Many popular British sea kayaking areas, such as Pembrokeshire, North Wales, and the Scottish Small Isles, are major breeding grounds for shearwaters. Over 130,000 Manx shearwaters nest on the islands in Pembrokeshire, and more than 100,000 are believed to nest on the Scottish island of Rhum alone. Another major colony is close by on Eigg. If you're paddling in these areas during nesting season, it's well worth staying out at night to hear the cacophony of sound accompanying the return of the birds to the nests. Be prepared to be roused in the night anyway by the noise.

The Manx shearwater, like the fulmar, has long been a culinary delicacy. The huge colonies on the Isle of Man were decimated by overharvesting of the fat young birds, only recently rebuilding into a healthy colony once more.

In the Faeroe Islands, where there has been a long tradition of conservation and wildlife management aimed at maintaining stocks for regular harvest, shearwaters are only taken when numbers are stable or rising.

On Nólsoy Island the size of the shearwater colony has always been limited by the lack of suitable nesting places. A local man took me out across the rough ground on the uninhabited end of the island to show me some tunnels he had constructed. He raised a long stone slab to reveal the ends of several carefully dug tunnels, each with the dark shape of a shearwater sitting tightly on her eggs. Each tunnel was at least five feet long. He explained that the soil on the island was too shallow for the birds to dig their own burrows, so each year he constructs more artificial tunnels, roofing them over with stone slabs to compensate for the paucity of topsoil. The ruse is working. Most of the tunnels are occupied. He also told me why these birds are nocturnal. The legs of petrels are more effective on water than on land, where they can only shuffle around with their feet and lower legs in contact with the ground. Consequently they cannot move quickly and have difficulty launching unless a breeze lifts them. It is nearly impossible for them to escape the nimble gulls.

The fulmar is the only tubenose in the British Isles to nest in the open, on cliff ledges and even on open grassland, although it still seems to prefer a shallow tunnel when available. Fulmars have pearly-gray colored backs rather than the more uniform gray of many gulls. The fulmar has no real enemy on the islands. Each female lays only one egg per year, and the survival rate of the young is good.

The fulmar's method of defense—spitting yellow stomach oil—appears to work well to deter predators. In a project to reintroduce the white-tailed sea eagle to the western isles of Scotland, the first birds released had been hand reared and had not learned from their parents about the dangers of fulmars. The subsequent death of these birds was attributed to the fouling of the eagles' plumage with fulmar oil.

On the island of Hirta, in the remote St. Kilda group to the west of Scotland, the former inhabitants used to rely heavily on the fulmar as a foodstuff and as a source of oil and feathers. They harvested thousands of young birds in mid-August before the birds could fly. The birds were salted and stored for the winter in wooden barrels, and the precious fulmar oil was contained in the inflated and dried stomachs of the Atlantic gannet. Men descended the cliffs using horsehair ropes and killed the birds by twisting their necks so that the oil would not be spilled. Each bird yielded up to half a pint of oil. The entrails were used as fishing bait, the bones for fertilizer, and the fat from boiling the bird was skimmed off and used as lamp fuel. When salt was scarce, the birds were simply hung in the many stone stores (*cleits*) to dry in the wind. The feathers and oil were also sold on the Scottish mainland. The feathers were used for bedding, while the oil, which is rich in vitamins A and D, was sold as medicine. The commerce in fulmars ended in 1930 when the islanders were evacuated.

Fulmars can suffer from psittacosis, a disease that also afflicts parrots. The disease is said to have been picked up by scavenging fulmars from a load of dead parrots dumped from a ship into the North Atlantic, and the disease has spread within the seabird population. I had always been told to avoid handling sick fulmars but had never heard of anyone catching psittacosis until last year, when a kayaker friend contracted the potentially fatal disease. It laid her low for many months before doctors by chance pinpointed the problem. The disease is caused by an organism partway in size between a bacterium and a virus and can be cured by antibiotics. Joan had not handled any seabirds, but she had been paddling close along the Scottish sea cliffs. There she would have been exposed to dust from the plumage of the thousands of nesting birds and dust from their dried droppings, either of which can carry this airborne disease.

I wait for the nighttime visit of shearwaters and storm petrels on Mykineshólmur, Faeroe Islands.

Fulmars appear stiff-winged in flight and sweep along cliff faces, banking-sharply, gliding tirelessly on air currents with seldom a wing beat. It is the fulmar that slides past the sea kayaker with one wing tip almost brushing the sea—so close that paddler and bird can stare into each other's eyes.

The pearly-gray back varies in shade from darker in northern regions to paler farther south, and wing tips lack the characteristic barring of gulls. The underside of the bird is pale, and the dovelike head is large. The silvery beak is adorned with two external tubes, found on all petrels. Because petrels spend such long periods of time over the ocean with only salt water to drink, they have developed the ability to desalinate, excreting the salt and dripping it out through the tubes on the beak.

In the tenth century the British coast was subjected to raiding Vikings in their long ships. The ancient Icelandic "Njal's Saga" recounts an event off the Isle of Man. The terrible clamor of shearwaters flying in dense clouds past the Viking ships and the crashing of the dark birds against the terrified warriors in the night roused the men into defending themselves with swords, axes, and spears. By morning there were a number of dead and wounded men, along with the bodies of dead birds. The saga describes the birds in the night as "ravens that came flying at them with beaks and talons that seemed made of iron." The birds were believed to be "… the demons you once believed in and which shall drag you down into the torments of hell." Strong stuff! But as I stood on the misty cliff edge on Mykineshólmur in the twilight, with dark shapes hurtling past in all directions and dropping from the sky toward me with hideous screams and cackles, it was all too easy to imagine how these gentle creatures might seem like demons.

4

BEAR, BE GONE!

The tides in Ungava Bay are some of the biggest in the world and can rise and fall as much as fifty-five feet. When the water recedes, it exposes a vast foreshore of rock ledges and muddy slopes studded with boulders. It's difficult to find an easy place to land that will also be a good place to launch from later. Within six hours a landing place at high tide can be left up to three miles away from the water. Halfway through the ebb tide, the water level drops at a rate of ten feet per hour. That's two inches per minute. If you stop ashore for a five-minute break, the tide will quietly drop ten inches: more than enough to expose rocks that can block your escape from shore.

Face to Face

We were ten days into our 675-mile journey from Kuujjuaq in northern Quebec to Nain in Labrador. My morning espresso from the stovetop pot had worked itself through my system, and I was ready to land. My paddling partner, Kristin, and I reached a group of rocky outcrops cut away from the main rock ledges by narrow channels of water. I cruised into one of these channels to seek shelter from the small chop and discovered a narrow slot between a steep wall and a gentle slope. This dead end was shallow, but it made an excellent dock. Kristin stayed in her kayak, so I left mine floating in front of her.

I strolled a few paces across the bare rock behind Kristin and stretched my legs and back. The slightly domed bedrock I was standing on swept upward in smooth, unbroken undulations to the low summit of the islet. The glacier that had pushed across this region in the last ice age had ground through the rock layers, exposing patterns

Polar bears roam the shore, Ungava Bay, Quebec.

of pink, green-gray, and black. The striations looked like the growth rings of a polished slice of tree.

My eyes casually followed the sinuous folds of a single threadlike band of dark rock as it meandered through clusters of bright crystals sparkling in the sunlight. I suddenly spotted a patch of ivory-white fur that appeared over a low ridge of rock about sixty feet away from me. In moments a polar bear came into full view. With its head held low, the bear walked straight toward me in long easy strides, its long fur swinging heavily around its legs and huge body.

I grabbed my float vest and spray skirt and turned away. Not wanting to provoke a charge from the bear, I walked steadily toward my kayak. "Back off into deep water now, Kristin!" I called. "Now!" She looked over her shoulder to see me walking toward her with the bear following only yards behind. As she attempted to back out of the narrow slot, I reached my own kayak and slid into the cockpit.

The water level had already dropped enough while I was on shore that Kristin's kayak was aground. Again I urged her to get away. She pushed hard against the rock with both hands, but her kayak was weighed down with a full load of gear and food. "I'm stuck, Nigel!

Should I get out?" I got out of my kayak and popped open my day hatch to grab my flare gun.

The bear stopped when it reached the stern of Kristin's kayak, its huge head extended toward her. It was close enough to reach Kristin with its forepaw, so it was unlikely she could escape to open water. I tried to stifle my fear of the bear's attacking Kristin and focus on loading the pistol. I fumbled with my flares, broke open the barrel of the gun, and inserted a red cartridge.

I snapped the barrel shut and cocked the firing pin. I aimed vaguely to one side of the huge animal, hoping to shoot close enough to startle it. A flare gun is not meant to be an accurate firearm, and I was worried I might shoot the bear and provoke an attack. I squeezed the trigger. "Poof," the flare rushed past the bear and bounced off the rock. In the brightness of day, the ball of incandescence seemed as insignificant as the muffled report of the gun. It was, however, enough to surprise the bear, which bounded a few yards away from us up the rock.

Kristin climbed out of her kayak. By the time I'd broken open the flare gun and pulled out the spent cartridge, the bear was back, standing next to us. I loaded another flare. Kristin tried to slide her kayak but stopped when the bear craned its neck to sniff the dry-bag strapped to her rear deck. The deck bag contained vacuum-packed freeze-dried food. Even if the bags were airtight, I knew we had probably transferred all kinds of scents to it from our hands.

Polar bears are said to have the keenest sense of smell of any mammal and have been known to pick up the scent of a seal from a distance of five miles and track it down. Kristin stood by her front hatch. I aimed at the rock beside the bear and set off the second flare. The huge white head turned, and the bear sniffed the rock where the flare had hit then turned back to look at Kristin. This time the flare had done little to distract the bear.

Kristin stood up beside her kayak and looked at the bear. "Bear! Bear, be gone!" she commanded loudly and firmly. It struck me as an odd thing to say. The words "Go away!" would have made more sense to me, but here was this slender woman looking up at a creature the size of a car, speaking to it in what sounded like Old English. "Bear—be—gone!" she demanded again, enunciating each word slowly and deliberately. Her choice of words seemed somehow absurd, but I was relieved that she was calmly facing up to this bear instead of screaming or running away, either one of which could provoke an attack.

The bear stood facing her just feet away, its mouth hanging slightly open. Its head was as broad as Kristin's shoulders. I was ready with the next flare. I had decided to shoot straight at the bear if it attacked, but I wasn't sure if the flare would deter the bear or just enrage it. The bear shuffled on its four huge paws. I fired again, just off to the side. The whoosh of red fireball flying close past the bear didn't get so much as a sideways glance. The bear continued to study Kristin. A polar bear can pounce twenty feet from standing, and this one was less than ten feet from us. "Bear! Be gone!" Kristin insisted. The bear looked at me, looked back at her, then half turned, shuffled its huge paws, and wandered a few paces up the rock away from us. Kristin instantly dragged her kayak backward until it was afloat, and with a single fluid movement she was in the cockpit and backing toward open water. The bear turned. I hauled my kayak across the rocks to the water and tumbled into the cockpit. My float vest and spray skirt stuffed on my lap, I started to push myself back. The bear fixed its stare on me, its head extended forward on its long neck. In a few steps it reached the water's edge, but Kristin and I were already a few yards from shore, paddling vigorously away.

Free from the confines of the narrow slot where we had landed, we now had to exit the channel between the islets to reach the open water beyond. I paddled close by Kristin. The bear ambled over the rocks, matching our pace with ease. Even steep clifflike rock faces didn't slow it down. It was elegant and graceful and seemed to gather momentum like a ball rolling down a hill.

When we paddled clear of the island and reached open water, the bear paused and stood watching us. It walked a few more yards, lifted its head to sniff the air, then walked headfirst into the water and submerged. The white shape of the bear's head appeared, pushing across the surface toward us and then vanishing again. Polar bears can stay underwater for as long as two minutes and swim at a steady six knots, so if this bear wanted to catch up with us, it was certainly capable of doing so. We hurried away and didn't relax our paddling pace for a couple of hours.

We had known there was a good possibility we might see polar bears during our trip. Polar bears hunt around the edge of the Arctic ice pack for seal, and when the ice breaks up and melts, they swim

Polar bears are agile underwater: swimming polar bear, San Diego Zoo, California.

ashore. On the Labrador side of the peninsula, the ice drifts south on the Labrador Current. Sometimes polar bears on the ice drift as far south as the island of Newfoundland before swimming ashore. Once they reach land, they typically wander back to the north. Bears that are working their way north during summer can be hungry, especially in years like this when the ice melts early.

We thought we might see a few bears on the northern tip of the Labrador Peninsula, but in fact we spotted our first two bears close to the mouth of the George River, just five days into our journey. Our face-to-face encounter was our third bear sighting, so we grew increasingly cautious and watchful. We also began to modify our paddling habits. On most trips I usually paddle close to the shore because there is so much to see and I can measure my progress as the scenery changes with every feature passed. The landscape changes much more slowly when viewed from a distance, but I thought we'd be safer paddling farther out.

We kept our distance from land, shying away from countless ambiguous shapes, uncertain whether we were seeing bears or merely pale boulders, patches of snow, or quartz outcrops. We made our rest stops on low, isolated rocks we could see were free of bears before landing and watched constantly for anything white.

Inukshuks

The territory along our route was uninhabited tundra, so there were no features like trees or buildings to offer any sense of scale. Some fifteen miles south from the mouth of the George River, we headed toward a sand beach that turned out to be a beach of boulders, each the size of a table. Distant islands sometimes proved to be much closer than expected and measured only a few yards across. To avoid getting disoriented by these illusions, the Inuit constructed *inukshuks*, stone cairns that resembled people in both shape and stature. They were often our only way to judge scale and distance.

About fourteen miles north from the mouth of Abloviak Fjord we approached shore intending to follow a long finger of rock to its outermost point. Kristin noted that there was a very prominent beacon on the highest point of the rock. It looked a bit like an *inukshuk*, but it was unusually pale, as if it had been painted white. Thinking it must be a navigation mark instead of an *inukshuk*, Kristin scanned her chart but found nothing marked, and I could see nothing on the topographical map. We continued paddling toward shore and had come close to land when the beacon stood up. It was a very large polar bear.

It climbed down from the flat summit and began walking toward us. We sped up and angled away from shore. The bear vanished behind a rock outcrop and reappeared much closer to us on the shore. We were paddling about as fast as we could, but the bear easily matched our pace. From time to time it got ahead of us, and then it would turn and watch us and wait.

It took us around twenty minutes to reach the end of the point. When we rounded it, the bear disappeared. We had no idea where it had gone. Kristin said she was more nervous being followed like that than when she had been confronted by the bear at close range the day before. Approaching shore ceased to be a pleasure.

The McLelan Strait

When we reached the northern tip of the Labrador Peninsula, we camped just north of the entrance to McLelan Strait, a narrow fifteen-mile-long channel separating Killinek Island from the mainland, waiting for the wind to drop and the fog to clear before heading through the strait. I was walking along the beach when I heard Kristin call my name faintly, like a loud stage whisper, but I could hear urgency in her voice. She had spotted a polar bear close to our tent. We skirted around to the back of a nearby hill, creeping low to keep from being seen. We watched from a high point while the bear wandered past our campsite, paying no attention to it. Walking slowly, it appeared to be sniffing at the ground to either side of its path as it slowly approached the inlet and was finally swallowed by the fog. We knew we would have to spend at least the night there waiting for the weather to clear, but there was little we could do except continue to be watchful.

The next day the wind dropped and the fog lifted, so we set out for McLelan Strait. Although we had arrived on a neap tide, the current would still run swiftly through the strait. On a spring tide it accelerates to ten knots through the narrow sections of the strait, where the channel is less than two hundred yards wide in places. With the tide against us, we planned to take advantage of eddies along the north shore, then cross to wait at an ancient village site for a favorable tide early the next morning.

We drifted over writhing fingers of kelp in the clear water, past outcrops of rock colored a brilliant orange by rusting iron ore. Across the swirling water, the steep slope of the Torngat mountain range ran down to a low green plain above the water. We cut into the fast water and paddled swiftly to ferry-glide across.

We had almost reached the far shore when I noticed a boulder near the shore that had an unusual glow about it. Suddenly I realized it was a polar bear crouching head-down watching us. Light shining through its thick white fur had created a bright edge around the large shape. We were heading straight to it. I called "There's a bear!" to Kristin, and in a single movement we pushed our bows around into a ferry-glide back in the direction we'd come from.

The moment we changed direction, the bear stood up and walked to the water. We were making headway against the current as well as moving away from the bear. It followed along the shore, matching our progress. It stopped at the land's edge, studied the water for a moment, and waded in. We could see its head on the surface and the large white lump of its back as it swam after us.

It took us a few minutes to regain the north shore, and we hugged the ledges to keep from the tide as much as possible. We rounded a point, and there on the edge of the water stood another huge bear. "Okay, Kristin! What would you like to do?" I had no desire to turn back toward the bear already following us. Kristin, sounding almost irritated by the bears, said, "Just keep paddling! We're not here to harm them, and they've got no reason to harm us! Just keep paddling!" As we passed this second bear, it turned sideways. It was the size of a Volkswagen Beetle. It must have been a male. The females are only as big and heavy as Austin Mini Coopers.

It strolled away from us, its rear legs spread wide beneath the immense bulk of its body, and vanished among the rocks.

Our fear of coming upon more bears kept us from using any back eddies, so we fought the current in the center of the channel, making our way along the fifteen miles of the strait against the tide.

On the Labrador side of the strait, the evening sunlight reflected off the water as if from a sheet of polished copper. Behind us the steep slopes flanked the strait, and their reflections seemed to pour the blue of the sky into the water. Ducks exploded into the air as we creased the water toward them. One duck remained on the water in front of me, but as we grew closer, it looked less like a bird and more like a fishing float.

"Can you make out what that is ahead?" I asked Kristin. "It looks like a duck, but it hasn't flown away, and the glare's too bright for me to make it out."

"I don't know. Are there otters up here?" she asked as we glided straight toward it.

"No!" I replied. "I don't . . ." Kristin interrupted me, "Nigel! It's got ears!" At that instant the bear let out a breath of air that expanded to a misty cloud above it. I could now clearly see the bear's dark nose and eyes, its rounded ears, and the wake spreading from its head as it swam toward us. We turned and sprinted away.

I had read plenty about polar bears, and I expected them to be well camouflaged against snow, but I didn't expect them to be impossible to spot on the water or among dark rocky landscapes. They often looked just like the pale boulders, snow patches, and chunks of floating ice that were scattered everywhere. I expected to spot them on flattish rock ledges or ice floes, but we spotted one halfway up a nearly vertical cliff. Whenever Kristin and I spotted bears, they had already set their sights on us.

I began to scrutinize every chunk of ice on the water, every floating object. But then, near the northern cliffs of Sapogatsiak Bay, toward the end of a rough day when our kayaks were launching over crests and plunging into the troughs, we almost collided with a pair of swimming bears. The bears appeared as startled as we were. It was the only time it seemed the bears hadn't already been watching us for a long time.

The Northern Limit of Trees

At the Okak Islands we finally reached the tree line and saw scrawny black spruce trees on the lowest slopes. We expected to see fewer polar bears south from here. We began to relax a little, although now there were plenty of signs of black bears.

Just north of Aulatsivik Island, we pulled into Village Bay, once the site of an ancient Inuit settlement. A single cabin stands there now. It belongs to Jim and Helena Anderson of Nain, the town where we would finish our trip about thirty-five miles to the south. They were staying that weekend to hunt and fish. As extra defense against both polar bears and black bears, Jim had put railings around the windows spiked through with long nails, sharp ends up, and spiked boards on the ground around the cabin. We dined with them on arctic char Jim had caught, with wild mushrooms Kristin and I collected. That evening we set up our tent near the cabin, and as night fell a green snakelike aurora writhed in the sky above us.

In the morning Kristin and I loaded our kayaks on the narrow ribbon of sand between the high tide and stiff, knee-high marram grass. Mosquitoes whined around our heads as we stuffed dry-bags into the hatches. The liquid whistling call of loons sounded loud across the water.

From the cabin along the beach I heard Helena calling "Nigel! Kristin! Nigel! Kristin!" We both stood up and waved. "There's a bear swimming toward you!" Helena shouted. A hundred feet away, the now very familiar shape of a polar bear's head was coming straight toward us. Aware that it had been seen, it changed course and swam parallel to the shore, eventually vanishing behind a low point of rock. When we left a few minutes later, we had to paddle in that direction, but we gave the headland a wide berth.

When we arrived in Nain after five weeks of paddling from Kuujjuaq, we checked into the local hotel. The windowsill outside our room was spiked with nails to deter bears. Tom, the Scottish owner of the hotel, showed us a photo journal left by Dullar Alfred, a frequent summer visitor from Austria. Whenever he camps in polar bear territory, he sets up a trip-wire alarm system around the tent. The wire is far enough from his tent to give him sufficient time to get out of his sleeping bag, grab his loaded gun and flashlight, exit from the tent, and locate the bear before it gets to him.

He notes that bears are so accustomed to the much louder percussive sounds of breaking ice that they rarely respond to the crack of rifle fire. In his experience they are often more startled by gravel jumping when a bullet hits the ground nearby. In cases where that didn't work, he'd fire a plastic pellet directly at the bear if it continued to approach; that apparently has been an effective deterrent.

On one night, however, he camped close to a streambed with part of the trip-wire circle stretched across to the other side. In the night a polar bear crept up the stream and under the wire. Alfred awoke as he was being dragged from his tent as the bear pulled the foot of his sleeping bag.

On our trip we had close encounters with sixteen polar bears and one very large black bear. The ever-present risk made it difficult to relax either on the water or on land. Yet the coast we traveled has been kayaked many times before by Inuit, and for them polar bears had always been an integral part of the landscape. The Torngat Mountains, which separate northernmost Labrador from Ungava, were named for the "Great Spirit" Torngarsok, who took the form of a large polar bear and ruled over all the creatures of the sea. If we'd paid more attention to the Inuit legends, we would not have been surprised to see him there.

Polar Bears

Polar bears are magnificent up close—magnificent and very intimidating. They may seem a little aloof in the way they behave. After all, they have no reason to fear anything. Imagine an animal weighing up to sixteen hundred pounds (as much as a small car) capable of standing ten feet tall on its hind legs. (The largest polar bear recorded was more than twelve feet tall and weighed 2,210 pounds.) As much as they are considered mascots, victims of global warming and habitat loss, cuddly creatures that tumble and slide in play on the snow, they are the biggest carnivores that live on land—and we are meat.

Their feet are larger than I would have imagined. Longer than they are wide, each foot measures one foot from side to side. This spreads the bear's weight for walking across snow. Their shield hairs mat together when wet to form an almost completely waterproof coat over dense fur and several inches of blubber that insulate so efficiently that a polar bear is almost invisible under infrared photography. That level of insulation is both good and bad for a bear. It allows a polar bear to roam around on winter ice and in arctic waters in complete comfort, so it does not need to hibernate. But it also slows a bear down. When running after prey, polar bears soon overheat. They can only sustain bursts of speed for up to a mile or so. If you can run faster than twenty-five miles per hour for more than a mile at a stretch, you might be able to outrun one! Even then the bear might catch you in the end. Polar bears can stroll at about 3.5 miles per hour almost indefinitely!

I'm sure most bears we passed knew we were coming. Polar bears have been observed making a straight line across the ice to the carcass of a dead seal twenty miles away. They can detect a seal's breathing hole in the ice a mile away beneath three feet of snow! They also have good distance vision and hearing similar to that of humans.

It is difficult even now for me to accept that in a landscape of dark rocks and water, a creature the size of a Black Angus cow—only creamy white in color—could be easily overlooked. Time and again we drew so close to bears that we were startled when we finally spotted them, while they calmly watched us approach. But that's part of the modus operandi of the polar bear. It is good at remaining immobile for so long that even attentive seals are not afraid. They are so good at being invisible that they survive by hunting creatures that are faster swimmers or faster runners than they are.

Polar bears live for twenty-five to thirty years. When young their diet is mostly protein-rich seal meat, and when mature they change to a diet of mostly calorie-rich seal blubber. When seals are not available, polar bears catch caribou, smaller animals, and arctic char and occasionally eat berries and seaweed. Less frequently they eat humans; thankfully we are not their preferred prey. There is little human population around the Arctic, so attacks on humans are rare. But whereas brown bears often maul a person then leave, polar bear attacks are more likely to be predatory and are almost always fatal. We did everything we could to avoid coming face to face with bears, but we failed. Thankfully our meetings left us intact, if a little scared! I have immense respect for this master of disguise.

Soon after we completed our Labrador trip, we flew south to California for a sea-kayaking symposium at San Diego. San Diego has a zoo with a polar bear enclosure. We spent the better part of a day there watching polar bears play endlessly, trying to dislodge frozen fish that the keepers had lodged in underwater crevices in the rock. The bears' paws were too big and their limbs too short to reach the fish, but that did not deter them from trying. They attempted to dislodge the food by emptying their huge lungs underneath so that the bubbles raged around the dead fish. They also tried to drag logs from the enclosure to use them to dislodge the fish. They would not give up. Their behavior reinforced for me how polar bears survive at the top of the food chain in one of the most challenging environments on Earth. They are intelligent, good learners, and tenacious problem solvers. They are supremely adapted to their environment.

5

MANATEES

Early morning is the coolest time to paddle in southern Florida, before the burning summer heat ramps up. I parked the ancient Cadillac that served me as the "Motel Coup de Ville" at a state park by the Intracoastal Waterway and slipped quietly onto the dark water. Closer to dawn than sunrise, tendrils of mist hung above the surface while the ghostly shape of a leopard ray cruised in the shallows across a sandbank, its wing tips breaking surface to warp the refracted image. I turned to find myself in a wider channel cruising between banks of mangrove and woodland interrupted by vast modern mansions with docks and boathouses and laser-level lawns. Egrets, herons, and ibis clustered in the mangroves like blown garbage, squawking awkwardly into the air if I passed too close.

Despite the human population density here north of West Palm Beach, there was vitality about the waterway as though America's wildlife had been spread disproportionately—half across the whole country and the other half crammed into the Florida marshes and waterways, feeding on the teeming life in and around the water. Mullet arched their silver bodies from the water and plopped noisily back time and again, as if practicing for flight. Spiders sat fat on their airy webs gleaming with droplets of moisture. The air chorused with the trills, bleats, and grunts of frogs and crickets. Then the golden sunlight began to catch the tops of the trees. I cut through smaller channels, backtracking toward the Intracoastal, speeding across the glassy surface with comfortable ease, increasing my pace now for the home run.

The sun glared now in my eyes and made the bark on the rods of red mangroves glow like hot metal. Then I struck a log, ramping onto it with a cushioned thump. But it wasn't a log! Water erupted from both sides of me as the creature exploded into action, throwing me off its back. I caught myself on my paddle, my body already in the water, and braced myself back upright. Water streamed from my hair. A glimpse of a giant rounded lily-leaf tail told me I had hit a manatee.

Manatees are the gentle giants of the Southern waterways and coasts. They cruise slowly, at about the same pace as kayakers, rising every few minutes to breathe and oblivious to surface traffic, whether slow like me or fast like speeding powerboats. It is little surprise that manatees get hit. They blend too well with the water and do not take evasive action. Powerboats slice their backs with prop blades, and impacts from hulls break ribs, which then rupture internal organs. Researchers identify individual manatees by the scar patterns on their backs, for although some survive their wounds, all have been marked. Perhaps the Intracoastal Waterway is not the best place for boats and manatees to mingle. Nor is it the most relaxing place to watch manatees. For that I prefer Florida's Gulf Coast.

North from Tampa and St. Petersburg is a series of crystal-clear streams and rivers that rise from the limestone rock as

Manatees swim past a kayak, Weeki Wachee River, Florida.

freshwater springs: the Weeki Wachee River, Homosassa Springs, Chassahowitzka Springs, Rainbow Springs, and Crystal River, to name but a few. Florida's wilderness is fast vanishing beneath roads and shopping malls, golf courses, and gated communities, driven by an economy that survives only on growth. Yet the vast reservoir of wildlife is not yet completely tamed.

I launched at a small state park into the tidal Weeki Wachee River and headed upstream, glancing cautiously above me at a dead tree, heavy with the rustling black foliage of a flock of vultures. Beyond the bend in the river were little waterfront dwellings, low-key, mildly tacky residences with model mermaids and plastic slides curving down toward the water. Staghorn ferns dangled in pots from trees heavy with local epiphytes: bromeliads, mosses, and tree ferns. There was a rich sweet-hot scent of saturated vegetation above the dark water, as though the land was sweating from every pore, as I was in the humid heat. Yet the water felt cool. In fact it remains fairly constant at around seventy-two degrees Fahrenheit warm in winter

A manatee approaches the camera, Weeki Wachee River, Florida.

and seventy-two degrees cool in summer. In winter, when the water temperature in the Gulf dips, the manatees hang out in the warmer water from the springs—or in the warm water from power plants. But you might find them here at any time of year.

I keep alert for movement and for shapes like the surfacing snout of a manatee, the smooth curve of its broad back, or the rounded tail flipper. I am looking for indistinct shadows too, for although large, a manatee is surprisingly easy to overlook as a sandbank or shadow. I watch too for the studded palm tree–log patterns floating on the water that are so often alligators, although this isn't a prime alligator river. My eyes dart from the slow-moving night heron stalking the marshy edge to a small powerboat moving fast around the bend toward me. Most river users here are friendly, if not thoughtful. They'll tell you what they've seen, even what they've scared away. This crowd just wave and tell me I'm going the wrong way, as if I hadn't noticed I was paddling upstream. Most rental canoes and sit-on-tops launch at the top and drift down with the current. But traveling upstream, the river gets ever clearer until at the springhead it is as clear as, yes, bottled springwater. I crank my kayak on edge to spin each corner of the snaking river, gliding across the current from eddy to eddy, sprinting up the straights and looking down through ever more clear water at the sandbanks beneath my hull.

Then I see a movement in the water. It is difficult to tell what I've seen. Manatees often look just like a bed of the eelgrass they feed on, but this shape is moving. It's a large manatee and a small one together! They drift slowly in a deep pool where the current eddies around. I press on by, hurrying upstream but watching carefully. I slip on my facemask and quietly duck upside down into the cool water. Seeing the riverbed speeding above my head I am disoriented for a moment. Then I see the manatees. I am drifting fast now with the current, but the calf approaches, nosing to within about five feet of me. It looks so streamlined and graceful, elongated like a torpedo with two small flippers at the head end and a curvaceous rounded tail. It hangs in the water, scrutinizing me with its tiny eyes. I'm enthralled, but I'm running out of air. In the end I am forced to move. I skim my paddle across the surface and roll upright. With the glare from the surface and the refraction, I can barely see the calf returning to its mother while I drift downstream. But if I see nothing more today I'll still go home happy, remembering that encounter and the river that flows on like a cool breeze through the sweltering day.

Mote Marine Laboratory on Lido Key, Sarasota, known for its shark research, its studies of sea turtles, and its more than fifty-year-long survey of Tampa Bay–area dolphin families, also teaches about manatees. The laboratory is known for its aquarium and educational programs. It also takes in injured and sick mammals for rehabilitation and, when they are healed, releases them back into the wild if possible. From the dry side of a massive tank, I watch a manatee scrunch its snout like a giant marshmallow against the glass right in front of a woman, who squeals of delight. Mote Marine is a great place to learn about Florida's wildlife before hopping into a kayak to explore. It prepares you for what you might see, where to see it, and how to behave should you do so.

6

GANNETS

The Atlantic gannet is a huge gooselike bird that cruises above the ocean on long, stiff white wings tipped in inky black. The biggest seabird of the North Atlantic, the gannet feeds on fish in the most spectacular way: circling the sky above the water watching for fish, then stalling abruptly, partly folding back its wings, and plummeting beak-first from up to one hundred feet above the water. With binocular vision, not typical for seabirds, it keeps on target as it plunges into the water at up to sixty miles per hour, surfacing to swallow its catch. Watching a single gannet plunge is spectacular. To see hundreds of gannets circling and raining down from the sky together is phenomenal.

Gannets nest on headlands and capes, often in huge colonies of thousands of pairs of birds that coat the cliffs white. To avoid predation they choose remote places like Grassholm in Wales, where twenty-two thousand pairs nest; Ailsa Craig in southern Scotland; and the great sea stacks of St. Kilda, sitting some thirty miles out in the Atlantic to the west of the Outer Isles of Scotland, where a staggering sixty-six thousand pairs congregate. Gannet nesting locations are destination gems for sea kayakers.

In 1984, with Alun Hughs and Sharon Foster, I paddled from Whitesands Bay in southwest Wales to the most remote group of off-lying Welsh rocks, known as The Smalls. Aiming west across a tide that carried us as swiftly sideways as we paddled forward, we crabbed sideways to the swell-swept rocks that are dominated by a stone light tower and the remains of an earlier, less-robust lighthouse. The swell surging around the slick, curving rocks made landing awkward. Alun slipped, skied down the slope into the water, and was swept through the channel between the rocks by the tide, searching for a handhold. It took a little time to secure ourselves and our kayaks on the top of the rock.

The Smalls lighthouse would soon become automated, so it was a timely opportunity to pay a surprise visit and deliver some fresh milk and a newspaper to the keepers. We whistled and shouted and climbed to the top of the fixed ladder up the side of the lighthouse to hammer against the sturdy door, but we failed to attract any attention. In the end a keeper sunbathing on the helicopter landing pad above the light thought he heard a whistle and peered down from the edge. We waited patiently until finally the door burst open and we could climb inside.

It was the first time the keepers had ever been visited by kayakers. We sat in the round tower, exchanging lighthouse stories and drinking tea with the keepers until it was time to leave for our nighttime destination. Then we slid down the rock into the slackening tide, cruised past the southern end of The Smalls, and turned east toward Grassholm, about eight miles toward the mainland. The island glowed in the low sunlight like a pale chalk cliff, but the white was from the gannets sitting on their nests, and from their guano. The broad shapes of gannets flew by, circling and attempting to land, even as we circled the island to choose our own precarious landing place. Beneath a darkening sky we prepared our evening meal with the island skyline dominated by the strangely quiet silhouettes of gannets.

In the morning we sat and watched the colony. The birds nest on steep mounds of seaweed and refuse, regularly spaced as if built on a grid. Each nest allows the minimum distance all around for a sitting bird to be just beyond the pecking range of the birds on adjacent nests. Understandably this causes problems whenever a bird wants to leave its nest. Gannets are big, and taking off isn't easy. If there is insufficient wind to lift them from the nest, they make a quick run through the gauntlet of nests down the slope to reach the steeper cliff. Long, sharp beaks peck from either side as they struggle downhill past the angry neighbors. But once they have launched themselves and are free in the air, they soar on the slightest updrafts and skim above the waves with ease.

I could have stayed to watch the gannets all day, but the spring tide was strong enough to dictate our timetable. We left the colony and headed north toward Ramsey. Elated by the sight of twenty-two thousand nesting pairs of huge white gannets, Alun eagerly persuaded me to visit St. Kilda with him to see the largest North Atlantic gannet colony.

Years before I had read in *Canoeing in Britain* magazine the story of the first kayakers to reach St Kilda and had ever since thought it would be a trip worth repeating. St. Kilda, some thirty miles west of the Outer Hebrides, was one of the last of the Scottish islands to be reached by kayak when Hamish Gow paddled out there in 1965. Gow had recently married and took his new wife, Anne, with him in a wooden double kayak with a sail, accompanied by a third member of the group in a single kayak who soon turned around and paddled back to the Outer Hebrides when the weather turned windy. The tandem continued alone with the help of the wind.

When the couple neared the island group, there was little to be seen. Poor visibility obscured the islands, and there seemed every chance they might sail past without spotting land. Luckily they saw the cliffs of Boreray, the northernmost island in the group, and crept close into shelter behind the gaunt thousand-foot-high cliffs. Boreray, along with two tall offshore rock pillars, Stac an Armin and Stac Lee,

Approaching the remote Smalls Lighthouse, South Wales, U.K.

is where you find most of the nesting gannets. It is a moody place, dank with the oily, fishy smell of birdlime. The powerful ocean swells rise and fall against steep cliffs with a slow, uneasy motion complicated by rebounds. For anyone with a hint of seasickness, the heaving of the ocean here combined with the pungent odor of the oily surface can be a powerful emetic. But with the main island, Hirta, just four miles away, offering the only places to land, Hamish and Anne sat until two in the morning until the mist cleared enough for them to see their objective.

Gow had previously garnered attention when American ships carrying Polaris missiles had first anchored in the Clyde estuary in Scotland. In protest against the nuclear weapons, he kayaked out to a ship and climbed its anchor chain. The harbor master confiscated his kayak as punishment. When Gow crept into Hirta late at night, his arrival was treated with suspicion. The remote St. Kilda, cleared of its residents in the 1930s, had since become the base for some forty military personnel operating a tracking station for test missiles fired over the water. A check with the authorities on the mainland revealed Gow's past record. "What are you doing here?" they demanded. The

A confetti storm of gannets surrounds nesting grounds on Grassholm, Wales, U.K.

disarmingly honest answer probably went something like "Oh, we just got married, so we're out enjoying a honeymoon paddle!"

During summer 1984 Alun and I paddled out twice from the Isle of Skye to camp on the Outer Hebrides, hoping to continue on to St. Kilda. Better weather on our second trip allowed us to cross. We decided to follow Gow's route, so we aimed at Boreray to circle that island before heading to Hirta. As we drew close, even a glance up at the dense, wheeling cloud of huge birds above my head and around me almost completely upset my balance. Gannets folded their great wings to plunge down, piercing the water's surface with their huge beak to vanish from sight, resurfacing almost every time with a fish.

It is surprising that a heavy gannet can impact the water at up to sixty miles per hour with no apparent damage. To minimize damage, gannets have developed air sacs between the skin and the muscle around the neck and shoulders. When preparing to dive, these sacs inflate to offer protection on impact. Even so, the repeated impacts can affect the gannets' startlingly blue eyes. Older birds often grow blind and become unable to fish.

Great skuas (*Stercorarius skua*) chased the gannets, trying to steal their fish. Sometimes a great skua landed on the back of a gannet, forcing it down. Sometimes one swooped beneath a gannet, coming up fast enough to push the gannet's tail up, tipping the gannet into a dive. Forced onto the water and accosted by skuas, a gannet seldom offered resistance. Once it had regurgitated its latest catch, the gannet was invariably left alone, while the successful skua now had to defend its plunder from a gathering gang of other skuas. Ignored by the peck-and-tumble of skuas, the gannet was free to rejoin the airborne kaleidoscope.

Creeping along in shadowy dimness at the base of the towering dark cliffs, we could gawp upward to the steep upper slopes of the stacks where gannets sat in row upon row in a snowy mantle that glowed even beneath an overcast sky.

With massive creamy-white, oily, fish-stinky droppings raining down all around us—and splattering us liberally—we finally crept into the shelter of Village Bay on Hirta, the site of the hamlet that once housed the population of these remote islands. Village Bay, the place where there is an easy landing, is where the military base is situated, and we had hardly unfolded our legs on the beach and rinsed off the bird droppings before we were intercepted and questioned.

If the questioning was not exactly hostile, I cannot describe our reception as welcoming. We were subjected to a barrage of personal questions. Then we were told we could only camp close to their building, in a small field surrounded by dry-stone walls in which storm petrels nested but adjacent to the base's ever-noisy generators. We were also directed to leave our kayaks in their boat shed, incidentally out of our sight, despite our protest that we wanted them conveniently beside our tent. And we were cautioned not to approach any of the installations on the hills of the island.

We learned that nobody had paddled out to the islands since Gow in 1965, and our unannounced arrival from the direction of Boreray rather than from the direction of the Outer Hebrides had aroused suspicion, especially as there were no vessels in that direction. However, despite their suspicion, our hosts did invite us to imbibe at the base pub, the Puff Inn.

The islands are such a magnificent haven for wild birds that little could dampened our enthusiasm to tramp the hills for a couple of days to gawp at the vistas and to wonder at the tenacity of the people who once scratched a living way out here on these volcanic remains.

Hirta was inhabited for a couple thousand years. Villagers rowed across to the precipitous stacks Lee and An Armin, the tallest sea stacks in Britain, and to the twelve-hundred-foot-high Boreray, leaping from the boat to scale the cliffs barefoot at night to harvest the nesting gannets. They tossed the dead birds down from the high ledges to be collected from the water into the boat.

Above the sickle curve of Hirta's beach along the base of the scooped valley crouched the ruins of the stone cottages of the last inhabitants, not far from where the military buildings now stood. Cradling the beach were grassy crags that rose steeply to the island summit at the thirteen-hundred-foot clifftop where we sat with our backs to the antennas and radar installations we were forbidden to approach. We looked north toward a broad ocean skyline beyond the gannet-splattered Boreray and stacks. With the biggest colony of North Atlantic gannets in the center of my view, I could not repress my smiles.

World Heritage Site

St. Kilda, inhabited for four thousand years, lay abandoned from 1930, when the last inhabitants were evacuated, until 1957, when the entire archipelago came under the ownership of the National Trust for Scotland. A small part has been leased to the military since then. St. Kilda became Scotland's first UNESCO World Heritage Site in 1986. The status was extended in 2004 to include the surrounding marine area, and in 2005 it became one of the few World Heritage Sites to be awarded mixed World Heritage status for both its natural and cultural significance.

7

SEALS AND SELKIES

There's a woman in the Western Isles of Scotland who rows her wooden boat out along the coast to a favorite place among the rock ledges. She stands in her boat and plays her fiddle to the seals. The seals gather round to listen, like shoppers at a street show, watching but keeping watch, diving and resurfacing. I too had a favorite place to visit seals. I went there throughout the years I lived in Wales, often taking other paddlers with me to share the special experience. I called to the seals. I talked. I'm not a big talker, so I struggled to keep my conversation going and often lapsed into talking nonsense in my attempt to keep going. I felt a little foolish at times, but most paddlers consider me a bit cracked anyway, so my monologues probably just confirmed what they already knew.

But the seals responded. They played chicken, creeping close behind me and splashing away in panic when I turned my head or made eye contact. Then gradually they gained confidence: Their curiosity overcame their fear, and they came close to sniff the toggles at my bow and stern or investigate my paddle blade as I rested it on the water. On one occasion when I paddled a kayak with a translucent hull, a seal slowly explored the whole length of the hull, on its back, one flipper visible at each side of the kayak. I could feel its gentle progress. I must have looked strange, my legs visible as a silhouette through the sunlit amber.

In time individual seals responded to my call and swam with our kayaks, darting from one kayak to the other, rolling alongside the moving hulls. Each time we stopped, they bobbed up to look at us and to listen to my voice, nudging the toggles and paddle blades with their noses. One had a habit of nosing my elbow, and the last time I visited, it remained motionless while my companion stroked its head.

I wondered whether the seals had become familiar with kayaks in general or whether they could recognize particular kayaks. Maybe they could recognize voices? It's hard to tell, but when I visited the island in a large group of paddlers, my familiar seals seemed to follow me around within the group when I called them. Yet I was seldom in the same kayak twice in a row, so it seems they must recognize me, perhaps by my voice rather than by my kayak.

This brings me to the legend of the selkies, or seal folk. Selkies live around the coast of Scotland and the Northern Isles, where "selkie" is sometimes a local name for the Atlantic gray seal. There are many different stories about selkies from the Scottish islands, but all have similar themes. Selkies occasionally come ashore, mostly at night; take off their seal skins; and mingle with the locals in their human form, donning their skins once more to return to the sea. The more commonly told stories involve selkies who have been trapped on shore by their human lovers, who hide the skins to prevent them leaving.

It is interesting to speculate how the legends might have come about. Imagine an adventurous Inuit hunter landing in an animal-skin kayak on a beach and socializing with the locals. Imagine a smart lover hiding the skin kayak, effectively grounding the new friend. Of course if the kayaker found his "skin," he could paddle away again.

A seal approaches my kayak in Gig Harbor, Washington. Maybe selkies have come to the United States too.

There have been documented cases of hunters in skin boats arriving on the Scottish shores, maybe driven by storm from Greenland, or perhaps escaped from captivity on a whaling boat. But it is more likely that the legends came to the British Isles from northern Norway. The Finni of northern Norway constructed and hunted from skin kayaks. Early pictographs from the arctic Norwegian coast portray craft that appear to be constructed from the skin of a moose, split along the back to accommodate three people, and with the head of the moose remaining at the bow.

The Finni arrived on the island of Fetlar, North Shetland, in skin boats before the arrival of the Norsemen, and there have been more-recent references to such people arriving during Norse occupation. Stories of the strange folk describe them as being humanlike above the waist, but when ashore and having peeled off their skin, their naked bodies appearing to be the same as humans'. If their skins were indeed skin boats or kayaks, then they would surely become waterlogged in time and need to be peeled off on the beach and spread to dry.

But in researching the selkie tales, I see a convenient blending of ideas. It is easy to anthropomorphize human feelings to an inquisitive seal, with its big expressive eyes. And in times of distress or sorrow, what better place to go to mourn than to the edge, the seashore? In some selkie tales, a woman bears a selkie's child and brings it up in his absence. When the child is older, the selkie returns to claim it and pays the mother the "Norris" fee customarily paid to a wet nurse.

Still other tales recount how fishermen who disappear at sea have been taken to live with the seal folk. It must be difficult to cope with the loss of a loved one if the body does not wash ashore, hope of ever seeing him again fading as the weeks pass but never having any final certainty. So it must be some comfort to the bereaved, repeatedly searching the shoreline and watched by the attentive seals, to believe that one of them might be the lost partner. Animals often respond to strong emotion. It could be why a particular seal follows and seems to show no fear.

But maybe seals really do come ashore, peel off their skins and then, appearing human, mingle with people. If so, I wonder who my pretty brown-eyed friends are that I meet with at my special island. Do I know them perhaps in their human form?

8

BIOLUMINESCENCE

"Did you have a good weekend?" my schoolteacher colleague asked as I arrived to work. "What were you up to?"

"I drove down to Dover Friday night and popped over to France to get some wine for a Saturday night party. . . ." That had just been the start to my weekend. I'd met my friend Jan, and we'd launched our kayaks into a dark night, slipping quietly and unseen from Dover Harbor between the ferries. It was something I thought would be a fun personal challenge—to kayak across the English Channel at night. We cruised from the beach, alert for the lights of ships.

The English Channel runs a little like a conveyer belt, roughly in one direction with the rising tide and in the opposite with the falling tide. More complex than this, the exact direction and rates differ depending on where you are in the channel. A few days earlier I'd worked out the vectors on the chart, plotting an hour-by-hour course to cross the tides so as to eventually reach France. The result: If we kept the compass needle steady in the same position while we paddled at a constant speed, we should hit France at Calais. I switched on my new flashlight. I was proud of it. Heavy with fresh batteries that would keep it beaming brightly for longer than this one night, it was a new sturdy rubber-cased flashlight with a stout plastic clip by which I'd tied it to the deck with line. I shone it on the deck where I'd written down the bearing we should follow. I read the number out loud to Jan, swung my kayak until my compass pointed me in the correct direction, and set off.

After a little while I heard "Nigel?" There was anxiety in Jan's voice. I was clearly the confident one tonight! "Nigel, should we be heading toward Dungeness?"

Now Dungeness lies to the southwest and is part of the shore of England. We were going to France. That's more southeast. "No, it's more the other way," I pronounced cheerfully, "nowhere near Dungeness!" There was a long pause.

The glow from an underwater entrance displays similar magic and color to bioluminescence.

"Then why are we paddling parallel to the shore?" I turned my head to see the lights of Dover now mysteriously alongside. "Ah!" was all I could say while I considered what on earth might have happened. Then I remembered returning home late the night before to see my chart and calculations on the table. I'd taken a passing glance and then recognized in a flash that since I'd be paddling south not north, I must have made a simple but easily rectified mistake. I made a mirror image in my head and calculated the number again, writing in bold on the paper. That was the figure I was using now. Clearly I'd been unable to think straight last night, so the bearing must be . . . I quickly recalculated and suggested, "Okay, Jan, let's try this bearing," and reeled off a new one. If Jan had lacked confidence in me before, she was surely no more confident now as we turned from shore into darkness.

With my flashlight trained on my compass, setting off on our new course was simple enough. But it's easy enough to wander off course even in daylight, eyes straying from the compass in the ever-vigilant watch for ships that could appear from any direction. It takes constant attention and focus to realign the kayak to the compass after each glance away. But at night, reading the compass by flashlight is more difficult. Once your eyes have adjusted to reading the compass, your night vision has gone, making it more difficult to spot distant ships with dim lights. While you scan the darkness for ships, you wander off course, and with two kayakers doing the same thing, it's inevitable that you steer each other off track.

The night was clear: no moon but a star-shot sky. So instead of watching the compass, we chose to watch the stars instead. I chose an easily identifiable star that lay directly ahead near the horizon. Now I could switch off my light and paddle toward the star. My eyes would accustom to the darkness around, and I'd be able to paddle with my head held high, which felt much better than paddling with my eyes dropped toward the deck. Jan's flashlight had already faded and failed, so using a star target was very convenient for both of us. But with Earth ever spinning in the sky, the relative position of my star would change. We would have to choose a new one, a little to left of the last, every half hour or so, or we would paddle on a curve.

As we pulled farther from the lights of shore, we could see the water around us was speckled with bright stars of its own. Unlike the stars above, these glowed green. I looked down to see sparks glowing on my deck and on my sleeves. Each pull on my paddle created a vortex of swirling sparks that gradually faded behind me. I was mesmerized. I looked toward Jan, who was keeping position alongside. She and her kayak were all but invisible in the dark, but a wake of brilliant green fire showed exactly where she was. The light trailed away behind her. Each paddle stroke she made created an explosion of light that drifted out as a vortex and then faded away behind.

This bioluminescence was probably produced by dinoflagellates—tiny single-celled plankton that, when together in such vast numbers and excited by movement into producing light, could create this stunning display. Although I'd seen bioluminescence before, I had never seen it glow in such density or with such intensity.

The English Channel, and in particular the Straits of Dover, is considered the busiest waterway in the world. At any time we could see the lights of several ships moving through or across the Channel. On the first part of our crossing, most vessels not crossing were heading toward the Atlantic, but later we began to see traffic traveling in the opposite direction, along the French coast toward the North Sea. This is according to a traffic separation scheme that acts roughly like traffic lanes on a road. It gave us confirmation of our progress and our approximate position.

It was essential we remained alert to ships. There was a chance, albeit very remote, we could be hit by one. In event of a collision course, we could not expect a ship to take any avoiding action. In the first place, it would be highly unlikely to spot us either on radar or visually. Even if it did, it would be too late for the ship to take avoiding action of any kind.

But in a kayak it is easy to stay awake and keep a good lookout. If we spotted a ship approaching on a collision course, its sailing lights would be aligned one directly above the other. In that event we would need to paddle directly across its path for just a little more than half the width of the ship to get out of the way. That's not very far, and by then the lights would already be out of line.

In the time it would take a ship to travel half a mile at thirty miles per hour, we could paddle our kayaks about one hundred yards, plenty far enough to be safely out of the way. However, we spotted and monitored the progress of ships when they were much farther away than half a mile and prudently kept well out of the way.

Everything went smoothly. Every so often I would switch on my light to see my compass and choose another star to aim at. Then during a brief stop, I adjusted my spray-skirt and dislodged the light. Thankfully it was attached by line! It felt so good to be prepared! I pulled at the line and up it came, but with only the plastic clip attached. Beneath me a pool of light shined up at me, growing gradually larger and fainter as my new flashlight sank steadily into the depths.

Now we had no way to see the compass. But by roughly estimating how quickly the stars had shifted out of alignment so far, I thought I could guess how much to compensate for the next stage. Besides, even though Calais was our intended destination, we would be fine so long as we found land.

After a couple more hours, we thought we should be getting close to France. But then our stars faded and vanished. We were running into a bank of fog. We stopped. It was not yet light enough to read the compass. As we sat, we heard noises. Could the sounds be from land? Optimistic, we paddled toward the noise. But then another sound began to mask what we had heard. It was the throbbing of a ship's engine, and a clanking. We stopped again. In the fog it was impossible to tell where the sound was coming from. It grew louder and louder and seemed to be coming from all around us. I felt helpless.

The Varne *lightship marks a shoal about halfway between England and France.*

We sat close together scanning the fog. Then suddenly a huge dark wall appeared on our left, pushing aside a breaking wave of white water. Shooting into action, we turned away and sprinted. Looking back I could see the rivets on the ship's plates as it sped past. Above the noise of the engines I could hear a voice making an announcement on a loudspeaker. We had almost been hit by a ferry!

Following the sound of waves on the shore, we found a beach. We had missed Calais Harbor but reached France. I gave Jan a hug. We would carry the kayaks up the beach and wait for a cafe to open for breakfast. Then we'd choose some wine to take home.

I had become so enchanted with bioluminescence that night, I began to kayak more on dark nights to see it, sometimes throwing handfuls of beach sand into the ocean to excite the plankton into sparking light. Sometimes I spotted the bright sparks of light in the water in daytime when I explored into the darkness of sea caves. My understanding of bioluminescence was that it was caused by tiny plankton. Then one quiet night, while camped on Rabbit Key in the Florida Everglades, I was curiously stalking a group of raccoons to discover what they were so loudly eating when I saw a number of greenish balls of light speeding up a small creek into the mangroves. Mesmerized I watched for a while before turning on my flashlight and aiming it into the water. I could see nothing. Perplexed I switched off the light, only to see the glowing balls reappear. I laughed!

When one of the glowing balls stopped in the shallows, I tried again with the flashlight. Now I could see an almost completely transparent plum-size jellyfish. With the agitation of the current, ridges of light flashed for several seconds in citrus-segment patterns down the body. In the still water the light then faded away, but in the jostling current the jellyfish followed one another like glowing lanterns up the turbulent creek to weave among the roots of the mangroves, finally drifting from sight.

So larger creatures than the single-celled plankton also produce light. Scientists estimate that about 90 percent of marine species have some capacity to produce bioluminescence. It's not every day (or night) that we notice the glow, but there's plenty of it out there!

9

SITKA HUMPBACK WHALES

Traveling north by boat is in many ways a better preparation for a kayaking trip than traveling by air. There's the slowing down of pace on board, where there really is plenty of time to get used to the idea that you're going away to have fun. There's the freedom to wander around, to gaze over the side at the water, to watch the gulls hanging in the air currents, being dragged along effortlessly. There's the comfort too in knowing that your kayak is sitting down below on the car deck, with everything you need for a journey lasting many long days. Or, in this case, knowing that at any rate much of what you need is down there. My camping gear was not there. No, that was here on the deck.

When we boarded at Bellingham for the journey to Alaska, our first concern was to roll the four kayaks on board as quickly as possible. There were only two of us with the kayaks. Les and Diane would fly to meet us at Sitka with whatever extras they had not already loaded into their kayaks. It took us two trips with our trolleys to get all the kayaks on board, unloading the first kayaks and then returning for the last two. The ferry does not linger in dock. We were almost the first on board and then almost the last, the ferry pulling away while we bedded the kayaks down and lashed them to the car deck in case we hit bumpy seas.

We hastened up on deck, but quick as we were, tents had already sprung from backpacks all over the semisheltered aft deck. Passengers without tents were busy staking their claim on the deck chairs in the shelter of the sun lounge. We pitched our tent at the edge of "tent city," choosing the spot that would catch the least amount of wind. Quickly finding our roll of duct tape, we taped the corners down onto the hot, gray-painted steel plates. The sooner we did that the better. Any wet salt spray on the deck could prevent the tape from sticking.

Then we piled everything we had brought up with us into the tent to help pin it down. Now, although less likely to blow away, we realized we'd lose much more if the tent did not stay put! There was nothing else we could tie to but the guardrails, but we would have to duct tape the line to the deck to prevent people from tripping on it.

As the ferry reached open water, a stiff breeze blew along the side of the boat, almost but not quite missing our tent. We ducked into the tent to find something more windproof to wear and found it calm and also balmy with the heat from the metal deck. After the rush to board the ferry, it was too tempting to lie back and relax. When we next looked out, the view was of a different place. This was the first time I'd ever gone to sleep in my tent and awoke with the tent somewhere else.

The Alaska ferry keeps as much as possible from the rougher stretches of open Pacific Ocean by threading between the islands that make an inside passage through much of British Columbia. True, there are a couple of open stretches where the swell rolls the ship and makes the tent a weird place to lie, but soon enough the calm channels offer the close-up view of forest, with rocky points and isolated cabins. Sea lions bark, people watch for whales, and climbers point out the peaks they can name. Soon enough it's time to eat and go sleep for the night.

Humpback whales accompany us near Sitka, Alaska.

The journey through British Columbia is both stimulating and relaxing, offering a chance to meet people on board and to share stories, but the boat does not stop in Canada. It stops at several places in southeast Alaska, not docking for long, but long enough for passengers to run ashore to pick up supplies or to sightsee. We bought a bottle of wine and caught a taxi to visit a totem display at Ketchikan.

Then finally the time came to peel the duct tape from the deck and collapse our tent. By the arrival time of 5:30 a.m., we were on the car deck with the kayaks, ready to trade the comfort of the ship for a cold concrete wharf seven miles from Sitka. It was a bleak reality to watch the ship sail away moments later, leaving us alone. We lifted all four kayaks down to the water, loaded them, and then drifted from shore. Each towing a spare kayak, we crossed the sound to find a suitable place to camp.

Finding an island with a low narrow neck sticking out from one end and rising to a rocky promontory, we landed in the bay to one side of the neck and lifted out the kayaks. Then we stretched out on our backs on a flat rock and fell asleep. I don't know how long we slept, but we were woken by a *"whoosh"* sound, quite close, and sat up. There in the dark water of the bay, just yards offshore from where we now sat, was a whale! No! Two whales! They surfaced again, one just before the other, and we could see that they were humpbacks. We watched for some time before they moved out of the bay, then we moved our friends' kayaks to the top of the beach and established our camp. Finally we were ready to paddle the several miles to Sitka to shop for food and supplies for the paddling trip ahead.

As we headed down the sound, we were suddenly aware that the whales had joined us. They swam parallel to us for several miles, always surfacing some distance to our right. Then one turned toward us. Next time it surfaced immediately ahead, so close we watched its body curve upward from beneath our bows, its huge blowhole opening strangely right in front of us. The long slope of gray skin flowed simultaneously out of the water and back in, until finally its tail swept quietly into the water and the whale was gone. That was the last we saw either of them. We assume they turned into the channel to the right while we took the left turn into town. The encounter made us feel very happy!

Russian Sitka

The Danish navigator Vitus Bering's expedition, in the service of the Tsar of Russia, is credited with Russia's first landing on the Pacific coast of North America in 1741. That was sixty-four years before Lewis and Clark reached the Pacific on their expedition. A landing party from the first of the two ships to sight land rowed to shore in Takinis Bay, one hundred miles north of present-day Sitka. They vanished, presumed killed by the local population. Bering himself died after his ship was wrecked during the return journey, but his name was given to the strait he discovered that separates Siberia from North America. Some of the creatures identified on that expedition were named for the onboard naturalist, Steller, such as a then soon-to-be-extinct sea cow, an eagle, a sea lion, and a jay. But it was the exploitation of the sea otters that opened up North America's west coast.

Baranof Island, on which Sitka is still primarily situated, was named for the Russian fur trader Alexander Baranof, who as governor of Russian America first established Sitka, originally a Tlingit settlement, as his administrative base in 1799. Sitka was retaken by the Tlingit briefly at the end of the eighteenth century before they were forced out, and the town was more heavily fortified by the Russians.

Sitka remained Russia's colonial capital of Alaska until the near extinction of the sea otter caused trade to dwindle. In 1867 Russia sold Alaska to the United States, which continued to use Sitka as the state capital until 1906. St. Michael's Russian Orthodox Cathedral is about the only building with a sufficiently different style to allow one to imagine how much this coast was connected to Siberia and Russia, rather in the same way that the older buildings in California reflect Spanish styles: Spain built its first mission in California in 1769.

Paddling the channel through Sitka itself, between the airport on an island to one side and fishing boats and float planes sitting on the other, we stopped to watch a large group of about twenty bald eagles fishing. It appeared the adults were teaching the juvenile birds how to fish, using fish scraps in the water outside a fish factory. The adults swooped down to grab a fish in their talons and climbed, only to discard the morsel, turn, and prepare to demonstrate another perfect grab. The juveniles imitated this behavior with varying success.

Leaving our kayaks on a beach, we explored town, shopping for food and finding a replica wooden blockhouse built in the style of the early Russian colonists. We also sought out the Russian Orthodox cathedral and the Russian Bishop's House. Besides sightseeing and shopping, today was our "test run" for our rendezvous with Les and Diane. Tomorrow we would tow their kayaks and meet them here.

Next day, almost as soon as the four of us had left Sitka behind, we felt we were in wilderness. We paddled the channels between scatterings of small rocky islands, landing here and there only to find each had a dense fringe of ruthlessly spiky devil's club preventing easy access from the beach to the forest beyond. Abandoning the idea of landing on a beach, we chose a rock ledge and found easy access to great camping.

It was a dry season, with few available freshwater sources, so we paddled to where an outlet from Redoubt Lake plunges over falls into the sea, creating an area of swift currents we could play around in with the kayaks.

If camping on the islands in such sunny weather was a treat, so were the butter clams and the fish that Les caught. Les prepared a fire and then dug a pit on the beach. He wrapped the fish in seaweed and foil and placed it in the pit on hot stones and embers from the fire. He then wrapped and positioned potatoes in the same way. Finally he covered everything over with pebbles and sand until the beach was restored and then walked away from it. I could tell he was sorely tempted to dig it up again to see how everything was cooking, but he managed to leave it there for the duration—and served up a wonderfully succulent and tasty fish supper!

Clams were everywhere. Scooping our hands into the low-tide gravel of the beach, we could easily find a couple of dozen perfect-size clams within minutes. We placed these in a net bag that we hung from a rock edge into deep water. The clams would filter clean water and stay fresh until we were ready to eat. Unfortunately for the poor clams, they were probably stressed by the arrival of starfish, whose crusty bodies of orange, brown, or purple completely coated the bag on the outside when we pulled it up. Luckily the starfish were unable to wrap around and feast on the clams inside.

We carried a small round grill about a foot in diameter. This we perched on three stones on the beach and scooped a hollow underneath for a small fire. Once the fire had settled to a bed of bright embers, we placed half a dozen clams on the grid at a time, waiting until they had cooked in their own juices and the shells popped open. Then we scooped out and ate the soft flesh, flinging the shells onto the beach and placing fresh clams on the grid. Our feast ended when the rising tide finally sent water hissing across the embers.

Drawn toward hot water from cold water, Les suggested we should visit Goddard. There was once a hotel there, built in the 1920s to take advantage of natural hot springs. We pulled up on the shore and followed a boardwalk across the marshy ground to where two big cedar cylinders stood sheltered beneath sturdy framed roofs but open to the bay.

These hot tubs are owned by the city of Sitka. We plugged one of the empty tubs and turned the water on. Pouring from a large-diameter hose, hot water flooded into the tub, but while it filled we hiked quickly back to where the hotel had been. When we returned our tub was full. We sank through the steam into the deep water, then peered out across the rain-gray sea to the islands. There are worse places to spend a drizzly afternoon!

Without kayaking far, we drifted near kelp beds to watch sea otters and watched whales slowly cruising along the shore. We hiked across forested islands, listening to the whistling chatter of eagles in the treetops. We took out painting boxes and sketched wildflowers we would identify later. We found collections of iridescent abalone shells and chiton remains left by otters on mossy hummocks.

Far too soon it was time to backtrack to Sitka, where Les and Diane checked into a hotel for the night and prepared to dine out with friends. Kristin wanted to have one more night camping. We retraced our route past the fishing eagles, on reflective calm seas past

slow-moving shrimp fishing boats back to the island we had chosen on our first arrival. It was Kristin's birthday. We lit a small fire
and cooked mussels. Then we rolled a rope of dough and twisted it
around green sticks, cooking it to aromatic bread over the embers.
Breaking it apart, we ate it hot with cheese and drizzled honey. Mist
edged across the mountains to the northwest. The snow on Mount
Edgecombe glowed with the last of a faint rose-pink sun. Forested
rocks and islands faded flat to shades of shadow, one upon another
upon another; green-gray on blue-gray on charcoal. Tomorrow we
would paddle across to the ferry dock to meet up with Les and Diane
again and wait for the ferry home. Tonight was our chance to savor
the last of our trip and appreciate the moment.

Woken early by the clamor of crows and eagles, we carried the
espresso maker to the beach. *"Whoosh,"* there was a humpback whale,
right where we had first seen one on the morning of our arrival! We
watched, captivated and enthralled. Another surfaced close by; curving slowly through the water until finally the tail flukes rose out, it
then slid almost without a ripple into the water. Slowly they swam
along the shore, as though tempting us back in the direction of Sitka.

The Pelican *floats by the dock at Sitka, Alaska.*

10

PEREGRINES

Kristin and I were exploring a stretch of the Washington coast known as the "Graveyard of the Giants." It lies on the west coast of the Olympic Peninsula, a part designated as a national park. Huge rock stacks, tombstones for ships and giants, stand in the ocean, breaking the power of the surf that rolls toward the partly sandy beaches. These stacks cause the waves to refract in bright curves. As the waves wrap around both sides of a stack, they meet obliquely behind, colliding in spectacular "zipper-runs" that throw up a plume of water that appears to race toward shore at breakneck speed. Beneath such "zippers" often form long narrow sandbanks that finger out across the water.

Forest clings to the shore, rising from the piled driftwood logs up the steep slopes that stand as cliffs where the rock is too steep or the ground too unstable to support trees.

We crept around a stack, cautiously. Our care was only in part because we didn't want to be annihilated by an extra-large breaker. No, we were looking for wild animals, and there on the flat ledges, only just out of reach of the largest waves, was a group of more than a hundred seals. We had seen sea otters today too, one lying on its back, bobbing buoyantly high on the water, with the meal of a crab resting on its chest. But we expected to see more if we were respectful and quiet as we approached, peering around each corner before making ourselves fully visible.

As we continued past the next stack, we were both aware of a gull gliding fast toward us. From behind our line of sight, another bird shot into view, flying in the opposite direction. Suddenly there was only one bird. Or was there? Something was wrong!

Winging toward us now was a peregrine falcon carrying the now-dead seagull that had been flying toward us! The peregrine had flown past us, hit the gull almost head-on, and was returning with it! It had all happened so quickly and efficiently, it appeared as though the gull that had been approaching us was still approaching, and it was the other bird that had vanished!

The peregrine landed with its prey on a small ledge on the face of the sea stack quite close to us. It immediately began ripping at the breast of the dead gull with its sharp beak, and down floated into the air. The falcon watched us cautiously, mantling its catch jealously with outstretched wings and regarding us fiercely as we passed. But it was not deterred long from tearing into its meal, even while we watched.

Peregrine falcons are more common now than they used to be, when DDT almost caused their demise. They've even moved into human-made cliffscapes and are found nesting on the ledges of high-rise buildings in my hometown of Seattle, where they find an abundance of their favorite food: pigeons. And in the city they seem even less fazed by people watching them. In Pioneer Square, right in the heart of downtown Seattle, I once saw a crowd of people gather to watch something. Curious, I walked closer to see what it was, expecting a public performer. It was a peregrine on the cobbles of the square between the trees ripping apart a pigeon—dining out in the city.

Camping between the storm-thrown logs at the top of the beach on the open Pacific coast at Point of Arches, farther north than the Graveyard of the Giants, we probed the rock pools as the tide fell, finding exotic crabs and giant many-pointed sun-stars. Then we noticed that all the juvenile gulls that had been scavenging the beach were running closer together and hunkering themselves down as if preparing for a chill wind. We turned to watch. What was happening? Then the wind came: A peregrine blazed into view in a low dive. I winced at the impact that floored the gull. The peregrine landed on the beach a few yards away, paused for a moment, and then returned to its prey. Moments later light balls of down and feathers were rolling along the beach in the breeze as the peregrine prepared its meal.

As soon as the gull had been hit, the other gulls straightened up and continued searching the sand for tasty morsels of seafood or whatever else they could find. Their moment of fear was over for the moment. We camped out a couple of nights in the same place and watched the repetition of both the behavior of the gulls and of the attack by the falcon. Each time the predator chose one of the gulls from the outer fringe of the group. From our few observations I concluded that the safest position for a gull was in the center of the crowd.

Peregrines are surely one of our more-spectacular avian predators. They can spot their prey from high above the land or sea, fold their wings back, and drop into a steep dive, or "stoop," that can reach speeds of 180 miles per hour. At this speed a blow from the peregrine's talons will instantly break the spine of its prey. Birds on the wing often have no warning. However, some birds seem more aware than others. Ravens seem particularly aware. I stopped one day beneath the cliffs of Anglesey in Wales, U.K., to watch a pair of ravens drifting around the cliff edges above me. I knew where they had nested not far from here the previous year and was curious to see if they would nest again in the same place or had chosen a new site. Suddenly I spotted the peregrine falling from the sky. I feared for the targeted raven, but at the seemingly inevitable moment of impact, the raven rolled

A peregrine falcon sits tight on its prey; Point of Arches, Washington.

upside down with a croak. Just as at the moment the curved horns of the charging bull lift to gore the bullfighter, his cape twists bewitchingly away for a moment and lets the bull pass, so the shape-changing raven had momentarily vanished from the path of the peregrine and the peregrine had fallen through the space.

Spellbound I watched the peregrine pull out of its dive, flap powerfully in a rising curve to gain height, and then wing away beyond the cliff. The ravens continued to float lazily around the face of the cliff.

But the show was not yet over. Once again the peregrine stooped, hurtling down from the sky. Once again the raven lazily rolled in the air to let it pass. After watching several dives, I realized the peregrine could not be hunting. No, the display must be in play. Croaking ravens, the rushing descent of the peregrine, the hiss of waves surging against the barnacles beside me, the breeze ruffling the surface of the water—I watched the performers rehearse for more than forty-five minutes. I was totally absorbed.

Finally I reluctantly drew myself away from this incredible aerial spectacle. I must leave now, or the tide would turn and deny me passage around the next headland. But I lingered to watch one last dive, imprinting the poetry of the movement in my mind one final time lest I forget. Then I turned away.

11

ALLIGATORS

Alligators abound throughout a large part of the southern United States, including Florida. The Myakka River, where it runs through a state park just south of Tampa, is alligator heaven. We parked beneath live oaks festooned in long gray drapes of Spanish moss. Huge golden-yellow spiders had spun wide orbs between the trees. A rustling sound made me look up. Dark plumage! A vulture, its stiff feathers whispering crisply as it slowly floated past on an air current. It was a warm spring morning, perfect weather to see alligators. If it's cold, alligators lay low, drifting around underwater, but when the sun heats up at this time of year, they haul out onto the banks to soak up the rays.

The river flowed brown and green, reflecting the tall vegetation. I paused to absorb the scene. A limpkin—a shy, brown, long-legged Florida bird—was stalking through the vegetation along the water's edge, probing with its long beak in search of breakfast. A little blue heron stood motionless in the shallows. A turtle, spotting my movement, abandoned its semisubmerged branch with a loud *Plop*. I watched its pie shape descend into shadow. We were about to enter a wildlife zone that might also be considered a snack bar. With a flash of movement the blue heron snatched a gleaming fish from the water. With similar ease an alligator might snack on a turtle or limpkin. Now watchful, we "intrepid voyageurs" were ready to explore downstream in search of giant lizards!

We drifted, scanning the banks for the telltale short or flattened vegetation and an easy launching ramp that could be a haul-out place for alligators. In England, think of the perfect place for a lunch break—perhaps an easy landing with gentle gradient to pull the kayaks out, with a flattish area of grass in the sun. Oh, and look! Perfect! There's even a big log to sit on! Now I think about it, perhaps that's what makes kayaking the Myakka so exciting for overseas visitors!

Rounding the next bend, I thought I could see an alligator on the bank, partly hidden by a fallen palm tree. I debated with Roland as we drifted closer, trying to confirm that it was an alligator. Then we both suddenly realized that the "palm log" was an alligator! And look at the size of it! When I spot an alligator, one of the first things I note is the length. This one looked about twenty feet long! To a surfer's practiced eye that translates to about eleven feet. An eleven-foot alligator is huge! Most alligators don't grow any longer than that, although they can reach fifteen feet. But this was a big one, with a massive girth!

I was unable to stop exclaiming about how big it was until it stood up. Then I was speechless! The beast was huge! It walked slowly to the water to slide in. Then, looking every bit like a floating log, it

Alligators rest like logs along the shore of the Myakka River, Florida.

drifted gently toward us. But before reaching us it silently slipped beneath the surface and was gone. Gone? Where had it gone? My fingers left the water.

The river is quite narrow in places, making it difficult to see around the bends. Suddenly there was an eruption from the bank a few yards from me. I'm always startled by sudden movement—and always surprised at how quickly alligators can move! There was a flash of dark, scaly body entering the water. I never saw the whole creature all at once; its head was underwater before its tail emerged from the vegetation. Moments later, all that was visible was swirling muddied water. Somewhere beneath me in the narrow river was another seven-hundred-pound alligator!

It's exciting to spot alligators on the riverbanks, but you generally see more swimming. Sometimes you spot the pattern of the ridges along their back and tail along the surface, making the alligator look like a half-submerged palm tree, but more often all you see are the up-kicked nostrils at the end of the snout and a pair of eyes sticking

Kristin leaves an alligator plenty of room; Myakka River, Florida.

up above the surface. There is a rule of thumb you can follow when you see approaching eyes: "The distance between nostrils and eyes measured in inches is roughly the length of the alligator measured in feet." For example, if the distance between the nostrils and eyes is ten inches, you're probably looking at a ten-foot-long alligator, which is big! If you're not good at estimating, don't forget to carry a tape measure . . . which makes me wonder: How dangerous *are* alligators? Might I be attacked?

Alligators are typically cautious around sea kayaks, but we once canceled a surf class because of a lack of waves and took to the Myakka in whitewater kayaks. That day we had more excitement than we expected. Alligators seem much less cautious around small kayaks than they are around sea kayaks. Either that or they've learned that the meat on the little ones is tenderer. Alligators mostly eat small prey such as frogs and fish, wading birds, and small mammals, swallowing them whole. They are said to be fond of dogs—but are not known to keep them as pets. Occasionally they'll take a deer, especially if it's swimming.

Alligators are attracted by splashing in the water and can swim at a top speed of twenty-five miles per hour to see if that splashing represents something edible. Alligators' conical teeth make for great grasping but not good cutting or chewing, so if they can't swallow the prey whole, they try to tear off chunks by violently thrashing and twisting. They use the leverage they can get by employing their massive tail. This is what's known as the "death roll," and it's how alligators rip limbs off human victims. With bigger prey they'll sometimes cache the body underwater until it rots and can be more easily pulled apart. And if you're still considering creeping along the bank to take photos, bear in mind that alligators can short-sprint on land at speeds up to thirty miles per hour. All in all, I'd say there are plenty of good reasons to be cautious around alligators, even though fewer people are eaten by alligators than alligators eaten by people.

We continued downstream cautiously, passing semisubmerged logs, watched by protruding eyes, and startled by sunbathing alligators suddenly taking to the water. By the time we reached the lower lake, it was time for lunch. But by now I didn't really want to land. I felt nervous. What if we ran into something big and scary in the tall grass? It's good to be cautious! There's nothing better than thinking ahead. "Russell! Why don't you go ahead and land? I'll join you in a minute. . . ."

"Waiter! Get me an alligator sandwich, and make it snappy!"

Alligators are farmed for meat, and you can buy tenderloin tail meat for about twenty dollars per pound. What does it taste like? Well, it has been described as a cross between turtle meat and frog legs, which might not help you much. I thought it tasted a bit like chicken, with a texture like veal. You'll often find "gator bits and fries" on the menu in Southern cafes along with deep-fried catfish and burgers.

12

NEWFOUNDLAND SQUID

In 1978 I arrived by kayak to Cottel Island on Newfoundland's east coast with my friend Tim. We walked with a local schoolteacher to watch the island car ferry load at Dock Cove. The ferry was an old tugboat from St. John's, and it carried four cars at a time. It moved farther along the wharf after each car had been driven across wooden planks onto the deck to allow a clear space for the next car to board.

While we waited for the ferry to leave, we watched a group of men and boys at work salting cod and hanging squid out to dry in the sun. I was fascinated by the squid, but I was distracted when the ferry pulled away, maneuvering through a narrow channel with little room to spare between the rocks on either side. The teacher told us there would be a new development at the south end of the island at Shalloway Cove. A new road was being built to the cove, and there would be a new fish plant and a terminal to accommodate a larger car ferry. If we came back, we probably wouldn't find the old tugboat ferry still operating. In the quiet following the departure of the ferry, we set off walking across the island.

Later we met another man, John, who was hanging out squid to dry. He told us squid are quite easy to catch, but messy with all the ink they squirt. He estimated he had caught more than a thousand the previous night. Each was a foot to eighteen inches long and a mottled reddish color. First he split each squid along its length and then draped the body over a pole. He then wound the two longest tentacles around the pole and flipped the body off the pole to hang from those tentacles. With the squid dangling like that, he could separate and spread out the remaining eight shorter tentacles like a flower to dry.

Apparently, if he left the tentacles clinging together, they would dry pink in color and the squid would not fetch full price.

When I asked him how much he got paid for squid, he said that dried they fetched between eighty cents and a dollar per pound, depending on the quality. Japanese fishing boats were anchored off-shore through the summer, and he could sell them as many dried squid as he could produce. It seemed to me a lot of work for little return.

"What do they taste like?" I asked. "I've heard they taste good." he replied. He'd never tasted one himself. Nobody he knew had ever eaten them.

Squid were drying everywhere on the island. Beside houses the sunlight glowed through neat rows of the parchmentlike bodies, held by clothespins on washing lines. In some places racks of horizontal wooden poles held hundreds of squid, and when those racks were full, the fishermen hung the squid from the branches of trees to dry. It was squid season!

So how were they caught? Originally the fishermen jigged with hand lines over the square sides of their fishing boats, using "jiggers"

Squid hang to dry at St. Brendan's, Newfoundland.

they made themselves by casting lead weights around a ring of upward-facing metal spikes. The spikes had no barbs. It's difficult to unhook a squid from barbed hooks. "When you grab them they squirt ink and wrap their tentacles around your hand. By the time you've got one tentacle off the hook and got your hand free, they're caught on the barbs again."

"So how do you do it now?" I asked

"We use a steel drum to wind up the lines, and each line has rows of jiggers, one beneath the other, and a weight at the end. The jiggers are plastic floats with a couple of rings of spikes that face up. As we reel the lines up, we pull each squid off into the boat. It's messy."

That afternoon at the tent, watching some small boats fishing not far from shore, I was inspired to try my hand. Finding the red case of a spent shotgun cartridge on the beach, I improvised a jigger by jamming a lead weight inside and sticking a single fishhook out through the side. Then I paddled from shore in my kayak with a plastic bag between my legs in case I was successful. But I had no luck.

Someone called to me from one of the boats, telling me I wasn't far enough out, so I paddled out to see how they were doing. They were jigging with hand lines, old style, pulling out squid as fast as they could throw out a line and pull it in again. They showed me how much line to use: about eight feet. I caught a squid almost immediately, and as I hauled it up, tentacles first, it squirted ink and water over the front of my kayak. It continued to make squirting noises long after it had run out of liquid. Its tentacles grabbed and stuck to anything and everything as I tried to free my single barbed hook from the tentacle. As quickly as I could, I pulled my hand free from the rest of the suckers and held the cold squid by its body. Its tentacles curled back, trying to reach me. I thrust the squid into the bag between my legs, where it continued to make an occasional squirting sound.

Heart beating fast, I dropped my line again and jigged it up and down in the water. Suddenly I could see squid completely surrounding it. Dozens of them came in from all directions, creating a reddish shimmering star shape in the water with the jigger in the center! First one would make a grab then back away, then another. Sometimes one would back away quickly, surprised by my jerking the line, and stain the water with a dark cloud.

Then one caught on the hook and I hauled it quickly to the surface, grabbing the body to try to aim the jets away from me. This creature was hooked in the side, but still those ten narrow fingers clutched and stuck, and the jets squirted and squirted.

I was afloat for less than one hour fishing and watching the men on the boats fishing. Curses and laughter mingled as the sounds carried across the water. When I paddled back to shore, my bag held nine squid—enough, I thought, for a good meal for both of us. Tim, however, was unimpressed. He didn't like the look of them. But I had caught these squid to eat. Nobody seemed to know what they tasted like, so I was determined to find out.

John showed me how to clean them, how to turn them inside out and push the intestines and a short transparent bone away with a finger. He pointed out that some of them had holes in them. I bent over to look more closely. They were neat round holes about the size of a penny cut clean right through the flesh. "That's from this," he said, pointing to a birdlike beak nestled deep among the tentacles. "When you grab a squid you have to make sure it doesn't get a good grip on you with its tentacles. If it can pull you close, it'll take a chunk like that clean out of your hand, sharp as a knife!"

I fell silent. When I thought about the thin plastic bag nestling between my thighs out on the water, I felt extra thankful that today the squid had bitten one another inside the bag rather than me, just outside.

Giant Squid

Newfoundland is one of the places best known for the appearance of the giant squid. Rather larger than the ones I had caught, giant squid grow to an estimated forty-three feet long, with a mantle more than six feet long! Their long tentacles are armed with rows of suckers with serrated edges that leave scars on the skin of sperm whales, their main predator. It is thought that pilot whales might also prey on giant squid.

The giant squid is probably the creature responsible for the Norse legend of the kraken.

Later in summer 1978, after hitching a ride on the schooner *Norma and Gladys,* Tim and I paddled south past Bell Island. There, in 1873, a minister afloat in a dory with a young boy was attacked by a giant squid.

PEOPLE

There's an English expression, "There's nowt sae queer as folk," and it sometimes fits us well! The wonders of character unfold when there's an ear to listen.

13

UNGAVA ENCOUNTER

In 1981 I made a solo journey by kayak from Iqaluit on Baffin Island, across Hudson Strait, to northern Labrador. Too late in the season, I cut short my journey when I ran into an oil tanker, three hundred miles from the nearest village. I hitched a ride to Nova Scotia but returned to Labrador in 2004 to complete the journey. The story is told in my book *Stepping Stones of Ungava and Labrador*. The following is a story from that book relating a precious encounter with an Inuit hunting party.

Our route in the fog was through a channel between an island and a point, but the channel made a right-angle turn from east to north. Three of my topographic maps met right here, the channel crossing the corners of all three, so I relied on just my nautical chart instead of struggling with four maps on my deck at once. I typically used both land and sea charts because each offered different details. Unfortunately this turned out to be precisely the wrong time to rely on the sea chart alone. Noting that it showed a clear channel between island and mainland unencumbered by shallows, I led us straight ahead, pushing into the tide that now ran powerfully against us. Rain splashed down, bouncing droplets into the air and creating blurry swirls as fresh water pooled on top of the salt water. The fog closed in around us until our view was confined to boulders sticking up out of rain-spattered water. The boulders just beneath the surface were more of a hazard than those we could see, as every now and then one of us would ride up with a screech of gel-coat against rock that, sounding like fingernails across a chalkboard, raised the hairs on the back of my neck. We slowed down to reduce the impact of any collisions, but it was difficult to tell the depth of the water over the rocks we approached because of the blurry surface and the refraction. We made progress against the current, but the water grew shallower until we caught mud with our blades while avoiding the boulders. We had almost run out of water. We crept along from eddy to eddy, boulder to boulder, in water little more than five inches deep.

"Is that a tent?" I exclaimed. Scarcely visible through the mist were two white tents pitched on the rock at the top of the muddy slope. We continued, paddling and peering up the slope. Kristin said, "There are people." I had not seen the slight figures looking down at us from the top. As we paddled they made their way down to reach the water's edge before we did: two boys and a man in his thirties. We scooted ourselves toward them, gripping against the mud with the edges of our paddle blades until we slid to a standstill.

There were a few minutes of shyness between us, mutual curiosity but uncertainty about the protocol. "The tide is still falling," the man said, sweeping his hand in an arc above the water. By his reckoning we

Me and Inuk hunter David; Ungava Bay, Quebec.

would be stuck there for a few hours. "Come up to the tent for tea." We lifted the kayaks a few yards from the water and then trudged up the slope. The slick, buff-colored skin of the silt punctured beneath each footstep, revealing black mud underneath. Boulders protruded everywhere through it. Near the top of the slope rested a long, gray freight canoe painted teal green above the waterline. A large outboard motor clung to the transom. An elderly man, his tanned face creased and wrinkled, stood leaning against the canoe gazing into it. Water streamed past his rubber boots and filled his footprints. Inside the boat lay carcasses of ducks, loons, and a seal. His party, he explained, had been out hunting from George River (Kangiqsualujjuaq) and had motored around the corner to find the tent here. It was raining, and the boys were cold and wet, so they had set up their own tent beside the first one to wait for better weather.

Higher up the shore was a second boat and two tall tents. Sewn of heavy white canvas, each tent stood like a low cylinder with short walls and a conical roof sloping upward to a point supported by a central pole. I have heard that sled dogs like to lift their legs to mark the outside corners of tents, making the inside corners damp and smelly, which is sufficient reason to adopt a circular floor and elimi-nate the corners. We lifted the entrance flap of the closest tent and stooped to go inside. It was warm and steamy. An elderly man with a smiling full-moon face framed in almost white short-cut hair sat on a plastic cooler with his back against the wall of the tent. He wore a thick blue-check quilted shirt and navy pants stuck into knee-length rubber boots. An old woman in a blue jacket and a colorful scarf pin-ning her hair lay on the floor on a pile of jackets, tending a fire in a metal firebox.

The man said something in Inuktitut and motioned to us to come in and sit down. I followed Kristin to crouch on a plywood board on the ground at the back of the tent. The two boys, in their early teens and wearing baseball caps, and a young girl piled in behind us, so we shuffled around to make room. Everyone settled down onto the ground, grinning. We introduced ourselves. The old man spoke. His name was David; his wife was Suzie. The boys were sons of the man who had just squeezed in at the entrance. He was with his father, the man who had been standing beside his boat. David and Suzie were camping with their granddaughter. The little girl smiled.

The man by the door translated. Suzie had cancer. She was ill. She couldn't walk anymore, but she liked camping here, so her husband had brought her out to camp for a few days. Now they had more or less run out of food, so they would go back tonight when the tide had risen enough to launch their boat. The other party would help them launch and would also leave at high tide. They asked if we wanted to camp there. We said no, that it wasn't easy for us to unload and carry our stuff up muddy shores. We'd much rather land on rock, so we waited for the tide.

Suzie poured water into a large kettle and set it hissing on the stove. She coughed for a while, awkwardly and apparently with pain. When she stopped I smiled at her and her eyes warmed. I looked around at our new surroundings. A rusty stovepipe ran up from the firebox through a hole in the roof, the cloth shielded from the heat by a metal plate sewn to the canvas. I pointed to this neat heat barrier and made a comment, and the old woman indicated with a smile that she had sewn it herself.

David had once been a seal hunter, hunting in summer from his kayak. His father had built his first kayak for him out of wood and sealskin when he was young. He had built others for him over the years, four in all. That was on the east coast, at Nutak, I think he said, in Labrador. He was proud of his skills, but now, he said, he was too stiff. He couldn't bend enough to squeeze into a kayak. The translator laughed and poked fun, saying "Too much television! Too much food!" and he patted the air in front of his stomach, suggesting a paunch.

David smiled and continued, "But we had to move away, some of us to Nain in Labrador, some of us to Ungava Bay, to Kangiqsualujjuaq and Kuujjuaq. Our families were split up, and the government told us we were to stay apart. We were forbidden from crossing to see our families. They didn't want people to keep moving from Quebec to Labrador and back. They wanted people to stay in one place. They wanted to know where people were. I came to Kangiqsualujjuaq with my uncle. My sister went to Nain, but we cross now to see them."

The girl was fascinated by Kristin's camera in its waterproof case. Kristin took her photograph and showed her the image, but with limited battery power for the five-week trip, she was reluctant to show a lot of pictures. She distracted the girl by switching on the little red emergency light she carried clipped to the shoulder of her float vest. The old man continued, "But things change. Always there is something good. If things are bad, then you can say things will get better, and they do." Optimism beamed from his blue eyes. He leaned his broad head forward and smiled. His tanned face, dark beneath almost white hair, radiated confidence. I glanced to my left to see the row of faces turned to watch him, waiting for his next words, but he just smiled, gazing as if into some inner thought.

The kettle was now boiling strongly; his wife struggled onto her side to lift it from the heat. Her deft fingers plucked off the lid and thrust in tea bags. She motioned to her granddaughter, who passed her several empty enamel cups, stained with rings of tannin, and she lined them up.

David continued, explaining how people crossed the mountains from Ungava Bay into Labrador in winter. When he was ten years old or so, he first saw a white man. "He was the best survivalist. When he first arrived the people didn't know how he would eat, but he ate raw meat off a split log like they did." David lifted a piece of wood from the floor to illustrate how they would use a newly split slab of wood as a plate. Then he handed it to Suzie, who slid the kettle aside and fed the wood to the fire. "Yes," he repeated, "that white man ate meat like us, using a split log, cutting pieces of blubber like we did, even eating stinky fish in winter. He was a survivalist."

Suzie lifted the heavy kettle and poured tea, passing the mugs first to Kristin, who was nearest. As Kristin reached to receive them, Suzie noticed the dressings on Kristin's hands and indicated that she wanted to see. She held Kristin's hands in her own and stroked them tenderly. She talked quietly to herself. David said Kristin's hands would become tougher as she paddled. "First you get blisters, and then your hands will be tough. You'll see." I hoped he would be right. As a ceramicist, Kristin's hands were constantly being abraded by clay, to the point that when she worked long hours her fingerprints wore completely flat. She didn't have a thick protective layer of hide to begin with, and her hands had blistered almost as soon as we began full paddling days.

David lifted the tent flap to look outside. One of the boys scrambled out, and moments later we heard the sound of an ax chopping wood. "We bring the wood!" our translator explained. "The wood for the fire we get in winter with the snowmobiles. There are no trees here. We go inland," he said, pointing. "We also bring the plywood." He pointed to the boards we knelt on.

David let the tent flap close and swatted at a mosquito, prompting Kristin to ask how they had managed with mosquitoes in the past. With a smile our translator pointed to a burning green coil near the door. Kristin said, "But you haven't always had coils. What did you do before?" David reached down and pulled a handful of leafy twigs from the ground. "We burned this." I tried to make out what it was. It looked like the aromatic leaves of crowberry. He continued, "But when we traveled, sometimes the flies were very bad. We couldn't sleep. We would keep going until there was some wind, and then we would all lie down on the ground and sleep. Without a breeze it was impossible to sleep with the mosquitoes. You can't sleep when there are too many flies. Sometimes we would keep going for days with no sleep. There is enough light in the summer to keep going all night."

David peered out from the tent again. He explained, "The tide, sometimes you wait for it to come. You are impatient. You say, 'Come on tide! Hurry up! I can't wait all day! Won't you come faster?' But it doesn't come. It comes, but very slowly. Then it starts to come, and you think, 'Good, now at last!' But it comes too fast. Then you say, 'Tide! Can't you come slower?'"

We smiled. This visit was precious. Although I had wanted to get through the channel earlier, our enforced wait brought us an unexpected and wonderful experience, so I understood his story. But I had missed his point entirely.

Suzie began gathering items from around her, pouring flour into a bowl and mixing a ball of dough. She struggled with a wide cast-iron frying pan, moving the kettle to reveal the fire through a hole underneath. The fire was low. One of the boys left again to chop wood, coming back with an armful of short, split chunks. Suzie fed some onto the fire and set the pan on top with a piece of white lard, which gradually melted until the tent was clouded with eye-stinging smoke. Then she spread her soft dough into the pan to form a pancake that rose slowly into a deep bannock. Flipped, it revealed a golden-brown underside. The bready smell made my stomach ache. I was hungry and eagerly accepted the piece she broke off for me.

Our translator began to ask about food. "Do you like duck?" "Yes," I replied. "Do you know what to do with a duck, how to cook it?" Again I said yes; I'd prepared and cooked animals often enough before. In Iceland it was ducks and puffins, fulmars and gulls.

He disappeared and came back with the gift of a duck. "You sure you know what to do with it?" he checked again. "Yes! This will be wonderful! And, yes, I do know how to prepare it." The duck lay on the ground in front of me, and the boy on my left and the granddaughter idly played with it, making the head peck at the ground and look around. They fingered the feathers and legs, as at ease with this dead creature as they would have been with a stuffed toy.

David opened the door again and peered out. "I can hear it now. It won't be long." He spoke of the tide. "Soon!" Then, "There is a place just around the corner where you can land in a kayak. You can camp there. It's a good place." To Kristin he added, "You will have a good journey. The current will be strong, but you can make it."

We continued talking, but a few moments later David spoke again. Translated he said, "It's time for you to go." I began thanking

Inuit boys welcome us at a hunters' camp, Ungava Bay, Quebec.

Suzie, saying good-bye, and then shuffled around to get out of the tent. Outside I shook hands with each person, saying "Thank you." But David interrupted. He pointed. "It's time for you to go!" I looked. The water had reached to within a few yards of the kayaks. I turned to speak to the uncle. "Nigel!" Kristin shouted. "The kayaks! We've got to go!"

I turned again to look; it didn't sound like her, and we were not that rushed for time. But Kristin had already gone. She was hurtling down the muddy slope with the jerky movement of someone not quite in control of her feet. Tripping on a rock, she flew headlong into the mud, then scrambled to her feet and ran on. Then I saw the kayaks. They were almost floating! A flood of water cascaded downhill from above the rocky dam to the north to meet the tide that had been rising from the south. The levels were so different that the current roared audibly as it rushed downhill. Kristin fell again then regained her feet. I hurried down the mud, clasping the duck in one hand. There was no way I could reach the kayaks. They were now drifting from shore, and the current was carrying them downstream. With a final burst of speed, Kristin ran right into the water and grabbed first one, then the other. The water was up to her thighs. She waded back to shore shaking her head. I held the kayaks while she pulled off each boot in turn to pour out the icy water.

We stowed our cockpit covers and climbed into our seats. Gliding from shore we pointed our kayaks against the current and paddled hard. Now each boulder that stood in the current offered us an eddy to ease our way. We sprinted from one eddy to the next, pausing for a moment then darting up to the next large stone, pushing upstream like salmon against a river. Up on the hill stood our friends, their figures now half obscured by the gathering darkness. They waved, and we waved back.

14

FAREWELL TO PHYLLIS

I sat there barely afloat in my kayak, drifting gently up against the sand and rocking back with the small waves. I waited. John had left his kayak at the waterline while he walked back to the campground, a longish walk. The beach was almost deserted, but I could see a party of four elderly people walking slowly toward me. As they drew nearer, it struck me as odd that they were all so smartly dressed. The two men wore suits, and the women wore skirts and jackets. Each sported a remembrance poppy at the lapel.

The group passed by me a little higher up the beach and crossed toward the rocks. I gazed around. It was a clear day, bright and warm. Maybe I'd walk out onto this headland later to look for field mushrooms. John seemed to be taking his time. His kayak was already stranded on the sand by the dropping tide.

At the rocks the two men in the group scrambled awkwardly across the wet wrack. One was wearing smart shoes and was clinging with both hands to the rock. The other, in calf-length green rubber boots, was stumbling on the weed, clutching a pale gray plastic container. It was a broad tube—a tall cylinder. I was mildly curious. Neither of them looked at ease on the rock. I smiled at the nearest lady when she glanced in my direction and called out to her. "Hello! What's going on here?"

She walked closer to me. "We're scattering the ashes of my aunt," she said. "She died last week, and she wanted her ashes to be scattered in this bay." I looked at her. She had warm eyes, a little wet in the corners.

I thought for a moment as I watched the awkward progress of the two men. "Would you like me to take her farther out into the bay?" I offered. "I could take her out in the kayak."

She appeared delighted. "How kind of you!" she said and called across to the others. "This young man has offered to scatter the ashes out in the bay, from his kayak!"

A few minutes later, the gray container was in my hands, and the little group had gathered around me as I sat. "What was her name?" I asked.

"Phyllis. Phyllis Haydn. She was my aunt. You know, she was lucid right up to the last," the woman said.

One of the men added, "She always said she'd live till she was ninety. She almost lived till she was ninety-one, but she was right in the end. Her birthday would have been on the fifth, but she passed away on the second. She was still ninety. She was a lovely woman."

"Her husband, Arthur, was scattered here, you see," the woman continued. "She wanted to be scattered with him when she died. They both loved it here."

I eased away from the beach and turned to paddle out into the bay. Suddenly I was aware of every rock, every mooring buoy, and every view. I headed for a place where I could see out of the bay between the island and the headland, near the spiky rocks that were just appearing as the tide fell. As the view opened I could see the mountains of the Lleyn Peninsula looking clear and close, although the more-distant summits appeared as islands. The horizon stretched like skin around those hills, hiding the land that joined them. A few oystercatchers flew rapidly across the water, heading for the island. It was quiet.

I turned to face the shore. The figures were grouped close together, distant now, small and out of hearing. I lifted the urn and held it out to one side of the kayak and thought hard. I could imagine her, a frail lady perhaps closing on death. Did death free her from the cage of her body? Was there something of her left beyond these ashes? I said a quiet prayer for her, hoped that she and Arthur would be together. Happy: together. I felt the peace and tranquility of her presence. I slowly tipped the container until the ashes poured onto the water and watched as the fragments drifted down into the clear, green depths toward the rippled sand way below.

When I returned, I passed back the urn.

"Thank you so much; you are so kind," the woman said. She need not have spoken. I could tell she was grateful. "Are we in your debt?" It took me a moment to understand what she was asking. "Do we pay you for doing that for us?"

"Of course not; it was my pleasure. You certainly don't owe me anything!"

"You know," she said, "Phyllis would have been so thrilled if she'd known that she was going to be carried out into the bay by a young man like you! She would have loved that! You have a kind face!" I was left with a warm impression of Phyllis. She sounded like a lovely lady. Now she would be forever in the bay, and I would remember her whenever I visited.

When John returned, I told him the news. "While you were gone, I sat a ninety-year-old lady on my lap for a trip in my kayak as far as the middle of the bay, over there." I pointed.

"But," I added, "she never made it back."

Children play in Rhoscolyn Bay, North Wales, where Phyllis and her husband rest in peace.

15

ESCAPE FROM HOLLAND

I met Mr. Henri Peteri at the gates to a campground in Holland. He was tall and slim, with a rapid, confident walk that belied his age of more than seventy years. As we sat talking at a table in the sun, I began to understand how he had managed to keep so young. Henri's blue eyes gleamed with enthusiasm as he described his latest project: manufacturing a new system to provide boiling water on tap, a system he had pioneered twenty years ago. But that wasn't why we had met. I had heard that this man had paddled across the North Sea from Holland to England in a double kayak in 1941. "Was this true?" I asked.

"Well, yes." he said. "But it was nothing special, you understand. It was wartime. The only thing that was special was that we found a way to escape from occupied Holland. Of course that was the dream of every man in Holland at the time."

Henri rummaged in his bag and produced a sheaf of papers. "I brought these to show how what we did was not anything extraordinary." He selected a page and pointed at the list of names and dates. "All these people left Holland in kayaks between 1941 and 1943. Look, here is a team that made it. These people here left but were lost. This team was captured and taken to a concentration camp. See? Ten kayaks. And you must remember that many others left Holland in all kinds of other ways in those times—by small boat or overland. You see, we were doing nothing special. We had no doubt about our ability to reach England."

I looked at the list. Ten kayaks, all doubles, of which just four made it to the English coast: eight paddlers out of twenty.

Why, I asked Henri, had so many of the crossings been more than a hundred miles, much farther than the shortest possible route between Holland and England?

He explained that the occupying forces expected escapes to be attempted from the part of the coast that lies closest to England, and they concentrated their patrols there. By leaving from a point farther north, escapees hoped they would have a greater chance of success.

As we talked the whole story gradually emerged. I recount Henri's story from my notes in English and a translation of his account in Dutch. I have attempted to retain his unassuming, matter-of-fact manner. The story, but not the exact words, is Henri's.

The Plan

It was a time in which the enemy occupied the Netherlands. I myself had been in the army, and we had fought for five days before surrendering. Under occupation life continued with a degree of normality, except for the armed troops, the patrols, and the curfews. I was studying, and the main questions in the minds of the students were "What can we do?" and "How can we get away?" If we could escape, then at least we could take some action. It was the obvious way to oppose the occupying forces. We had to get away. Nobody would consider our opposition extraordinary. No, the only extraordinary thing was that I had come up with the plan that my brother and I should escape by kayak. The distance itself wasn't that big, in context.

The students at the university went on strike, and we suddenly had a lot of free time. I was reading philosophy. I preoccupied myself with rowing, but I was also reading a romantic epic in which a man crosses from Iceland to Norway by canoe. The idea appealed to me. When I was a child, my father used to take me to the beach at Katwijk, where I gained some experience in surf using rental kayaks. So my brother Willem and I went into Rotterdam and bought a folding kayak.

I should say we had an advantage: In contrast with other kayakers, we were free to choose the timing of our escape. We were not wanted by the Germans; we were not monitored. We didn't have any reason to leave in a hurry, so we were in a good position to wait. We had to establish what circumstances we needed. The night should be very dark, preferably with a new moon. It should not be summer, for with the longer hours of daylight, it would be more difficult to get away from the coast. Ideally the wind would be from the east, to help us, and there should be a stable weather pattern. Nowadays of course, you are able to find out a few days in advance what weather to expect, but in those days there were no weather reports at all.

It was September. We had waited a very long time, hoping for perfect conditions. I went to work in Delft, and looking out of the window one day, it occurred to me that if we continued waiting, we wouldn't get away that year at all. We really should try to get away as soon as possible. So I took my pushbike to Katwijk. Please keep in mind that we were occupied by the Germans. Although the coast was barbwired, in daytime people were allowed to go onto the beach, and people still went as holidaymakers.

There was a small entrance to the beach through the barbed wire, so I set out to find a room to rent that was as close as possible to that hole. I told the people we wanted to stay there for a week and asked whether we could rent the room for that time. Of course we had to find a room that was big enough to hold the assembled kayak. It also had to be easy to get the assembled kayak out unobserved. I didn't care about the beds they showed to me, but I pretended to show interest anyway. My brother had just started a new job. He'd only been working for seventeen days. When I went to him and told him he would be leaving the next day, he was exasperated. He said, "But I can't! What about my job?" In fact he worked there for only one more day.

We transported the kayak from Rotterdam to Delft by train. That was one of those experiences I really treasure. The kayak packs into one sack, which could be mistaken for a tent or something like that, and a backpack containing the skin. I also had a suitcase full of food and stuff because, well, we wanted to take a few things along. We got on the train in Rotterdam, and some German soldiers entered the carriage with us. One leaned against the big pack, which in a way was comforting, because it made it look as though the pack belonged to him and gave the impression that I had less baggage.

We took a tram from Leiden to Katwijk, and from the station carried the load into the house. There my brother and I wrote a little note to our parents. It was difficult to leave without telling anybody what we were going to do. It was in our minds that if something went wrong, they would never know what had happened. But on the other hand, if they knew nothing, it would be safer for them. I sent the note with my food ration coupons to a girlfriend, with the request that she inform my parents two weeks later. Betty, that special girlfriend, was sixteen years old at the time. She later graduated as a lawyer, and we married in 1951.

Our rented room was big enough to assemble the kayak. The room had a door toward the sea and was not too far away from the exit through the barbed wire. You may not have any idea of total black-outs. Try to imagine there were no lights at all. In the darkness we assembled a kayak that we had only assembled once before—and one that we had never paddled before. We really didn't know this kayak at all. You may ask why we didn't pay much attention to this point. I think maybe we had good fortune sent to us from above, because we had so little experience with it that when we put it together, we left out one of the pieces of frame in the bow by mistake. We had put the whole thing together, including the skin, and pressurized the frame to make the whole thing more rigid before we realized we had a piece left over.

We had to take the whole thing apart again before we could place the missing piece. This took us another hour and a half. Instead of leaving as planned at midnight, we were not ready to leave until 1:30 a.m. I should say that was lucky, because the barbed wire would have been better guarded at midnight than at 1:30 a.m. If we had left at midnight as planned, the guards might have been more awake. Later the guards probably were sleepier. Yes, it was probably our good fortune!

We went to the beach running. But in our haste to launch quickly, and trying at the same time to keep our shoes dry, we capsized getting in.

In addition to getting wet and filling the kayak with water, most of our gear had fallen out. We quickly searched around in the dark for the missing items, but it was very dark, and we dared not use a torch for fear of being spotted by a German patrol. In all these circumstances, one needs a little bit of luck. We had two compasses, just simple ones; one survived. We had three flashlights; one survived. We were left with only two shoes between us, but we didn't really need shoes. A lot of food got lost, but that didn't matter because we had taken far too much anyway. We emptied the boat, reloaded, and launched again.

We paddled quickly for a bit, anxious to get as far as possible from the shore. We needed to paddle west, but being very inexperienced we thought it would be very easy to go off course. We had decided that we would keep within approximately thirty degrees variation going on west, but then you need a device to indicate the direction. Our compass soon failed, but we found out how easy it can be in a kayak, even for very inexperienced paddlers like us, to keep your course.

When we left we had beautiful weather. All that first night we had beautiful weather. The next day we came across a convoy. But to be spotted from the air or from such big ships was almost impossible, as we hardly came over the crests of the waves. We had some wind, so there were waves. When we saw the convoy in front of us, we turned and paddled in the opposite direction for a while.

Paddling by Ear

The wind was from the east, so we tried to keep it behind us in order to paddle west. We had no concept of time; we had no idea about maps. It made things easy. We didn't have a sail, and we didn't try to be fast. We had the simplest aids one can imagine, and I think that became our fortune. If we had used an outboard motor, we would have attracted attention, but we were prepared to continue slowly until we reached England. With just two of us, we were not of any size.

The second night was quite strange. We had misplaced one of the bow ribs, and therefore the spray deck didn't fit properly. We left without the spray decks on, as we thought we were going to paddle on absolutely flat water. We thought we would put the spray decks on later if we needed them; we didn't notice that we had also misplaced one seat. When we launched the second time, we also broke that seat. We put it back together, but it was not comfortable. Therefore a large sea was quite an unkind thing to us. We sat there all the time with a towel between our legs, trying to mop the boat. That was the best solution, because with a large towel you can mop quite a bit of water. It was a wet, poor activity. Our food started to smell rotten, and we paddled on with it for quite a while. It was interesting to discover how you use your ears in the wind to keep course. With the wind from the east, we kept the wind coming from exactly behind us using the sensitivity of our ears.

Arrival!

Finally we became so tired we discussed what we were going to do. We decided that we would take turns closing our eyes for approximately one thousand strokes. We were exhausted and had great difficulty

Henri Peteri poses with the kayak he used to escape occupied Holland with his brother during WWII.

keeping our eyes open. Our arms kept going far longer than our eyes. Then in the fog we heard a sound as though water was running up against a ship. It turned out to be the water inlet for the Sizewell power station. We paddled along the coast, calling out for someone to help us. We dared not land because we expected the whole coastline and beaches to be full of land mines, but we were also worried that we might be mistaken for the enemy and be shot at. But finally a soldier came across the beach to help us. It had taken us fifty-six hours to cross from Holland to England, a distance of over one hundred miles.

The events and emotions that followed are indescribable. It felt so good to have escaped. We were first taken to the local police station. If you ever get taken to an English police station, I would advise you not to carry much in your pockets, because everything is noted down. They put down large sheets of beautiful white paper, and everything we were carrying was put down on them. I happened to be carrying a ball of wet string in my pocket. They wrote down "One ball of string." They asked why I carried three tram tickets. Why on earth would they want to know why I had three tickets with me? They just happened to be in my pocket. I answered, "Because my girlfriend brought her sister." Of course we only had two shoes between us. Two left shoes.

After the interview in the police station, we were taken to the Royal Victorian Patriotic School for interrogation. Every piece of "driftwood" coming into England was investigated there. And every story we heard there gave us the shivers. We had undertaken what we thought was the safest way across to England, but we were to hear of many other routes across, some through busy overland routes where one cannot be afraid of people. There were people who had done all sorts of things: escape routes across the Pyrenees, people traveling in all sorts of boats. It was fantastic to see such a bunch of vagabonds—and extremely difficult to tell whether there were any spies among them.

One very interesting thing happened. Just ten days after we had set off from Katwijk, another double kayak left from the same beach to arrive safely in England. We met the team during an interrogation. We discovered that they had stayed in the same room of the same house that we had used, crept through the same hole in the barbed wire, and left from the same place on the beach! Throughout it all, the people of the house knew nothing of what was going on. I later discovered that following our departure, the supplies that had spilled onto the beach when we capsized had been spotted by the morning patrol, and the whole area was searched. Another kayak was found hidden in the dunes, and an escape plan was foiled. I met the man whose kayak it was. I met him for the first time a couple of years ago.

What happened afterward has little to do with paddling. My brother and I both joined the Navy (the Dutch Navy was under Allied command). I serviced radar on my ship. Initially we left the kayak on the beach, but after a few weeks we thought, "Why leave it there?" I kept it with me all through the war and had some good trips in it now and then all over the world.

The trip itself has only drawn attention in the past five years. It's strange, but after the war we put the memory aside and got on with our lives, although we did paddle the kayak once or twice after. The overview of the whole story has only begun later. People who were young during the war have started to show interest. There is a man who searched for all these kayakers and listed them. He has found out how many more attempts took place.

When you look back, it was a very risky adventure, mainly because people got caught just off the coast and because a number of people who tried to get away were in a hurry, or left in the wrong season, or launched from the wrong place. The launching spot was very important. Katwijk didn't have the greatest interest for the Germans; it had no harbor. They showed more interest in the area of Hoek van Holland. There were patrols there. A number of people got caught and put into camps; others were killed at sea. Because all of us enlisted after arrival and some didn't survive, only two of the four crews that crossed the North Sea survived. I mention this because it was the whole emotional drag of those wartimes that was exceptional, not the paddle journey itself.

Paddling Like a Twenty-Year-Old

Henri wanted to paddle in a sea kayak to see if he could still do it. We drove to the coast and set a couple of kayaks on the sand beach. A modern sea kayak is totally different from the double folding kayak that Henri and his brother used in 1941. Henri slid easily into the small cockpit on the sand and adjusted the foot braces, then, with a quizzical look at the crank-shafted paddles, he took off across the harbor at high speed. His kayak rocked a little, and in the stiff breeze I was concerned he might overturn, so I leapt into my kayak and followed at full speed. He was fine, handling the kayak as if he were a twenty-year-old who paddled daily rather than a man in his seventies who hadn't paddled for years. I was impressed and felt honored to paddle with this man. We rounded the harbor arm and, leaving shelter behind, headed out onto open water. Sunlit spray flew from the paddles. "It's good to recall that feeling again! Being in a kayak!" he called across to me as his kayak lurched over the waves. His white hair blew in the breeze, and satisfaction beamed across his face. I could imagine that same expression on his face fifty-four years earlier, when he and his brother arrived on the shores of England.

Henri's Historic Kayak

In the small upstairs room of his house in Holland, Henri unfolded the kayak skin onto the floor. "See!" he pointed to a shining white crust in the folds. "There's still salt on it. Of course that's not from the crossing. We've used it since then."

He spread the dark wooden frames and ribs on the floor for me to see. Spotting the bow section of ribs, which hinged apart on dull brass brackets, he knelt down beside it in his fine tweed jacket and smart trousers and inserted the end frame section to show me how it would look.

"We had to do this in the dark." His hand gestured across the pile. "It's not surprising we missed a piece the first time around!"

16

FLATEY FISHERMEN

Surfing our kayaks east along the north coast of Iceland we crept into a tiny stone harbor on Flatey Island at around two in the morning. There, moored against the quay in the cool light of the August subarctic night, we found the varnished hulls of some wooden fishing boats, a small white open boat, and a small whaling vessel from Akureyri, its harpoon gun prominently mounted on its foredeck. We were cold and tired and quickly hauled our kayaks up to the grass. I changed into dry clothes with numb fingers before helping Geoff tether the tent against the wind with a kayak on either side and boulders at the ends.

At some time in the early morning, I heard the sound of boat engines, but I was not prepared to crawl out into the cold to watch. When we did get up, we found the whaler had gone. It was a chill rainy morning. We hung out in the shelter of the tent until we heard voices: The owners of one of the fishing boats and their young children were looking at our kayaks. We invited them inside, and they crouched in the entrance for a few minutes before continuing on their walk.

A later visitor, Guđmunder, offered us a tour of his boat, the *Aron*. We followed him to his vessel. It was maybe fifty feet long, the full hull varnished below and painted white above. He showed us the tiny bridge with its radar, echo sounder, and controls and a half-size chart table. He told us the boat did ten knots under full power. Then he took us down to show us a spotless engine room.

Guđmunder's own cabin was accessed by a separate companionway. There were a couple of built-in cupboards, a sink, and a table; basic but sufficient. Two bunks were hidden behind the bench seats, the curtained spaces cozy, if confined, with racks for books and other small items. His ten-year-old son used the second bunk in the summer when there was no school.

In the forecastle were the crew quarters—six holes in the walls for bunks and two long wall benches at a table. At the wide end of the triangular space was a large cooker with a huge pot held in place by metal rails. At sea, one man was normally the cook, doing nothing else while the other men took turns on deck fishing, using the hydraulic reels with seven cod hooks on a line with a three-kilogram weight at the end.

Between the crew quarters and the bridge was the hold for fish. The boat typically leaves Húsavík for three to four days at a time, sometimes for a week, returning when the ice starts to melt rather than when the hold is full. Guđmunder usually fishes between Grímsey and the mainland (Grímseyjarsund) or around Langanes, so he was able to tell us with certainty about the tides and currents around Langanes, or "Long Head." The Gulf Stream flows around Iceland to the east and the west, the flows meeting at Langanes and heading out to sea as a considerable tide race. The flow is always out

Me standing by an old Willys jeep on Flatey Island, Iceland, 1977.

to sea, but the direction depends on the state of the tide. The safest and most comfortable place to be, he advised, is right under the cliffs, where there is only a short stretch of rough water.

Outside the bridge of the boat, fish hung, strung by the tail from the rail. Guðmunder grabbed a couple and wrapped them in a plastic bag for us to take. "These will keep for about a week. You'll need to boil them for about ten minutes," he explained. He added that cod is easily dried if split and left out in the sun, or by salting and then drying in the sun. But to flavor fresh cod and firm up the texture a little on the boat, fishermen often hang it for just a few days, like these fish.

Disembarking, he led us to his small warehouse near the other harbor arm and gave us a salted fish, which would keep much longer but would need to be soaked for a couple of days in fresh water to get rid of the salt before cooking. In the warehouse were racks of dried cod. He explained they are left for three months to dry bone hard, and then they are sold to an Icelandic company that sells them to Nigeria and Italy. These are the smaller fish and what he called the "bad" fish. Icelanders don't eat these. I wasn't sure whether he meant these fish were in some way actually bad or were just types of fish or sizes of fish that Icelanders do not prefer.

Guðmunder returned to our tent with us but invited us to join him for coffee and to hear the weather forecast on the radio. We waded across the wet grass to his house. In a living room cozy with the heat from a stove, he introduced us to his father, wife, his brother and his wife, his sister and her husband, and numerous children. They hung up our dripping jackets and handed us towels for our faces and hair. Then we sat, warm and happy to be indoors. The old man, who had said nothing, suddenly began to rise. He struggled out of his chair and walked across the room to where I sat. He reached down and felt my feet. My socks were thin and damp. Saying nothing, he returned to his seat and removed his own socks and brought them to me, indicating I should put them on. They were thick wool socks, hand-embroidered in green at the top with his initials. Encouraged by the others in the room, I slipped my feet into the already warm wool, while the old man sat with bare feet.

Over coffee we heard the weather forecast, which promised worse weather. They said they would leave before the storm arrived. Nobody lived on the island nowadays. They had all moved to Húsavík, a larger town on the mainland, but this had been their old home, on the island, and they maintained it and used it as a holiday cottage. They proudly showed us around, explaining how their father had built the house about the time Guðmunder was born. Now the family is slowly rebuilding it over two or three years to make three rooms upstairs. Some of the island houses are maintained as summer holiday cottages. Others are used occasionally by fishermen who shelter their boats in the small harbor when caught out in bad weather. As we looked out from the window, the clouds cleared and revealed fresh snow coating the mountains on the mainland. When it was time for us to leave, the old man insisted I keep his socks.

We helped the family carry their bags from the house to the harbor, stopping first at the old harbor arm, where Guðmunder looked over another boat, his old one, also called *Aron,* which had moored up there for shelter while the men on board gutted their catch. Each head or coil of guts thrown over the side was fought over by a flock of fulmars waiting on the water below. As soon as each morsel hit the surface, there was a scuffle of feathers as they all dived beak-first into a tight knot of writhing gray bodies.

Guðmunder's brother opened up the warehouse where he stored barrels, offering it to us as shelter until we were ready to leave. He handed us the padlock to snap shut when we left and wished us "good luck!" Then he set off in his boat, speeding off into the distance. Guðmunder waited with his family on *Aron,* peering down from the side until the tide finally lifted the keel from the bottom. Then he pulled slowly away, towing his father's small open boat. Everyone stood on deck, waving until they were well clear of the harbor.

Now alone on the island, Geoff and I moved our sleeping bags and stove into the warehouse and cooked the chicken curry, rice, and potatoes that they had left us. We were cold. While we waited for a pot of water to boil for hot chocolate, we put on our extra sweaters and huddled in our sleeping bags.

The storm hit with howling northwesterly winds blowing straight from Greenland, raking up lines of white breakers and gusting with snow and cold rain. We sat in our sleeping bags, chilled to the bone. The warmest place, we agreed, was actually in the well. But to get there we had to sprint through the snow and rain and would arrive thoroughly chilled and wet. The water pump did not work, so to get water we had to slide aside the lid of the well and climb down the rough stonework, sliding the lid closed once we were inside. It was not far down to the water, and filling our water bottles took little time, but the enclosed space felt quite warm, so we always delayed climbing out for a few minutes until our arms tired of clinging to the inside wall.

The storm blew itself out one afternoon a few days later, and the cloud base lifted to reveal a dense white carpet of snow on the mountains of the mainland. We decided we'd sleep on Flatey for one more night, this time in the tent, and leave next morning. That left us a fine afternoon to explore the island. We found the old school, a locked church, and a lighthouse.

Geoff left the tent first next morning. Fully encased in my sleeping bag, I could hear the metallic sound as he rummaged with the stove. Finally there was the comforting roar and the slightly sooty smell of the gasoline jet. I savored the extra minutes of comfort until, having boiled water, Geoff called to me to pass him one of the dried fish the fishermen had given us.

I reached an arm from my sleeping bag to feel for the plastic bag, and thrust my hand in to take out a fish. I felt an immediate tickling sensation on the palm of my hand and jerked my hand back out again. Wide awake now, I looked into the bag. The fish were writhing with fat maggots. I quickly screwed up the neck of the bag again and without a word handed it out to Geoff.

17

MULDOAN AND MAXWELL

Kayaking solo around Cornwall in 1975, I turned my head and saw a huge black fin cruising along right beside me. It slowly rose to a height of several feet above a dark shadow in the water. Startled and thoroughly scared, I had just begun to recover my composure, heart racing, when I saw a second large black fin following several yards behind me. Two sharks!

It took long moments to realize both fins belonged to the same shark. A giant shark! Still trailing mackerel hooks I had been towing in the hope of catching supper, I sprinted toward shore! It was only later that I learned that what I had seen was a harmless basking shark, or "muldoan." It is a plankton-sifting shark and, as a fish, is second only in size to the whale shark.

Had I known what it was, I might have stayed out there to watch it. Apparently they cruise along slowly with their mouth gaping wide, straining plankton from the water. Their propensity for cruising just below the surface led to the name "basking" shark, as they appeared to bask in the sun. But then again, alone and surprised by a fish that can equal the length and weight of a city bus, I might not have.

The following summer, exploring the western isles of Scotland with my friend Dave, we aimed our kayaks toward an island called Soay, which translated means "Sheep Island." There is more than one island with this name, presumably because sheep graze everywhere in Scotland. This particular Soay lies off the southwest coast of Skye. As we approached, Dave described to me an elusive shark-fishing factory he wanted to look for; a place we never found that year because we didn't know what to look for or exactly where. We explored the wrong side of the island. But afterwards my curiosity led me to find out more about both basking sharks and that historic shark-fishing factory.

I've revisited Skye many times since, but it was not until 2007 that I seized an opportunity to explore Soay again and follow up the story. We landed on a wrack-covered beach of angular stones and exposed rock and climbed up a short, steep cliff. There stood the ruins—a small stone house and the roofless remains of the factory—blurred by the pouring rain. These were the ruins of an industry destined never to succeed, ruins of an idea grasped at by a man desperate for a way to make a living in the wilds of Scotland, far from the memories and reminders of the Second World War.

Toward the end of World War II in 1944, Gavin Maxwell, spending his leave on his thirty-foot lobster-fishing boat, the *Gannet*, caught sight of a basking shark. Such huge creatures had in the past been harpooned by Scottish islanders from small boats for the oil in the liver. Maxwell's inclination was to shoot at it. So far into the war, he was well accustomed to death and killing, and with the light

Maxwell's shark-fishing station.

machine gun mounted at the bow for shooting drifting mines, he fired three hundred rounds into the side of the shark before the shark finally lay wallowing at the surface. As soon as his crew had made fast to the shark with a boat hook, the shark took off like Ahab's Moby Dick in "a boil of white water"; the boat hook flew from the water several hundred yards away, and they saw no more of the shark.

At the close of the war, Maxwell bought Soay Island, but by an administrative oversight he was not able to secure the lease for the commercial salmon fishing by which he had intended to make his living. Left to his imagination how he might survive there, and remembering the basking shark incident, he decided to try his hand at hunting sharks for their liver oil.

Maxwell's research revealed that very little was known about the basking shark. In fact there appears to be little more known today than when he began his commercial venture. His bald plan was to cruise the sounds, harpoon sharks, and tow them back to Soay for dissection. With this in mind he built a slipway from the bay on Soay with a bogey on rails. Each huge fish would be floated onto the bogey

This rusting boiler was used during Maxwell's shark-fishing years on Soay Island, Scotland.

and winched up the rails. The carcass would then be maneuvered onto a flat concrete platform for dissection. The liver would be removed, cut into pieces, and placed in barrels. Steam from an eight-ton boiler directed to the barrels would render the oil from the liver. The liver accounts for up to 25 percent of the body weight, and as much as 590 gallons of oil have been taken from a single shark.

Maxwell's initial plan was to try to use every part of the shark, if he could find people willing to buy the products. The meat would be cut up and placed in an icehouse under the dissecting platform. The fins and tail would be removed and placed in tanks to extract a liquid to be used in glue production. There would be a plant to produce fish meal; chopped and minced shark residue would be loaded onto trays and fed along rails into an eighty-foot tunnel through which a fan blasted hot air from the boiler furnace. The cartilage would be spread out on the grass behind the factory to dry, ready to be shipped in bulk as fertilizer.

The plan did not proceed without a hitch. In 1946, before completion of the factory, the buildings were demolished by 120-mile-per-hour winds. And then there was a problem with the icehouse. It was not sufficiently insulated to keep ice from melting, so the meat would spoil. In a change of plan, he converted the icehouse into a huge "pickling tank"—in essence an enclosed vat, or bath of brine, into which chunks of meat were dropped. But the pickling process went spectacularly wrong. The meat took on a life of its own as a sea of millions of writhing maggots hatched in the meat. He was haunted throughout that summer by concerns that he might let loose a plague of flies across the Hebrides if he opened the access hatch once the maggots morphed. In his attempts at damage control, he poured kerosene through the hatch onto the meat and later attempted to bury it all in quicklime, but the seething mass lived on underneath its top coats.

Maxwell's shark-fishing venture was short-lived. By the end of the decade it all was over. The effort and expense of dragging dead sharks back to the shore base for dissection and then finding markets for the various products was far too unwieldy. Had he harvested the livers at sea and dumped the carcasses, he might have been more successful, but there really were not enough basking sharks to support such an industry. It takes up to thirteen years for a basking shark to reach maturity, and the gestation period is three and a half years.

At thirteen years old a basking shark attains only half its potential length. Not only were sharks now difficult to find but also prices had fallen as the market for lamp oil dwindled.

The North Atlantic basking shark population has yet to make a full recovery and probably never will. The worldwide population is currently estimated to number only eighty-two hundred, and it has been found that the sharks travel vast distances. The same individuals that appear off Scotland may be spotted at other times of the year in South America or in the Caribbean, so hunting in one area will simultaneously affect the population elsewhere.

Only the ruins of the factory remain. The concrete dissecting platform, first moss coated then grass matted, now has a fringe of encroaching bracken. The steam boiler still stands, but so much metal has rusted and flaked away that rain now drips in and trickles out through countless holes. The steel rails have not seen the cleaning grind of wheels in years. Down through a brick-bordered open hatch, we peered into the stark cellar that was the icehouse before it served as the maggot breeding pit. The roofless factory now shelters from the wind a colorful collection of fish boxes and floats, nets and ladders.

We retreated from the cold summer rain and relentless midges into the stone house that predates Maxwell's interest in the island. Inside, nets and boxes and floats served us as makeshift furniture, while lobster pots stacked neatly against the outer wall barely diminished the breeze through the glassless window. We ate our lunch with steaming cups of bitter tea from stainless-steel vacuum flasks. Then, stiffly, we tracked across the yellow-brown wrack, pumped the rainwater from our kayaks, and began to warm ourselves again by paddling our kayaks back over the sea to Skye.

Gavin Maxwell's book *Harpoon at a Venture 1952* makes interesting reading that offers insight into life on a Hebridean island following World War II and the demise of the second largest fish in the world, but Maxwell is better known for his later work, including *Ring of Bright Water*, an autobiographical account of his experiences with otters. Maxwell died in 1969.

18

TREES WITH KNEES: BOATBUILDERS IN NEWFOUNDLAND

Newfoundland, England's first colony, developed as a summer fishing ground for fishermen from Europe, including Britain. For a time British fishing companies persuaded Parliament to discourage settlement on the east coast to reduce competition, and the Admiralty benefited from the pool of seamen who honed their skills on a triangular route from the U.K. to Newfoundland, to Spain and Portugal with dried and salted cod, and then home to England with wine, olive oil, cork, and fruit.

But although homesteading was forbidden for a time, timber and supplies could be gathered near the shore, and shore stations were used every season for drying and salting fish.

It is little wonder that many of the people who eventually colonized Newfoundland had shipbuilding skills, were sailors and fishermen, and passed their skills down from generation to generation.

When I was kayaking there for the first time in the late 1970s, before the cod fishery collapsed, there were huge areas set aside for drying cod, which was gutted, opened like a book, and spread flat in the sun to dry. Most of the fishing boats were built from local timber, cut from the forest. Many of the older men I talked with had spent their lives on a seasonal timetable, cutting timber in the interior every winter, sealing on the ice off Labrador and northern Newfoundland in the spring, and fishing along the coast through the summer. Somehow they also managed to build a house and raise a family!

Hiding in our tent from a rainstorm not far from the nearest village, Carmanville, we emerged at the sound of voices outside. Two men stood examining our kayaks. They had learned from a fisherman who had spotted our tent that we were camped here and had come out to find us. Our tent was not very weatherproof; Tim's sleeping bag was soaked by rain blowing under the side of the tent in the night, and both of us must have looked wet and bedraggled. When the men invited us to return with them to get warm and dry, we gladly accepted.

We were driven to the house where Ray Butt lived with his wife, Pearl. It was a small two-story wooden house that Ray's brother had built a bit farther down the hill and that he had dragged up to its present position to be in line with some other houses. Fortuitously there was a spring beneath the house, and it turned out to be the only water supply in the area that never dried up in summer.

It felt good to be under a roof, and no sooner had we arrived than Pearl began frying a lunch of salmon for us. While she cooked, Ray explained he had built several of the other houses nearby and that he also built wooden boats. "Of course you'll stay a few days till the weather clears?" It was not difficult to accept their warm invitation.

Ray enthused about his boats and later proudly rowed us in a small wooden dory to the twenty-six-foot-long slender sailboat he

Boatbuilding on the beach in Newfoundland, 1978.

had also built himself. He started up the twelve-horsepower engine and took us farther from shore, into the wind and tide until after every leap into the air, the bow would pitch so deep into the next wave that water deluged over our heads. Then we turned, the boat rolling crazily as we took the sea from the beam, and headed back. It was a short and damp run! It was clear that Ray loved boats, and he delighted in telling us tales of his childhood aboard various boats in the area and of the sailing schooners that used to trade along the coast when he was younger.

Then we got to talking about whales. We'd seen a lot already during our trip. Ray told us of a bay not far from here with more than one hundred whales in it. In the past the whales would have been killed to prevent damage to the nets, but now that a government ban protected the whales, the fishermen were experiencing a lot of expensive damage to the nets. "There are sharks too," he added. "There was a boat capsized near here, with two men clinging to it, and moments later one got his leg bitten off." I made a mental note to keep my toes out of the water.

Ray explained that his next project was to build a long-liner, but he needed some timber. The straight logs for the planking and the ribs he could cut in winter, along with firewood, dragging it over the snow behind his snowmobile to store by his beachfront sawmill. It could season there till he needed it. For a two-dollar permit he could cut twelve cords of wood, for firewood or for building. A cord is the stacked volume of timber, four feet by four feet by eight feet. With the purchase of an additional special permit, he is allowed to cut the angled timbers he also needs to build a boat. Those are more difficult to find and bring home. Newfoundland is a land of conifer forest, so angled boughs like the ones the British once used to cut from their oak forests are simply not available. Instead such timbers must be located and cut from the base of a tree, where a large enough root projects out at the required angle. In winter that part of the tree is buried under snow, so these timbers must be cut in summer and carried out of the forest by hand. Ray suffered from a bad back, so he could not carry the timbers himself.

Of course we offered our services, and when the weather finally cleared, we climbed into his pickup truck. Ray got ready. Driving a distance from town, Ray turned off the highway and drove a few hundred yards into the forest along a small track. (The government doesn't allow people to cut timber within one hundred yards of the highway.) Soon we found ourselves following at his heels into the forest, where he blazed a trail by chipping bark from an occasional tree so we could find our way back out. It was a windy day, but in the forest, where the trees cut the breeze, mosquitoes gathered around us in hordes, whining around our ears and settling on our exposed arms and faces.

Then we heard a sound like an electric shaver approaching and finally spotted the small radio-controlled helicopter approaching fast! That's not entirely accurate: The "helicopter" turned out to be a copper-eyed stout, named for its stout size no doubt and its copper-colored eyes. I swear it was the size of a small bird when I looked down as it perched on my hand and stared back at me. Then I felt the sensation of a blunt nail being driven into my hand and I was spurred into action. I whacked at it with my other hand and felt a certain revengeful satisfaction when it fell with a damp thud into the moss at my feet. Nursing my wounded hand I crouched down to look more closely at this vicious creature. Yes, it truly did have huge bulging coppery eyes, but it also had a stout proboscis with which it had punctured my hand. The beast was large enough to have escaped a horror movie. And horror movie–like, it had the ability to come back to life after a blow that would have killed a bear. It twitched, shook itself, and moments later launched into the air again. Buzzing like an angry chainsaw, it began circling my head. My arms windmilled wildly, and it was all I could do to stop myself from running! "Where's that stiff upper lip, Foster?" I demanded reproachfully. "Just above this loose flabby chin," I heard myself quiver.

If the stouts were about, at least we could hear them coming, and we could hear them circling. But as with World War II doodlebugs, the tension began whenever the noise suddenly stopped. There would be just enough time to brush every reachable part of my body in an attempt to dislodge the creature if indeed it had landed on me before the stab wound reached through my T-shirt into the middle of my back—the part I hadn't reached. Now I knew why Ray had climbed into a sturdy boiler suit before entering the forest.

We examined a number of possible trees before Ray found one he considered suitable and pointed out to us what he had been looking for. Firing up his chainsaw, he bent to the task of carving out the piece he needed. Then pulling it aside he trimmed it a little to make it lighter to carry. It was an L-shaped slab of wood about four feet tall by three feet long and eight inches thick. It stood beside the now-fallen fifty-foot spruce tree that had the misfortune to have once owned a "knee." "What about the rest of the tree?" I asked. Ray shrugged and said he'd probably return with his snowmobile in the winter to collect it.

Leaving the timber where it stood, Ray strode away, checking tree after tree until he found another, slightly larger, tree that looked good. Scraping away the blueberry undergrowth around the root with his ax, he eyed it up for size before once again grabbing the toggle at the end of the starting cord on his chainsaw and tugging the engine into action. Soon he had his second timber. That was enough for now, he announced. We could start carrying them back to the pickup. Grabbing one end each, Tim and I heaved the first piece up between us, surprised at how heavy it was. Then, like a four-legged pantomime horse, we stumbled from tree root to mossy man-trap, stirring the mosquitoes and stouts from the undergrowth as we went. Now we knew how Ray got his bad back!

19

WHEN DEAD SHARKS HAVE THE LAST WORD

I was exploring a section of coast in northwestern Iceland with a group of teenagers from Cambridge, England. Several days into the trip, in late afternoon, we cruised into a short fjord toward a shallow basin at the end. To the north side was a house, and on a spit that crimped the south side of the bay was a second house, with outbuildings. A narrow road ran along the north shore to follow a beach that almost separated the bay from a tidal lagoon beyond. A bridge crossed from the beach to the south shore. We headed under the bridge up the river that connected the lagoon with the fjord and chose a place to land and camp.

While everyone else set up their tents, I paddled a little offshore and dropped a line. A fish would be good for dinner, if I could catch one. As I drifted and jigged my line, I wondered what was causing a disagreeable smell. With only one house on this side of the fjord, it smelled more pungent than a sewer outlet, especially one from a solitary house. Perhaps something had died. I jigged the line for a while longer but landed empty-handed.

As we sat in the evening, two burly men and three boys approached from the nearer house. Reaching the river, the boys cast lines from the bridge with fishing rods. The men continued walking till they reached us. "Did you have any success fishing?" one asked after our initial greetings. "Nothing," I admitted. The boys had now joined us. "You can borrow these," they offered, handing me their rods. "We can pick them up later!"

The men said they were from Reykjavik; brothers taking time with their sons at what had been their parents' home. Both men were truck drivers, and although Reykjavik was the best place to get work, they liked to come back to the old farm whenever they could.

They strode off to where a small boat was hauled up on the shore of the lagoon. Soon the boat left shore, one man rowing, the other feeding out a long net from the stern. Completing a semicircle, they then hauled the net to shore from both ends. Apparently it was a more-assured way of catching fish than with a rod and line. The fish I had watched from the bridge were still there, but the Icelanders returned carrying a bucket of gleaming sea trout. They handed me four or five. Promising there would more for everyone in the morning, they turned homeward.

It was still dark when the sharp sound of a car pulling up abruptly on the gravel road woke me. Doors slammed, and there were loud voices. It was the Icelanders back again. I struggled from the tent to greet them. "How many fish would you like?" they asked. "We have enough for everybody!"

We stood chatting in the wet grass until one man offered, "Come back to the house for coffee with us!" So we followed them around the shore to their house. But just as we were about to be shown inside,

The Icelandic brothers pose with a hunk of rotten shark meat before we go inside to sample it.

one of the brothers stopped abruptly, turned on his heel, and said, "Wait a minute! Before we have coffee we must have *hákarl*!

I had no idea what he was talking about but followed as he led us quickly to one of the outbuildings above the beach. The hut walls were made of vertical wooden slats to let the breeze blow through, and the interior was protected from rain by a tidy roof. He flung the door wide, revealing rows and rows of chunks of creamy-yellow meat, some hanging on loops of green string, others from steel meat hooks. "Shark meat," he explained. Each piece was about a foot in length by about eight inches, with a layer of coarse black sharkskin on the back. There was a rotting stench. Now I knew the source of that disgusting smell I had noticed on the water.

He explained that the shark was left buried in the beach for six months then dug up and the pieces hung to air and dry for up to another six months. They had buried this shark last October, and it had been hanging for four months.

He showed us the rectangular bordered areas where they bury the sharks. The boards indicate where the sharks are buried but have no lid. A pool of greenish water had gathered over one enclosure, but he didn't seem to worry about that. I assumed it would be impossible to spoil the meat more.

He lifted down one heavy amber chunk in his huge hand, took a knife in his other hand, and sliced off a large piece. With a big grin he thrust the fresh-cut surface to my face for me to appreciate. The intense putrid odor hit me with an immediate feeling of nausea. He laughed and led us back to the house—and the kitchen.

Here he made a number of deft cuts through the creamy flesh as far as the skin, creating small cubes still hanging to the skin. Now, before coffee, he encouraged us to try an appetizer.

Backing down was not an option. I stepped forward to take the first piece and popped it straight into my mouth. If I was going to vomit, I would get it over with! However, to my intense relief, the flavor was more akin to that of an overripe Camembert cheese than what I was led to expect by the odor of the rotten meat. It melted away in my mouth like a marshmallow but left a wad of gristle. This I wrestled vainly with, unable to swallow it or reduce its bulk and unable to speak with it there. In growing panic I watched for any indication of what one could politely do under the circumstances. Nobody else seemed to have the same problem, although truthfully not everyone managed to get the morsel past his nose. I finally gagged the gristle down, feeling it squeeze down my neck with a mixture of apprehension and relief. Never was coffee more urgently needed!

Greenland Shark

The big chunks of meat suggest that the shark must have been huge. In fact it is the Greenland shark that is used for *hákarl*, and they grow to more than twenty feet in length. Left alone they can live for up to two hundred years. They are inedible when the meat is fresh, as they contain too much uric acid, which accounts for the strong smell and taste of ammonia. The meat also contains the toxin trimethylamine oxide, which breaks down into trimethylamine. This chemical is not only poisonous but also causes the repulsive odor people associate with such things as fish going bad, some infections, and bad breath. When "rotted" and dried, the meat becomes edible and it is often served in Iceland with an aperitif—typically Brennivín, a popular brand of Icelandic schnapps also known as "black death."

PLACES

Precious are moments spent in reflection—time taken to assimilate the sounds and scenes, to taste a place.

20

SEARCHING FOR MERMAIDS' TEARS

I paddle automatically, feeling the load in my kayak steady its action on the water, savoring the crisp air. I'm back in Scotland. I'm back among the rocks and the islands of the west coast. I am among friends too: Barbara, Evelyn, and Ed. We are an international team: English, Dutch, and German. We cross toward Mull, feeling the speed and motion of the water change as it focuses toward the narrows. In places close to here, the islands concentrate the tidal flow into jets that run to eight and a half knots. We'll be there later in the trip. We begin near Oban, the fishing port on the mainland at the end of the "Road to the Isles."

The Sound of Mull weaves a watery channel north from Oban. Fort William lies down the loch to the east. There's always a sheltered alternative should the weather break. We snake north, running the tide through extensive but harmless rips, watching the black backs of porpoises surface silently in the chop. This for me is the lead-in, the warm-up, a chance to ponder the history of the ruins, such as that of the stark lookout, Duart Castle, that we pass by.

Near the north end of the Sound of Mull, Tobermory lies on our left—a steep town of pink, dark blue, and yellow houses rising from the reflections beneath a slipway. The distillery here has produced single malt scotch whisky since 1798. Giant copper onions distill what in time will be imprisoned as amber nectar in broad-corked bottles.

The wind has shifted and I can smell a blend of seaweed, windblown salt, and seabirds. Gone is that musty rankness of the estuary, the fine mud smells, the still water and salt marsh. The sea is on the move in the air. Soon I will feel its surface muscling gently beneath me. The wind on the move, however, is not necessarily a good sign. I scan the sky for more clues to the change.

The Treshnish Islands

By the time we cross to the Treshnish Islands, the wind is blowing hard. We paddle close together, a tight group of bright kayaks. Rainsqualls run across our line of sight—dark staining curtains that are more imposing than the islands, even Mull, lying behind them. Without thinking, I keep direction by the most prominent landmarks but find myself straying as the walls of rain move. I rebuke myself and steer by compass.

The Treshnish are a row of green islets laid out in a finger toward the south, culminating in the enigmatic Dutchman's Cap. With Netherlanders in our party, we must visit this outlying island, but for the moment our target is Lunga, "Long Island." We thread past the first rocks and islands in the group. There are castles on two adjacent rocks. Neither turns out to be impressive to look at. The builders had been subtle. Each gully that could lead up the cliffs is headed off near the summit by cunningly hidden walls constructed of boulders. Stand on the top and there is no sign of the defenses, just a tall sea of grass shot through with flowers. My wet leggings become festooned with the hinged anthers from the grasses.

Barbara and Evelyn probe their kayaks quietly between the rounded rocks in the midst of the island group, sheltered from the wind. Sand is visible way down below. Seals have hauled out on the rocks. There are seals in droves around every corner. Rounded heads appear from the water then vanish with a splash.

We come to land on a finger of shingle at a "corner" of Lunga. This can be a good place to camp. There is some flat grass nearby, although there's a beach on the other side of the rocky point that hoards seaweed, dead seaweed by the truckload! Besides, I know the position of a hidden well that will provide us with sweet water.

Lunga is a favorite island of mine. I could spend a whole summer here just watching birds. To begin with there are puffins (*Fratercula arctica*). They land on the cliff edge within a couple of feet of you when you lie there on the short grass. Then they turn and give you what could be construed as a disapproving look from mournful painted eyes—and walk toward you! The cliff edge is peppered with puffin burrows. Birds pop in and out incessantly. Then there's the sea stack separated by a narrow chasm from the cliff. The side of the stack facing the cliff is occupied by vast numbers of guillemots, razorbills, shags, and, dizzily below on the steepest part of the cliff, kittiwakes. The clamor from the birds drowns out even the sound of the sea thundering through the chasm below.

Suddenly awake in the night, I hear a haunting cry—the wail of a shearwater flying past my tent. I slip outside and listen as more fly past. I've not heard them here before, so I creep across the island and up onto the cliff, ultimately reaching the top of the island. I still cannot discover if these birds nest here or are just passing over, but with so many rabbits burrowing into the turf, the conditions must be ideal for shearwaters. As I make my way back, stumbling down the steep path, I catch the gentle *churring* noise of storm petrels in a dry stone wall. It's a comforting sound, almost like purring, emanating from every crevice, from beneath every stone.

Dutchman's Cap

We leave our tents behind on Lunga and head for Dutchman's Cap. On the way we cannot resist the challenge of the narrow route behind the bird stack. I enter first, gingerly, for the swell breaks here and there over boulders that sometimes stick their sharp heads through the surface. The echo of screeching kittiwakes rises frenetically above the hubbub of grunting guillemots. It is an incessant, reverberating noise. I time my turn around the end of the rock with care and surf for a moment toward the exit, tense until I am in deeper water once more.

At the end of Lunga we discover the tide is running in an unexpected direction. Sometimes the tidal information doesn't tally with what you observe from the water. Ahead is Dutchman's Cap, the shape of a round-topped, broad-brimmed hat of a style I have only seen in paintings by artists such as Brueghel.

We land carefully from deep water in a gully onto an awkward ledge some feet above our heads, lifting the kayaks up onto precarious perches out of reach of the rising tide. The next stage is a climb. The rancid rock is slimy from passing birds, with patches of vegetation clinging on. Most of the plants are dark green with thick, tough, shiny leaves splattered white with birdlime. One at a time we scramble over the top onto a huge spongy mattress of dense grass. Ruins of buildings ride like ships on waves as gusts of wind make a sea of the meadow. Nothing grazes here, so the turf is deep enough to bounce on. Out of a sense of duty, we scale the summit, but the view from the crown is mostly obscured. Yet in the distance we glimpse Staffa.

Organ Pipes

Staffa is a strange island. In 1832 the German composer Felix Mendelssohn was inspired by a visit to Staffa to write his concert overture "The Hebrides." The feature that inspired him was Fingal's Cave, an organ-pipe cave worn in among the polygonal basalt columns. It's hard to accept at first sight that these regular blocks are not man-made. From a well-rounded base of smooth rock, the basalt intrusion manifests itself on the south end as a wall of dark gray rods of rock resembling baleen in the open mouth of a whale. Above, another layer of columns blossoms out in all directions like garlic from a press.

We stop at Staffa on our way to Iona. I have only paddled into Fingal's Cave a few times, and only once to the very end. A swell thunders across the smooth, rounded rock at the base of the cliff. At the cave entrance there is a constant crash, slap, and a rain of spray as the waves buffet and rebound from the rows of dark pillars.

Mermaids' Tears

While Staffa is a part of an extensive dark basalt intrusion that almost caught the corner of Iona as it spread from Northern Ireland, Iona is composed of different stone. In the evening the rounded granite glows with rosy warmth. Beneath our hulls lie pale, sandy shallows— silver ripples against jade, turquoise, and aquamarine. My eyes are screwed tight against the brightness but captivated by the rich color and the dancing patterns. Mesmerized and cruising fast, I slam into a barely covered rock. Back to Earth! I reverse off the rock, grimacing at the shriek of tortured fiberglass. The glare is intense. I check my hull when we reach the beach close to the Iona ferry ramp and Iona Abbey. At least my kayak is less damaged than the solid structure of the centuries-old abbey that stands nearby!

It is the massive stone Celtic crosses that impress me most when I visit the abbey. Slabs of stone are carved with sailing ships, surrounded by stone knot-work. Yes, the crosses, and the tomb that is carved from Iona marble, its alabaster translucence studded with glowing green globules. It is said that the translucent green-and-yellow gems can be found on one particular beach on the island, not far from the abandoned marble quarry. Sea-worn, these pretty pebbles are said to protect the wearer from drowning. We decide to seek out these "mermaids' tears."

The sea off the western coast of Iona is almost always a little or a lot rougher than might be expected given the general conditions elsewhere. I'm not sure why that is, but it provides us with some excitement as we weave between the stacks and play the swells that peak over submerged rocks. There are some really inviting sandy surf beaches, but we pass these by; we are seeking a pebble beach. Finally we find it and land through waves laden with minced seaweed. This is the stuff that clings to clothing and kayaks for weeks if once left to dry. We fan out across the beach, faces to the ground as we scour the pebbles for stones that almost resemble fragments of misty-green

The sea washes around the basalt formations of Staffa Island.

sea-tumbled bottle glass. I hear the excitement mount as one person finds a gem, then another.

Bay of Eagles

Eagles fascinate me. In British Columbia there is a bald eagle on every dead tree branch, but golden eagles in Scotland are scarce enough for them to make you stop and gawp. There's a cove on the south coast of Mull with a rough pebble beach that rates as one of the least-inspiring stopping places. I first used this isolated bay as a shelter when the weather forecast suggested all the nearby alternatives might be untenable. As we stood by our kayaks that time, an eagle sailed along the cliff edge nearby, majestically hanging on a breath of wind until a diminutive sparrow hawk fretted around it, making the golden bird twist a ragged wing tip and circle up into the clouds, a fading speck.

We stayed that night because of the eagle, despite the sea-delivered rubbish that littered both the beach and the small valley beyond. Plastic: endless bright plastic stilling the tiny streams into stagnant ruts. A friend suggested we cleaned up the beach. He lit a fire. We found plastic fish boxes and filled them time and again, heaving each load onto the pluming fire. Molten plastic ran alight like lava as dense black smoke billowed. Then the eagle returned, sailing in the gloom along the cliff edge again. Since then I've always stopped at this stony beach, and I always see the eagles. This time we find the valley is relatively clean. I suggest a concerted effort, and the others pitch in. By midnight the valley is pristine and its sparkling streams run unfettered.

We hit rain. Scotland can be like this. Evelyn is cursing the wind that is making her kayak difficult to handle, but she crosses the awkward sea with stubborn energy that gets her to the Garvellachs anyway. The name "Garvellachs" means "rocky islets," and at first glance they are prickly rocks. Yet, like Iona, this place was home to early holy men, who built first a group of domed beehive-shaped monastic cells and later a monastery, all from the stone they found.

There is warmth about the southern Garvellach Island, Eileach an Naoimh, that gives me peace, despite the fact that it stares across to Scarba and Jura. For the gap between Scarba and Jura is held in awe by mariners, including sea paddlers. The planning skill required to time a passage through that channel at precisely the right time to avoid the heavy overfalls is matched by the paddling skill required if you get the timing wrong. Not that Corryvreckan is ever still, or its water easy. There are almost always churning white breakers and swirling vortices somewhere in the strait, even when the tide is supposedly slack.

We camp at the head of a small bay, inside the mouth of Corryvreckan on the Jura shore. It is a classic place to camp, looking out toward the summit of Scarba across the white-ripped entrance to Corryvreckan. It's a sandy beach, with a clear-running stream and a patch of golf course–flat grass on which to set the tents below a slope of dense bracken. From the sky comes the haunting cry of a buzzard circling in search of carrion.

Toward the Whirlpool

We launch into the sheltered water of the bay, hanging on clear water above the sandy bottom. It is a spring tide, and by now the tidal stream is approaching its peak rate of about eight and a half knots. We are going in the "easy" direction this time. The overfalls are usually less severe when running west to east. This could be a straightforward run for once. We group loosely, chatting as we approach the gap between the islet of Eilean Beag and the rocky, gull-white shore of Jura. It is only now that our speed is apparent. We are still warming up, not paddling at full strength, yet we are being hauled toward the narrowing gap. Sheets of smooth, gray water slope visibly downhill. Boils erupt. Eddies swirl and catch Ed in a sudden spin, taking him sideways toward a diagonally breaking wave that seems to roll and roll without moving. We point our kayaks toward the north and the coast of Scarba and begin to paddle hard.

The fast tidal stream in the Gulf of Corryvreckan is caused by the barrier of islands that runs roughly northeast and southwest, causing the coastal run of tide to funnel and accelerate through the many narrow gaps. Corryvreckan is notorious for the eddy line just south of Scarba. On the flood tide an eddy forms, running eastward at about eight knots, bordering the main stream flowing in almost the opposite direction at about eight and a half knots. The eddy line, not surprisingly, sets up some fierce vortices. At one point, at the top end of the eddy, there is an underwater pinnacle that directs the current into a vortex called The Hag, about which there are many legends, and into which I care not to explore. I look across toward that spot, but the feature only forms during the flood tide.

The water seethes and churns noisily. A whirlpool develops at my side, keeping pace with me as I paddle. The greenish depth gurgles and bubbles with froth that rolls and rolls and rolls—and still remains alongside. I glance around to see two kayaks engaged in a dance together, each backing or pulling forward, sweeping to try to get back on course but neither achieving anything, locked by the whim of the rotating water.

We are through, but the water still churns around us. The vista rapidly widens to reveal Shuna and Luing, the islets in the Sound of Jura. We are paddling north; the current is taking us to the southeast. We approach a string of islets and bounce through a tidal rapid at the northern end of Reisa an t'Struith to spin one after the other into the eddy behind. Sloping slabs of rock tempt us ashore with sun and shelter from the breeze, but some ragged goats make us hesitate. But it's a good time to take lunch while we wait for the tide to turn. Wildflowers blossom in the crevices in the rocks. Sun-crisped lichens crackle when we sit.

The Race of the Grey Dogs

We discuss Corryvreckan while we drift north. There's a fresh westerly breeze now, so I try to discourage the others from a return trip. I persuade them to take the shorter "Race of the Grey Dogs" at the north end of Scarba instead, where a tiny channel runs between Scarba and Luing. The speed of the tide will be similar to Corryvreckan—about eight and a half knots—but the race is more compact and more confined, with forgiving eddies.

The entrance is innocuous: A small island sits midchannel and with land enclosing the view is lakelike. The sound of pouring water in the narrow confines is reassuringly like a river. But the race itself is hidden around an S-bend, hidden until it's too late to change your mind. We speed around the corner into sight of steep walls of leaping water. Crests burst apart with resounding power and leap together in clapotis. I grin around at the others, hoping this rapid will satisfy their yearning for adrenaline. Then we are in it! Now there is no staying dry. I am buffeted by breakers and, for a while, cannot see anyone else. I fret lest anyone is having trouble. Then I spot Ed close behind me as I run the steeper waves to the right. He appears to be in control. I glimpse Barbara and Evelyn together over to my left, closer to the far eddy line. They will have to cross the main race to reach the northern eddy, but they look fine.

The walls of water are packed so tightly one behind the other that my kayak rears skyward from one wave then plunges deep into the base of the next. I am being pounded! The rapids are as punishing as Corryvreckan but nowhere near as long. On a crest, I wave a "Come over here" to Barbara and Evelyn. Then I drop and turn and slice a wave across the current toward the northern eddy. The spray flies from my blade as I hold my kayak on course on the wave, then the wave dissipates and I cruise into the eddy. Ed slides in behind me, a big grin on his face. Several minutes later Evelyn and Barbara appear, bouncing across the waves toward us. We regroup. The experience was what everyone had been after.

Belnahua

We drift north, the Garvellachs to our left, the tide helping us along. Belnahua lies three miles north of the Grey Dogs, and to get to it requires a little crafty positioning. Tidal streams of up to seven knots cross in various directions to render preplanning an exact route futile; it is one of my favorite "seat-of-the-pants" routes. I seek transit points and read the water to identify the fastest stream in the best direction, avoiding countereddies. We dawdle on. It's great to cover so much distance with so little effort, and it's a personal challenge to try to hit the island where the water parts around it. It takes all my attention to keep my kayak from being taken either left or right around the island. I begin to drift sideways left and correct quickly. The tide is so strong I have to sprint the last few yards, ferry-gliding to hit the island near my target but nevertheless downstream of it. I look ruefully at the missing yards that I failed to make and wonder when I'll get another chance to try.

Belnahua is a mixture of man-made and natural history. Here a slate quarry carved away the heart of the island, replacing the gold-flecked, steely slate with a pool of aquamarine that is deeper than the island itself. Otters leave their spraints on little mounds of slate sand around its edge and flatten paths around the protective rampart walls that hold the storms from the workings. The jagged-tooth skyline of the island is also man-made, although nature has assisted in the removal of the roofs and the lowering of the walls of these quarry workers' cottages. A knee-deep eiderdown of soft springy grasses surrounds them now, ungrazed and dotted with the white droppings of the gulls and fulmars that nest beside the walls. Fluffy chicks bumble around, while anxious parents swoop and chide. Elder trees have sprung up in the confines of the house walls and, with the nettles, help create an almost impenetrable barrier.

The quarry workings used to be pumped to keep them dry. We discover the remains of the massive boilers and the pumps and drainage ducts. Stooping through one underground duct, I recognize the footprints of otter but fail to figure out how this maze of ducts and pipes once operated. Outside, the ocean swirls past the island at seven knots, dividing at the bow of the island and pushing onward toward Seil and Kerrera and farther to Oban.

Lazy Morning

I wake to the scent of the white flowers of sea campion and the musical sound of slates sliding and scattering as Ed makes his clattering way along the beach. I emerge from my tent, set my stove on one flat slab of slate, and seat myself comfortably on another. The dark stone is already hot from the sun. Seals stretch inquisitively from the water as the tide sweeps them by. My view is of islands. A couple of yachts drift under white sails toward Luing. The Garvellachs stand steep and forbidding, with the thousand-foot-high cliffs of Mull beyond to the right. The sea is gleaming, metallic blue-gray, hurting my eyes with its brightness. And time? Well, the time just sort of lingers.

21

KAYAKING BELOW SEA LEVEL

John draws a map with his finger in the dust of the ferry sign, "Capital D for Delft." He stabs near the top of the D. "We are here in the north. Turn right from this canal when you've gone a little way, and all the turnings lead into town."

It's time to leave my Dutch friend and slide the white Legend from the grass to the dark water. A tugboat muscles a large barge past carrying a dozen containers toward The Hague. The water bounces, rushing into the vegetation on the bank. An angler catapults live maggots, white into the waves. He has set his tent beside the canal, by the cycle path. There are more maggoty fishers ahead, lines strung like spider webs to snag the unwary boater.

I'm keen to quit this water road and explore the "delfts," or drainage channels, within the city. I lie flat on my deck to squeeze beneath a low bridge and exit the main canal. This reminds me of ducking into a low sea cave. Beyond this arch is a completely different world: a narrow canal, a houseboat to the left—nothing more than a clapboard box in pale, unpainted planks. To the right a brick wall rises from the water to white-painted iron railings. A row of green trees separates the narrow road from the water, and the gabled brick houses stand side by side by side. Geraniums sprout out from pots and window boxes.

It is a gentle cruise into town. Church bells ring in the still air. People sit in the sun outside a cafe drinking beer. I enter a damp tunnel and discover a side tunnel. My paddle strokes sound crisp in here. I am alone in this private space. A few kayakers suddenly appear and pass me, their faces alert in this underground world. I greet them, noting their jeans and shirts splashed with water. "Hi!" I cannot understand their comments in Dutch.

I take a corner into a ribbon of water between the street and a wall of buildings. Through windows a couple of feet above the water, there's a fleeting view of washing hung up to dry, a sink full of dirty plates, and a man wearing only underpants in a dim hallway. The ribbon runs to a low bridge that it's just possible to limbo beneath. But then there's a dead end. I am behind the tourist office by the square. The channel is too narrow for me to turn around. To climb out to turn around would be too awkward. I reverse out, smelling drying laundry and garlic cooking as I pass the windows beside the water.

It's just possible to turn around immediately beyond the low bridge, hemmed in by brick walls. One mistake and this happy crowd will hear the crash of fiberglass against ancient baked clay. It's the 750th anniversary of this town. This land has been sinking over the years. All these waterways are below sea level—more than fourteen feet below sea level. If it weren't for the dikes and canals, I would be paddling on salt water, on the sea. The leaning church tower would stand in water. It has a strange lean. The tower slopes one way, but the top angles the other way. Why? One local told me it was built on cowhides to prevent the building from sinking into the soft earth. But it sank a little toward the canal anyway while building was in progress, so the architect made a few adjustments to the top section to balance

Barges along the canal, bright with geraniums, offer cool beer.

it. It is the oldest church in Delft: Built in 1246, it still stands beside the old canal. The architect's adjustment must have been about right!

The waterway widens and there are white water-lily flowers, great green floating leaves and green beer cans. There are also bottles and bikes. Seems there are only the white railings around the canals to prevent bikes from ending up in the water. A distorted wheel hangs by a chain locked to the railing. What happened to the rest of the bike? When the town decided to dredge the narrow canals so that tour boats could operate, they hauled more than two thousand bicycles out of the mud.

My plan had been to stop for coffee at the cafe on the barge, the one with blue umbrellas, but it is closed. It's Sunday. I suppose I could find another, but I'd hoped to sit in the sun and let my damp clothes dry. Besides, I like that cafe. It sits across from an elegant house beside tall reedlike iron railings. This was once the home of Antonie van Leeuwenhoek, the man who observed the magnifying power of a drop of water and went on to construct the first microscope. We owe our modern lenses to Leeuwenhoek's initial observations.

Close by is a tunnel. BOTERBRUG says the sign. I pass into cool darkness. The sound of my paddle strokes echo a little. I feel pleasantly alone here, surrounded by brick, moving toward the circle of light that is the exit. Butter Bridge is the widest bridge in town at one hundred yards from side to side—or a tunnel a hundred yards long, depending on your viewpoint. This structure of tiny clay bricks, more than four hundred years old, was built to accommodate the flat-bottomed barges that carried butter. In the heat of summer, the barges were tied up under the bridge to keep the butter cool. Nearby were the old weigh-house and the butter market.

The low arch makes for a cambered street above that scarcely hints at the canal beneath, or of me on the canal. I pause in this man-made cave to savor a moment's peace away from the clamor of the streets that line the canals. Turning into the bustle and sunshine once more, I drift again, this time to view a series of arched bridges, one beneath another, and a bridge inside that one, and so on until the bridges become very small in the distance. It's a city of echoes. Each canal seems to echo the previous, and each intricate rooftop gable that reaches in steps and curves—tight, tall, and narrow—is reminiscent of another in another street.

I come upon a barge moored against a wall: a black wooden hull topped with white umbrellas and boxes of bright red geraniums. It offers extra seating for a pub. I wouldn't mind a pint of the locally brewed blond beer, sharp and refreshing with a slice of lemon. As the canal system was extended from the thirteenth century onward, Delft was perfectly positioned as a center for import and export. In particular, it was the production and export of butter, cloth, woven carpets, and Delft beer that brought prosperity to the town. Almost two hundred breweries were built beside these canals!

A duck swims beneath a brick arch. There's the clatter of a bicycle chain and the noise of tires on cobbles. I turn. The young woman cycling the road beside the canal grins at me. She has a nice face. I smile back. Her long fair hair drifts out behind her. She leans the corner and pedals up and over the arch of the bridge then turns to freewheel down the cobbled street, weaving between the pedestrians. My eyes follow her progress down the road beside the canal, her long legs and straight back soon lost behind the pollarded lime trees. As I paddle on, a splash of water trickles down my shoulder. It feels good.

At Witches' Water, a window box overflowing with brilliant red geraniums overhangs the river from a house where an artist once struggled to make a living and finally died. Upon his death his paintings soared in price. At this corner, behind the church, women suspected of being witches were thrown into the water. If they were able to swim, they were declared to be witches and were dragged into the square and burned to death, along with any daughters they had. If they were unable to swim, the population watched them drown, whereupon they were declared innocent. Are those dark fingers that now grasp toward the surface really waterweed?

Near the north end of town once more, I find my low bridge by the houseboat and lie flat against my deck to squeeze under. I'm back on the main canal. The charm of the old city has suddenly vanished. An oarsman passes me: Pull and surge, pause to reposition, pull and surge. Another is approaching in a long, slender scull, oars scooping the water.

There is a small canal on my left, threading between some trees and a factory. Houseboats sit beneath the trees, moored alongside the bank with more space than most of the houses on land. The factory gates are closed. Quiet. Ducks scoot out from beside the boats. Here I come to another dead end and drift backward, my kayak finally stopping among the water-lilies. Beer cans begin to rock as my wake spreads slowly out. I stretch, arching across the back deck. There's a sweet smell of flowers. Above me is blue sky—blue sky with just a couple of clouds going nowhere, like me.

Some Delft History

"Delft" means a "dug" waterway, or canal. The old delft from which the present town takes its name is thought to have been dug in 1100, when the town supposedly grew up around a castle built after the capture of Holland in 1070. Newer delfts were dug parallel to the old one, with connecting channels between. The town received municipal rights from Duke William the Second in 1246.

Like many medieval towns, Delft was periodically hit by disasters. A major fire in 1536 destroyed all but the stone buildings in two-thirds of the town; a year later the population suffered badly from the plague. In 1654 the gunpowder in the town's artillery depot blew up. At that time Delft was one of only seven armament suppliers in Holland, and the demand for munitions was great, with shipping companies defending themselves against the Spanish Armada on the one hand and on the other pursuing a lucrative trade in piracy against the English and French. The fire destroyed part of the town, so after that the munitions factory was repositioned a little farther away.

Delft is probably best known for its pottery: "Delft Blue" with its distinctive blue glaze on white, frequently depicting scenes of sailing barges, windmills, and girls in winged hats and clogs.

Winter temperatures often cause many of the canals to freeze. Residents wearing ice skates cruise above fish frozen in the transparent layers. Possible thin ice beneath bridges and in tunnels is all that might deter wintertime exploration on foot where I cruised by kayak.

22

SUMMERTIME IN SWEDEN

Grasshoppers spring before my feet from the parched grass. As the evening flies gather, the predatory dragonflies crackle past, sometimes crashing against the windows behind me. A bat darts across the luminescence of the sky, excited wing beats living a tempo much accelerated from our lazy, wine-sipping evening. I am in Sweden, on the deck outside the forest home of artist Håkan Jernehov and his wife, Lena. The apricot scent of newly gathered chanterelles mingles with the deep red wine on the table here and the penetrating tang of pine resin from the surrounding trees.

"Rock-hopping": Håkan points out this phrase familiar to me and printed in English in the text of the Swedish newspaper. The article explains what the term means and announces that the event of the following week will be the first of its kind in Sweden—that's if this beautiful, sunny, calm weather will allow us some waves! But first we will explore the west coast islands near Mollösund, close to Sweden's border with Norway: a social paddle before the more serious stuff.

Sweden here is woodland, fields of golden-ripe barley and wheat, wooden farmsteads painted rust red, fine yellowing grasses on parched land and then smooth slopes of rock. The coast here is naked, bare rock. It is here that the work of the ice sheet that flattened this land becomes apparent. Sensuous curves in pink granite are combed with fine grooves, all running in the same direction. As the ice moved, thousands of pebbles and boulders beneath its weight ground against the bedrock, smoothing and grooving it. In the sheltered shallow waters of the innermost bays, marshes are slowly taking hold and channels are narrowing.

We launch into shallow water, our laden kayaks sucking at the muddy bottom until we reach a deeper channel. We pass a village of red-brown buildings, fishing huts spidering out over the water on wooden pilings, boats tethered and floating as though ready at a moment's notice to be away, off to the islands. We are still in sight when a handful of people laugh into one rocking boat, start the outboard motor, and follow us, easy as a car to a road with no traffic. Their laughter ripples across the still water like voices in a dream.

The island chain here on the west coast is quite narrow. A few miles of paddling and we reach one of the outer isles, sheltered by the archipelago on one side and exposed to swell on the other. The maze of islands is so dense it is easy to understand why nobody knows how many there are. How do you count islands anyway? Some of these are quite large, some small enough to be holms and skerries, but what of the smaller rocks? Who chooses what to call an island? It's like looking at a map in a newspaper and then scrutinizing the map under a magnifying glass; thousands of dots appear. The closer you focus on this island chain, the more islands there seem to be.

We weave between rocks with sunlit, rippled sand several feet below us. Thin blond grasses haze the contours of the islands between the flowing slabs of rosy granite. We pass sunbathers, lizardlike on the stored heat of the rock, perfect harmony of curves on curves; naked bodies on bare Swedish rock, blond hair and fair grasses. Most Swedes care for their land as they care for their own bodies. The individual's care for the islands makes it possible for the islands to remain unblemished as the crowds retreat.

Camping could not be simpler. Sweden's people's law, or custom, permits access and camping overnight almost everywhere. We could pull up on any one of these sloping rocks or on any of these hidden sandy beaches.

There's no tide, or at least not enough to notice. And yet there is the smell of the sea, salty and tangy, familiar. I investigate the gaps between the rocks, the narrow passages. The water is still. Not much today to offer the rock-hopper.

Next morning the waves are here. The wind is blowing a swell across the rounded granite heads. This is not a place of jagged rock. Everything is curvaceous. Lacy tendrils of foam spread thin across the cheeks of rock and channel down the grooves in rivulets.

"Watch the wave, watch the rock, measure the spacing between the narrowing gap in the trough and the turbulent channel as the sea rises through. Measure in your head the paddle strokes you need then go for the gap. Rise with the swell over the hurdle to rush down the other side, accelerating onto sheltered water."

We work the coast, in and out between the rocks, playing on the waves until we reach the gap between two islands. Here rock ledges heap the waves into a surf break. The unrivaled summer has brought the sea temperatures to twenty-three degrees Celsius (seventy-three degrees Fahrenheit). We surf the waves across the shoals in sunshine, laughing at each others' antics as the kayaks twist into "enders" or speed off into the bay in a plume of spray.

Stockholm

Stockholm is the capital of Sweden. Paddling west from the island of Lidingö toward the city at a leisurely pace could take me an hour. My hostess, Agneta, kayaks to work this way. To cross the city, kayaking is quicker than driving. There are large wooden sailing vessels under way, moving from Stockholm. I have been told that the owners of these magnificent vessels receive free moorage in the city, for the city enjoys the character enhanced by this flavor of history. It's a nice touch.

My choice is to kayak through the narrow canal that runs to the city center. It's a contrast to the city canals in Holland. Here it's grassy, with many trees and a few buildings. I wave to small children feeding the ducks, their mothers chatting nearby. A tour boat passes in the opposite direction, scattering the ducks. I move aside too. Then the canal widens to reveal a view of tall city buildings, square shapes adorned with towers and spires, ornate masonry, copper cladding and ironwork—substantial buildings overlooking the waterfront. Moored along the shore are old steam tugboats and wooden fishing vessels. Ornate iron bridges are embellished with statues, and there are rows of tour boats and local ferries. There are broad squares flanked by massive stone buildings sloping up from the quays.

Eventually I hit a dead end at a sluice. This is one of several that define a boundary halfway through the city between saltwater on one side and fresh on the other. The lock that allows boat access from one side to the other is bustling with traffic.

This area is the old city, built at the point where narrow channels once flowed freely from the vast inland freshwater lake system into the salt water. Here were the small islands, or holms, where the local people hauled ships against the flow or guided them down, drawing them against lines of wooden stakes driven into the canal bed. It was profitable business at a strategic point for trade and led to the site of the stake-holms (Stockholm) becoming the capital of Sweden.

Today I limit my visit to the saltwater side of the city, if this barely salty Baltic water can be classified in this way. Here the salinity measures about 1 percent, compared to 3 to 4 percent in our oceans. The saltwater city waterfront is crowded with cruise liners and the gigantic Finnish ferries, but it's less formal around the islands in the center of the city harbor area. Here trees overhang the water, people sunbathe, and children play at the water's edge. I pull my kayak up onto the grass of a park and watch a group of kayakers cruise past. There are kayaks to rent beside the bridge to this island. It's a perfect way to explore the city.

Close to my friend's home island of Lidingö is a small, uninhabited island. I make camp here with a group from the Brunnsvikens kayak club. The island is steep, rocky, and wooded. I linger beneath an old oak tree, studying a cluster of ants clinging motionless to the underside of a leaf on an aspen sapling. Suddenly aware of the loud throb of engines, I look up the slope. A huge white wall dotted with windows is moving steadily behind the trees. Above the treetops is the top of the gigantic ferry with its upper decks, superstructure, and funnels. I am spellbound. It must be passing within yards of the shore! As the ferry passes I hear the sudden sound of cheering, the roar of a football crowd above the pulse of the engines. I discover later this is the spontaneous reaction of the hundreds of tourists lining the rails of this ferry to Finland: One in our party had poorly timed her exit from the water after skinny-dipping.

We cook and eat our evening meal on the clifftop overlooking the shipping channel to watch the sunset and look up at the ferries as they thunder past. Someone on the next island is having a party, and the music is loud when I fall asleep beneath the stars. I awake in the glow of sunrise to hear the music still shouting across the water: "Girls Just Wanna Have Fun!"

The Stockholm Archipelago

Nobody could tell me how many islands there are in the Stockholm archipelago, but they number in the thousands, many more than on the west coast. We depart from a sandy ramp into a reed-bound creek near Stavsnäs, southeast of Stockholm, and meander beneath overhanging trees toward more-open water to join the rest of our companions. There is no watery horizon here, yet we are as close to the open Baltic as is possible from the mainland near Stockholm. The islands that form our horizon are wooded. Square-walled wooden huts and small houses peek from the woodland edges. Short wooden jetties run out over the still water. Tiny inflatables, little wooden rowboats, twenty-foot-long sailboats, open canoes, and smart little motor launches all find a place here.

It's quiet and the air is motionless. The light is low in the sky despite its being almost lunchtime, for it is now late summer and Sweden lies at an Alaskan latitude. We move as geese across the inverted sky, our wake spreading across the stillness till Göran guides us gradually to a narrow place between walls of twisted volcanic rock. I reach out to finger the gnarled surface as I pass. It's slippery with a fine algal growth. It's not the weed growth that my friend Mikael Rosén has watched spread out from the clean rocks at his kayaking center near Nyköping, a little south of here. But it too is probably encouraged by pollutants in the water, the fertilizers running off the land into the lakes and down into the Baltic. I've noticed the difference during the few years that I've been visiting Sweden. I've watched the spread of the weed in the creek where Mikael's "run and leap" jetty ends close to his "après-kayaking" wood-burning sauna. The bottom was clear when I first took the plunge. Now weed obscures the rocks. Even in an island paradise such as this, things change.

As the day progresses we pass islands that have few trees, lower islands, then islands almost bare of vegetation. They appear like boulders, generously curvaceous, yet they are bedrock. The land here is still rising after the melting ice sheet released its massive load at the end of the last ice age. In this part of Sweden the land is rising at a rate of about half a meter per hundred years. In a few centuries there will be more islands here, and many of the islands here now will have joined together.

It takes most of the day to reach the outer isles and to at last view a water horizon. Now it seems more like the ocean, but the familiar salt-sea smell is missing. As we weave between rocky islets, Ragnhild points proudly at the place we are to land. Adventurous, like many Swedes, she has spent many years roaming these islands, and this is a favorite spot. A polished slab of granite rises at the edges in steps and rolls into lichen-dusted vantage points. I slide from my kayak and lift it nine inches sideways onto a ridge of rock. I don't need to haul it farther. There's no tide here. But as we unload our camping gear, the rain begins. It's a brief storm. The rock runs with water as I erect my tent and boulder it down onto the rock. But when I crawl inside, I am in a steam bath. The rainwater is evaporating with the stored heat from the rock. As the shower passes, tendrils of mist float from the rock across the entire island.

We use this island as a base for a couple of days, exploring the bewildering labyrinth of channels between the thousands of rocks and islands. I ask Göran how he can find his way. He unerringly seems to know precisely where he is all of the time. He smiles and tells me he comes here a lot. He really knows all these places and carries his own personal map inside his head. He loves it here. Even

The night is quiet on Utterkobben in the Stockholm archipelago.

when the winter ice is almost complete, he finds channels to explore, places to stay, beauty to see.

Is this a typical Swedish phenomenon, I wonder? All these paddlers I'm privileged to paddle with seem obsessed by the beauty and magic of their environment. Peter tells me the Swedes are not particularly religious people, not in the "church" sense, but these islands are their "holy place." Here they feel complete, restored, rejuvenated. I see the care they take of their holy place. Every boulder they've used to hold down a tent they replace where they found it. In Sweden there are few restrictions on camping, but there is a deep personal sense of responsibility toward the land. The place is pristine when we leave.

Pristine, that is, except for two deep scars on the flat rock. At some time in the past, fires were lit here. A few flakes of rock had split from the surface with the heat, creating small craters. Since then, every year the craters fill with water, splitting further with each winter freeze. It seems incredible how fires could cause such deep pits—but it's only a matter of time. They will grow bigger every winter. I feel saddened, yet I'm glad to have seen this example so that I might pass on the message to others not to light fires on the rock.

We move north between the islands, talking across the calm water, to an island south of Sandhamn, close to an area where we hope to find more swell. I'm delighted by the springy mattress of moss and lichen and the aromatic scent of juniper where I have placed my tent. From where I stand, looking south, blue-gray misty islands stretch into the distance.

I stand on a dome of crusty lichen-patterned rock, sucking the bitter juice from lipstick-red rowanberries. It's been days since I've worn anything on my feet, weeks since I've worn more than shorts and a T-shirt. There's a call from the water. Some members of the group are setting off for a late-evening paddle to visit Sandhamn, the "sailing capital" of the outer islands. I decide to join them.

We have to cross the shipping channel where the Finnish ferries weave their way toward more-open water, so we paddle swiftly. Suddenly Göran stops and reverses. He has spotted a greenish-brown bladder floating on the surface. It's a toad, swimming slowly out in the middle of this shipping lane. It's puffed itself up into a bloated ball, skin taut, its little legs stiff drones from a bagpipe. I scoop it onto my deck. "How can it survive out here?" I ask. "Oh, they swim around between the islands," replies Göran. "The water's not too salty. They survive." We offer it a free ride to Sandhamn, and I paddle the rest of the way with this mealy pudding staring from its bubble eyes as it sits motionless on my chart. At Sandhamn I resist the impulse to kiss it. Maybe a kiss would turn it into a beautiful princess. On the other hand, it might turn me into a toad. As though happy to avoid kissing me, the "princess" crawls quickly away to vanish in the vegetation.

The town of Sandhamn is a contrast to the bare islands and the inconspicuous fishing huts that appear to sprout spontaneously like wild mushrooms. Sandhamn exudes an air of wealth and leisure. Huge modern sailing yachts ride against the floating pontoons in front of expensive restaurants, and the people on the yachts are aloof as they ignore our greeting waves. So we find a little hidden beach between the rows of jetties and then make a landing. I am reminded what another Swedish paddler told me: "The sailors regard sea kayakers as the cockroaches of the archipelago." And this really is the realm of the sailor. It is the main starting and finishing point for races in the Stockholm area, and many of the racing yachts are modern and sophisticated state-of-the-art vessels. However, there are also the more traditional wooden boats here too.

An inflated toad, perhaps an enchanted princess, gets a ride on my kayak but not a kiss.

I change quickly in the hope of finding a shop still open to replenish my food supplies. But when I reach the little store, it has long been closed. I turn away, but a cyclist is pulling up. It's the shop owner. Just for us, she opens the store and waits while we select our provisions.

There is a restaurant near the store. It looks more down to earth than the one beside the large yachts, so we investigate. But the people dining there are well dressed, and my companions are still in their wet kayaking shorts and T-shirts. Downstairs, however, is a bar that also serves food. While the setting is casual, the fish stew I order rivals any I've eaten anywhere in the world.

I watch a man in the corner opposite me sitting with his head in his hands, talking to himself. He seems a little crazy, but then I realize he has a tiny portable phone. Sweden in 1998 has the second-highest number of portable phones per capita in the world, following Finland. We even have phones with us on our kayaking trip.

After dinner it's dark as we speed back across the flat water toward the shadows that could be our island. But we could be anywhere. Suddenly there's a shout of alarm. Somebody has spotted the Finnish ferry. *But why the rush?* I wonder. It's far off, just emerging from behind an island. But when I realize how fast it is traveling, I too begin to sprint. We are barely across before it passes behind us, lights ablaze, engines throbbing. Another ferry is following. They run this route in pairs since a recent ferry disaster.

When we reach land, I don't recognize it. One ledge of rock seems like the next in the dark, and there are so many here. I am thankful to see the lights in the tents as we round the point.

It is morning. We weave between exposed rocks, dodging the waves and surfing through narrow gaps. The breeze has given us some swells to play with. I sit beside a wall of rock, a few feet from a shoal that has caused an occasional heavy break, but it's been quiet for a while now. I watch as one by one my companions emerge from what appears to be solid rock. There is a crevice there. They bound over the steep waves, curve in a wide arc, and then surf, riding a wave in through the next gap. Here the sea is joyful, alive, and almost frantic. Just on the other side it is serene, placid. I don't notice that one from the group is behind me. A bigger swell approaches, breaking abruptly over the shoal beside me. There's a shriek and I turn my head. There's a kayak locked in the breaker being swept sideways past me and up the cliff. There is a pause and then the swell retreats, but the kayak is left standing almost vertical against the rock. And my friend is bracing against air. There is something odd about the scene, almost comical. She has landed flat against the rock, but the rock is not horizontal, so she sits with her bow pointed skyward. It's all in the wrong plane—about eighty degrees wrong! But the next wave puts it right. Gravity returns and she rattles back down the rock, hull scraping, to vanish in the foam. It's all over in a moment.

We thread along the coast, in and out of the rougher water, then through narrower gaps and winding passages back to our tents. It's my last day. A few days here have seemed endless, but the dew-laden spiderwebs in the mornings and the red tinge to the leaves, the ripe berries, and the longer nights are hints of a passing season. It's been the hottest summer since they began keeping records in the nineteenth century, but all things end. From here on in, the wind will carry us toward the mainland on a following sea—an opportunity to swoop along with the waves, steering toward the distant trees, then the bigger islands, into what seems like lake water, then back to the winding creek, poking our kayaks into the reed beds.

For me this is the end of my sun-drenched, watery summer in Sweden. From here I must travel by road. But my Swedish friends will be spending their weekends out among the islands in their kayaks right up until the winter frosts bind up the Baltic. And then they will strap long blades to their boots and follow the same kayak routes on foot, gliding over the frozen meniscus. People say "to know is to love," and I can tell how deeply all my paddling companions love their archipelago. But having spent just a little time here, I can also believe there is such a thing as love at first sight.

23

QUEEN CHARLOTTE ISLANDS

I took stock of my position. The Queen Charlotte Islands lie to the west of British Columbia, Canada. I was floating up to my neck in water, my kayak at least a hundred yards away from me. I looked across an expanse of bay toward sunlit mountains cloaked in forest and adorned with bright mist. An eagle cruised overhead, quite low. For a moment my head lolled forward under the water, my breath silver bubbles and my ears rustling. I had scarce an ounce of willpower left. I wondered where the others were. I knew they were in the vicinity, but they were out of sight; Martin, Sue, and Simon. Ah! The self-indulgent joys of hot springs!

We'd flown from Vancouver to Sandspit in a small plane and checked into a motel room while we bought, sorted, and packaged our supplies. Then we made use of the local tour operator, Moresby Explorers, to ferry us south to their floating cabin, where the rented kayaks awaited us. There, while the others packed with maniacal determination and haste, I fed the bright aluminum tubes and white nylon frames into a teal-green kayak skin until my struggles with the Khatsalano rewarded me with the desired shape. This was the first time I had assembled a folding kayak, although I'd attentively watched a seamlessly efficient demonstration back in Vancouver at the Feathercraft workshop. I almost remembered how to do it without referring to the instructions.

Martin, Sue, and Simon had paddled with me many times before, in places including Wales and the Scottish Islands. They'd watched with awe my finely tuned rapid-loading techniques—skills I honed while paddling the Scottish Islands in "midge" weather, when the little biting no-see-ums can drive a man crazy enough to take up Highland dancing in the dews of morning. Yes! I knew they'd watched me with dismay! On those Scottish excursions we'd agree each evening on a time to be afloat in the morning to catch the tide. From the smug comfort of my sleeping bag I'd hear the sounds of banging pans, flaring stoves, voices cursing the midges, and the desperate slap of palm against skin. Later there would be the sound of kayaks being moved, of tent fabric being shaken to shed the dew.

At about that time I'd emerge immaculate from my tent, gently closing my reading book around the page marker and brushing the crumbs of breakfast from my beard. I'd stretch and look around at the morning, breathing deeply the fresh morning air.

All around me the others would be in a frenzy of frustration verging on panic trying to stuff clothes into dry-bags, collapsing tent poles, and feeding bulky sleeping bags into small hatches. All the time they'd be cursing and rubbing, prising tiny flies from the tender corners of their eyes, experiencing pain from a thousand tiny cuts.

Within minutes my own tent would be down and stowed, my reading book neatly secured in the day hatch, and I'd be slipping my kayak quietly from the sand onto the water. I'd be the first afloat, the first to ripple the still water and escape the hoards of hungry midges. I'd relax a few yards from the beach and watch the dance on shore. If I hadn't been humming some little tune to myself, I'd have been sure to hear curses from the shore. "Damn Foster's done it again!" But I was oblivious to their envy. I was simply fast and efficient.

So here I was on the end of a gently rocking floating platform in the Queen Charlotte Islands, the air heavy with the crusty smells of damp forest. Huge loops of orange-brown bullhead kelp floated on the salt water beside me. I held a length of shining metal tube in my hand and wondered if this might be a spare piece or if I could possibly have missed a step in the assembly. As I unfolded the assembly instructions I sensed everything had gone quiet. Suddenly the gleam vanished from the tube as I was immersed in cold shadow. I looked up.

Above me towered the Terrible Trio, hands on their hips. Their faces beamed with some evil expectation. I felt totally vulnerable. For a moment I thought they were going to swing me shoulder high and fling me far out into that cold water, but no! They were not going let me get away that lightly! A barrage of "Having a little trouble there are you, Foster? Ha! Mind if we watch you? This'll be fun! Not even started loading yet? Better get a move on, Foster! We're all ready! Ooh! Let me suggest a place for that piece! You know all that stuff won't fit in there, don't you! You'll have to unpack it all and start again!" made it impossible for me to focus.

Then there was a dark chuckle. "You don't mind if we brew up a little espresso for ourselves while we watch, do you? I'd offer you some, but I can see you're busy! I'll let you smell it. But don't let me distract you! You're not getting flustered are you?" At that moment I knew my time was up. They were hitting where it hurt!

We couldn't pass by Hotsprings Island without taking the opportunity to soak for a while. Paths through the forest were marked with bright seashells, with boardwalks over the marshy sections. Steam rose from the bleached rocks in the vicinity of the springs, and there was a smell like hot towels. There was nobody else on the island. This late in the season we had the place to ourselves to enjoy the rare sunshine from the deep pools of hot water. Martin and Sue wandered off along the shoreline in search of their own private Eden. Simon turned the opposite direction, so I hopped into that first pool we'd found. It was right to set the tone and pace early in the trip.

It was a moment for me to take stock of where I was and to know that I had arrived. The Queen Charlotte Islands are situated to the west of mainland British Columbia, north of Vancouver Island, south of Alaska. They enjoy a constantly mild, humid climate that encourages the growth of a temperate rain forest, with its lush ferns and mosses, lichens, and liverworts that cling to every surface as a dripping coat of green and gray. Dripping, after all, is the essence of rain forest.

We paddled on clear, cool water, skirting kelp beds and keeping close to shore where possible so that we had more to watch. Big crusty starfish in jellybean colors clung to the barnacled rocks amid lustrous emerald-green anemones. Bald eagles sat on virtually every treetop and bare branch. They swooped out over the water from the hillsides with oddly high-pitched squeals and squeaks.

The water remained placid and dark and cool, yet the hull of my folding kayak flexed around me in a way that was both strange yet familiar. It took me a little time to realize where the familiarity came from. It was from my very first kayak, a rigid canvas kayak in which I'd explored the waterways of Southern England as a teenager. That had moved and flexed in a similar way, the water pressing the canvas against my legs and the framework moving with the waves. "Rigid canvas kayak" sounds like an oxymoron. It was anything but rigid! But in those days there was a distinction between folding kayaks and rigid ones. Ironically the only kayaks I'd ever folded (unintentionally) were supposed to be rigid—fiberglass, and plastic, whitewater kayaks.

We landed where deer grazed at the water's edge. They drifted slowly to the edge of the forest until suddenly all we could see were shadows. "Why don't you select your camping spots first?" I offered graciously. "I'm not in a hurry, and there are plenty of good spots here." They looked at me with a mixture of disdain and pity. They would open their kayaks like cupboards and their gear would all but fall out by itself. For me to tease my bags from the recesses between the frames would take longer. They knew they had the upper hand today, and they were going to extract the greatest possible enjoyment from it. Martin and Sue chose the center of a mossy glade with a waterfront view. Simon chose the other mossy area close to the beach, with a choice of seafront logs to sit on. We had the whole forest to ourselves, so there was little point in camping right beside one another.

I scouted out my options. The remaining beachfront real estate was encumbered by logs that had grown into the ground, pinned down by a sheath of saturated moss. But a little farther into the shadow of the forest were flat areas of leaf mold between huge straight trunks. I picked a spot at random and set up the tent. It felt as though I was putting up the tent inside a house, which I have done before. The forest surrounded me so completely I felt I almost didn't need a tent at all. Every sound I made was swallowed by the absorbent surfaces around me. The experience was so eerie that I hurried out to join the others in the daylight on the beach, where suddenly I found I could hear again, as though I had just removed earplugs.

We cooked at the water's edge as the smooth sea reflected the pastel-pink evening sky. Simon related how he'd been hiking once with friends and they'd hung their food from a cliff overnight because there were no trees. A bear had found it and left them without food and with several days' hiking ahead to the road. Starving on the trek out, they met another group hiking in the opposite direction and explained their misfortune. "Oh, bad luck!" was the response. "They didn't even offer us a Mars bar!" bemoaned Simon.

So after we'd eaten, I helped Simon sling a line over a long, high branch. We all hauled together to raise the heavy food load well out of reach of any normal bear. But even so, I was more alert that evening as we sat on logs at the forest edge with a tiny crackling fire, watching the thin gray smoke drift out across the water. There were a lot of shadows that could be bears if you watched them long enough. Not even a Mars bar? No bear was going to get my food!

That night I lay on the flat ground, the musty smell of rotting leaves and the pungent tree resins in my nostrils. I was comfortable. I'd enjoyed my meal, a few gallons of coffee, and a wee dram of good single-malt Scottish Island whisky. Even with one ear listening for the footsteps of a bear, I was quickly asleep.

Some people call it a Chinese alarm clock. I don't know what it has to do with China, but I know what it has to do with porcelain. I had to pee, and I couldn't put it off any longer. I crawled from my sleeping bag and out of the tent. As I stumbled naked into the darkness, my eyes gradually focused on nothing. Nothing? That's right! I couldn't see anything at all. I stumbled onward, slowly coming to terms with this new idea, and then a few more paces before I confirmed I was awake and my eyes were indeed open. I couldn't see anything. Instinctively I looked up, but if there was a sky above me, it was completely black. Of course! The forest! The forest canopy was so dense it had been almost dark in there when it was still light on the beach. I turned and looked up again, then took a few more paces and looked again. Yes, it was really dark. Interesting! Suddenly I looked around for the tent. It wasn't there. I turned again, slowly this time, looking all around me for a trace of light that might tell me where the beach was. There was nothing. The forest was silent. Not even the crackle of a ripple on the shore. I reached out with my arms but couldn't feel anything, so I peed.

I felt helpless. My tent must be quite close, just a few yards away, but I had no idea where. I felt around for it, reaching down and around in all directions, then taking a pace and doing the same again. I began to feel desperate. There was a chance I might come out onto the beach, but what if I worked my way deeper into the forest? I didn't want to spend the rest of the night out in the open stark naked. But equally, I didn't want to shout to wake the others up to announce, "I've lost my tent! Will you shine a light so I can find my way back please?"

Why, the story would be all over toy-town with a million perverted versions by morning! What a dilemma. I took a couple more steps and cast around with my arms again, then a couple more. Eventually I stepped on the tent and breathed a silent prayer of gratitude.

A rain forest needs rain to grow and thrive. But it never seemed to rain hard: It simply rained often. Fine rain sprayed like a heavy mist to coat everything it touched with myriad sparkling droplets. When it wasn't raining, rainbows sprang up across the misty mountains, and everything remained damp. After a week of traveling, everything felt damp even after we'd hung it in the sun to dry. Molds began to speckle the surface of all my gear. But molds are fungi. That gave me cheer. I began to look for bigger ones.

Every morning I searched in the forest and returned with apricot-colored chanterelles in my pan. I cooked these and ate them alone, not out of greed but because the others regarded my finds with more than a little suspicion. I'm sure Martin and Sue, both of whom are doctors back home in England, were biding their time in the expectation they'd be called to rustle up a little professional sympathy—to announce with grave finality some "told-you-so" diagnosis of untreatable amanita phallotoxin or other. Part of me wanted to educate these ignorant Brits, but another part felt a little smug. Then one day I tempted Simon to taste one. After all, I'd been eating them for days and I was still alive, right? Then the craze spread. Four people searched the forest for free treats as though on an Easter egg hunt. But finding fungi requires a combination of skills, observation being the key one. You have to observe where they like to grow and how they appear camouflaged among the dead leaves on the ground in different weather and lights. It's easy to walk right by them and search an area where they're not. Skills come with time and practice. Of course luck is something else. As I brought back another pan full of gleaming golden fungi to their hands, I wondered how soon they'd get their eye in.

We paddled an eastern route among the rainbows and the squalls, stopping to view the remains of Haida homesteads. Sometimes there were elaborately carved totems, sometimes the remains of lodges with massive timbers becoming one with the earth and the living trees. Here it's impossible to miss the intertwined nature of life itself. The timbers that fall in the forest become coated in thick moss. Seedlings grow there, sending roots through the moss, sometimes for many yards, to reach where the log touches the ground. Other roots hang down until they contact the earth. The new trees grow around the old remnants, and through them, but the shapes of the fallen "nurse

Remains of Haida longhouses grow back into the forest on Moresby Island.

tree," or the stump around which they grew, remain preserved in the bases of the new trees long after the original timbers have rotted to dust. They hold the history. The young trees use the nutrients left by the dead ones in a cycle of replenishment. Haida lodges and totems follow the same cycle. Trees! It's the trees that make the place what it is, and it's the trees that wake you in the night when a portion of dead lumber thunders to the ground, or when the rising tide floats the log pile from the beach until the logs jostle in the swell with a musical clunking, like giant wind chimes.

I took every opportunity to walk in the forest between the colossal trees, but it seemed wherever I went I found beautiful mother-of-pearl abalone shells gleaming with a deep luster, and the strange butterfly-shaped white bonelike objects that I later learned were the bleached exoskeletons of chitons. They always seemed to be laid out in prominent display on some hummock of deep moss or right beside a tiny path. I wondered how so many could be found so far from shore. It remained a puzzle to me how or why birds might carry them there. Then I saw an otter and it all fell into place. The otters were bringing abalones and chitons ashore to eat.

Forecast bad weather prompted us to paddle for sheltered water to the north of Louise Island. Here the trees had been cut around the time of the Second World War, and the area had since become reforested. Somewhere in there, so we had heard, was a kind of parking lot. We poked our kayaks up streams until we found a hidden and overgrown graveyard then, nearby, a bottle dump. Next we found the parking lot: a number of ancient trucks parked so tightly between trees that we knew the trees hadn't been there when the trucks were abandoned. There were rusty metal skeletons, steel-shod wheels with wooden spokes, leather boots with nailed soles, and the remains of a boardwalk. There were large rusty boilers and the remains of wooden skidways along which logs were dragged. Long curtains of Spanish moss hung veiling the trees, and the light that filtered through was dim and green.

We surfed on a following sea toward our final destination, with sea lions powering past us with an ease that put us firmly in place as landlubbers. Sea lions can be so big that the mere sudden appearance of an open mouth beside my kayak brought shivers down my spine. I imagined the flexible black hull of my kayak might seem like the living skin of an animal to these exuberant beasts. I felt afraid in case they were tempted to give it a nip.

We found the vehicle Moresby Explorers had said they'd leave for us. It was the tail end of the season, and the place was empty. We sponged out and racked the rental kayaks with the others. Now we'd left the water, I felt the cold and dampness in the air more than before. While the others gazed out across the now gloomy water, I began my extra task of carefully dismantling the feathercraft, slipping each length of tubing and each nylon frame from within the skin until it lay like a distorted sack on the ground. I was surprised at my efficiency, but in my moment of pride I heard a chuckle. I looked up to see the others watching me. It wasn't going to be over until it was over! *May they all be afflicted with Scottish midges!* I thought.

We were soon on the bumpy road back to town, and it was there, not in camp, that we spotted a black bear lumbering between the trees. I mentally noted my appreciation for Simon's "not-even-a-Mars-bar" care in finding good places to string up our food each night. After all, we were from England, where it's more common to cook and eat at the tent entrance and store food in the tent at night. And I remembered Martin and Sue's generosity in sharing their single-malt Scotch. And I remembered why I had invited them to join me on this trip and what great people they were. And I looked forward to the next time I would paddle with them. Perhaps next time we'd all use folding kayaks. I by then of course would be practiced in assembling and taking them apart and in loading and launching them. Next time, I vowed, I would have the upper hand!

As it happens we never will return to the Queen Charlotte Islands, for they no longer go by that name. In June 2010 they were officially renamed Haida Gwaii as part of a reconciliation protocol between British Columbia and the Haida Nation.

24

SHETLAND BY SUNLIGHT

The ferry turned to dock at Lerwick. Turning away from a sky full of screaming, wheeling gulls, from the view of stone houses climbing the rounded green hills, I dragged my feet from the brilliant light into the gloom and dusty diesel fumes and fish-water puddles of the car deck. I wanted to enjoy watching the ferry berth once more, but I felt self-conscious, anxious not to hold up proceedings as I had that morning by arriving late to catch the ferry.

Wolfgang waved me down on the Lerwick quay. I was sleepy after several late nights of folk music and Irish beer during my visit to the Orkney Islands, so when I wound down my car window to greet him, I was dismayed to hear words like "later tonight" and "pubs."

Next morning Wolfgang was up with the dawn, fishing in the lake; it gets light early in Shetland. Wolfgang has boundless energy and an insatiable desire to use every moment to the fullest, so we were soon out on a warm-up paddle around the Burra Isles, southwest of Shetland. By lunchtime we reached the shelter of the northern end, surrounded by low moorland hills. To the north sat the bright green dome of Greenholm. If ever an island could be a landmark in such a maze of small islands, this one, with its greener than green color, is it. Probably it was the nutrients from the seabirds—puffins most likely—that nested there that built up the soil to support such plant growth.

We cruised into the shelter of a shallow bay and sat for a moment, drifting on the clear water. The sun scrolled patterns from the surface onto the sand, which danced in waves beneath us. I caught sight of a raven's nest, well disguised among the many cormorants on the low cliff back of the beach. The young ravens were off the nest, exploring the ledges, experimenting with newly feathered wings but not yet flying. As I drifted into the shallows, I dragged my fingers in the sand to stop my kayak and spotted a whirl of golden sequins shimmering in the clear water. I flicked the sand up with my fingers again to watch the tiny mica discs sparkle in the sun as they settled.

Keith was the next to arrive in Shetland. A quiet, dark-haired man who worked hard and really appreciated his time away, Keith had recently equipped himself with camping gear especially for this trip. I watched his tent climb onto the flower-shot turf and then flatten again in a web of thin poles. Keith sat with a sheet of paper in his hand, concentrating.

We headed north at a formidable pace, weaving between the shallow islands and sandy points in a warm-up that led us swiftly to the cliffs. There we looked for a good place to camp. A pebble beach sheltered by a red cliff appeared an ideal spot, but when we landed to check it out, a horde of terns took off and turned aggressively toward us. It was as though the pebbles were turning into birds before our eyes! We retreated down the beach, our ears stinging from the piercing *"Cree-ya!"* threats from the terns as they rained at us.

Papa Stour, off the west of mainland Shetland, was a tempting target; it was another twenty miles along the coast. We would camp for the night then leave our tents standing while we spent the day circling the island. Papa Stour is best explored with an unladen kayak; the cliffs are riddled with deep caves and tunnels. We cruised on calm water, probing between massive blocks, threading narrow slits, and drifting into gaping caverns where the sun sent reflections undulating across the roof. Down long, cool passages, moisture beaded up on our salty hair. I was aware of the sounds in the darkness: water slapping like a hand on a thigh, burbling, pouring, gulping, and gasping. There was the occasional clash of a paddle blade against rock. Then it started getting lighter. An exit gash expanded to reveal the other world: warmer drier air, flower-sweet and dusty with the feathers of fulmars. My eyes screwed against the glare. Cries of seabirds mingled with the background rush and hiss of waves upon the rocks.

Cut into the cliff of Papa Stour is a particular cave that I'd heard about and wanted to find. We took care not to miss a single entrance. Eventually we found a cave that fit the description: a split finger of rock in a high-sided gash in the cliff, with a tunnel behind. We crept through the tunnel into a high-walled canal, open to the sky. The roof must have collapsed here. The cave continued beyond. As our eyes readjusted to the darkness, I made out several routes. A central passage continued onward, and there was a curtain of rock to the right,

I'm approaching the exit of a tunnel beneath a cliff on Mainland Shetland.

which had broken through in several places to a parallel passage. A tiny slit led off to the left. I took the left-hand route, which twisted in a tight dogleg to reveal a view of the end chamber. There a hole in the roof let down a single diagonal bar of light. It burst through the surface of the clear water to illuminate the bright pebbles beneath and simultaneously shattered upward to throw a shivering pattern of warm light against the reddish roof. I sat stunned. All the routes ended in the same domed cavern. But it was not until I had explored the other routes that I discovered the shaft of light only showed when viewed from this one spot.

Katy and Fred, the last two members of our party, were due to arrive from London. We left our kayaks and tents on a beach on the mainland and hitchhiked to Lerwick to collect our vehicles and be ready to pick up Katy and Fred early next morning. We had some people to meet that night: a sheep shearer from New Zealand who was planning to cycle around Iceland and a couple from Glasgow I had met on the ferry. I swear I hadn't expected a party, but at 4:00 a.m. I found a spot at the head of the stairs and feigned death for an hour and a half. Wolfgang and Keith took the whole night in stride. By morning, however, they looked as though they had risen from the grave. Keith declined a second opportunity to circle Papa Stour, but Wolfgang, with Germanic fortitude, was ready.

The weather was the calmest in years, locals were delighted to inform us. We could explore even the lowest arches and the longest tunnels. Some of the caves had submerged exits, and only the deep, almost iridescent green light glowing from beneath told of a watery way out. Sea urchins and starfish lay on the bottom or clung to the pink encrustations below us. There was a small island with a tunnel running from end to end, crossing at the island's center with another tunnel that ran from side to side. The tide sped through the shorter passage like a river.

But then the weather hiccupped and a blustery wind raised the spray from our paddles as we skidded almost out of control beneath the arches around Eshaness. An offshore breeze carried squalls of rain. We landed by some ruined farm buildings and used the shelter for our tents. Stone walls looked as though they had grown into position; the chimney breasts rose from the low-arched fireplaces supported by long, irregular slabs of cold rock.

The next day we reached Fethaland. My sister, Debbie, had recommended I stop at this narrow neck of land with a beach landing to the east and another to the west. The cliffs rose to the north to encircle the final headland, which is topped by a lighthouse. Nobody lives at this end of Shetland now, but a circular mound of rocks shows sufficient detail in its interior layout to suggest historic origins. More recently this remote landing site was used by fishermen from villages farther south in Shetland. Rowing their "sixareens" forty miles out to the west to the richest fishing grounds, they would set their long, thousand-hooked baited lines, sometimes a mile in length, and haul in their catch before rowing back to land. At Fethaland their canvas-roofed summer dwellings housed family members who helped split, salt, and dry the fish they caught. Nowadays the silky rocks glisten with silver, not of the scales of fish but of soft mica. The tiny cottages cluster along the raised bank above the beach, and the slabs of warm rock offer places to sit and watch the seals play. The cottages are now open to the sky. The windows are without glass, and one or two are framed with shrinking wood and sweet-smelling sea pinks.

We installed our kayaks in the ancient nousts cut into the alluvial bank. The rock-lined nousts must have sheltered boats from the violent winds on many occasions. I've seen Viking boat shelters in the western isles of Scotland constructed in a similar fashion, and yet more in the Faeroe Islands that had walls and roofs built above them to form boatsheds, but these, the simplest, seemed perfect to me: a groove in the shore up into which a boat could be hauled to shelter it from the wind, lined with rock slabs and boulders to stop the vegetation from taking over and the sides from crumbling in.

We spent two nights at Fethaland, savoring the haunting cries of ringed plovers nesting among the rocks, the graceful gliding of the fulmars along the many cliff edges, and the crackle of a driftwood fire as we stood around sipping rum and chocolate. On the silvery rocks as smooth as silk that make up the western beach, I stood barefoot to view the whitecaps on a dark blue sea around the bird rocks to the north.

From Fethaland we launched into Yell Sound. I'd heard tales of fast tidal streams and raging rapids, but although we were rushed through from the east to the west, the water was kind to us. Yell Sound runs about fifteen miles between green rolling hills. There's low land, low islands—a soft contrast to the gash-cut cliffs of the west. We camped on Yell, opposite a tiny island almost totally covered by a Pictish broch. These ancient fortified shelters, scattered thickly across the Orkney Isles, are remnants of times troubled by the threat of attack. There's an excellently preserved broch on the Shetland island of Mousa that stands a full forty feet, with its cavity-wall construction gradually tapering as it rises. For the many centuries that building has stood, not one scrap of mortar was ever used to bind stones that were laid bare one upon the other. On the tiny island across from us now, the broch stood in ruins—concentric circles of banks and ditches around a fallen tower, home to starlings and fulmars.

Wolfgang wanted to try for a beer at the ferry ramp where the small roll-on, roll-off car ferry reaches the narrow road on Yell. When we got there we discovered that the shop was closed, but the owner opened it up and let us buy beer anyway.

Back at the tents, the others were absorbed in watching otters, which had swum from the broch to Yell and wandered across the headland past them. When we returned, the otters were in the water just off the shallow headland. We followed their progress for ages before they

Fred approaches a pour-over by the cliff on Mainland Shetland.

swam far enough downwind to pick up our scent. This section of coast has one of the biggest populations of otters in all Shetland.

Fetlar Island, a fifteen-mile paddle north, is known for its bird life. Much of the island is managed as a reserve. We strolled along the deserted singletrack road that traverses the island. Dim shapes on the asphalt scuttled aside with mournful wails and plaintive cries. I love the calls of the moors: whimbrel and golden plover, curlew and redshank. The island stretched bleak and low into the distance with one dark, sinuous thread across it.

Near the crossroads we stopped. "What's the marquee for?" asked Fred. We could see a large tent on the flat ground at Tresta, between the beach and the lake below us. Cars were parked around the lake, and there seemed to be a crowd of people. The binoculars, brought for the birds, turned onto the shore. The events there looked worth investigating.

"All the meat you can eat for a fiver!" a lady announced cheerfully as we approached. It was an impromptu community barbecue: a choice of rabbit, mutton, pork spare ribs, burgers, and fresh-caught sea trout with rolls and onions! "Take a bit of everything! And come back for more."

We strolled along the beach, following where the majority appeared to be moving. There on a flat area a game of soccer was in progress—vigorous "take no prisoners, give no quarter" stuff. It was islanders versus non-islanders. Ages ranged from about ten to forty-five, and there was no going easy on the little ones, I noted, as I watched a boy ricocheted to one side from the charge of a two-hundred-pound man. The goals at each end were marked by piles of clothing discarded in preparation for the exertion, but the game ran well past the goals to the natural boundaries: the rougher ground, wherever that lay, the sea, and the lake. The game continued for hours, and I doubt anyone was keeping score.

We left the party soon after a massive fire on the beach was lit. We had paddling to look forward to the next day. We trudged back across the moor, tired, stomachs heavy with meat and beer.

"Today should be a gentle day!" decided Fred and Katy next morning. My casual "Oh, it's only about fifteen miles to paddle a circuit of Yell" cut no ice with them. They knew how to measure the distance on the map themselves. Fred planned to go fishing.

Wolfgang set off at Olympic pace into the mist that day. *A circuit of Fetlar before breakfast?* I wondered. The fog curtained the land from us, and we crossed the bays by compass when we strayed from the cliffs. But around the eastern shores we began to pick up a little more swell. That made exploring behind the stacks and between the rocks more interesting. I get absorbed by that sort of thing sometimes. I spotted a big stack with the swell mounting high behind it and gestured "After you!" to Keith with my hands. Keith grinned and set his head to one side. He followed Wolfgang's back.

I was on my own. Not wishing to lose them in the mist, I sped straightaway into the gap, grinning with satisfaction as I reached the high point where the swell from both sides met and heaped up in the middle in the darkness of the narrow gap. I was positioned just right. From there on it was downhill, accelerating out the other side. But no! As I turned the corner to freedom, there was a waterfall ahead of me: a ledge of rock with the water pouring over it in a drop of several feet.

I shut my eyes and waited for the impact of hull against rock. Then I was chest deep in water as the next wave piled toward the cliff. The fall reversed, and moments later I was paddling hard forward as my tail rose with the spread of water against the cliff. I made the drop once more and was then thrown back to the cliff again. Reversing falls can be disconcerting. I was bounced against the rock in both directions. Of the others, all I could see was mist.

When I finally caught up with Keith, he made just one brief observation. "Your hair's wet!" He's a man of few words.

Later, much later, that evening we sat around the fire Fred had lit to help us recognize our landing. I overheard someone mutter "twenty-five miles," but it wasn't Fred or Katy. We ate fresh fish and dough twisted onto slender sticks and toasted above the embers. That and Fred's favorite drink: hot chocolate with rum. Around us we could hear the drooping flute calls of golden plover. Out in the bay, red-throated divers splashed and called. The sounds seemed amplified by the mist.

We had parked a vehicle at Brae, where a narrow neck of land separates the Atlantic to the west from the sheltered Sullom Voe to the east. We returned up the Voe into increasingly calm water, past buildings that house special oil-retaining booms that can divide the Voe into many segments in just minutes. And that was just one of the rigorous safeguards at this, the largest single oil and natural gas depot in Europe. A vast tanker sat at the quay, bristling with gleaming pipes. The refinery itself is relatively well disguised, hidden low between the green moors. A quarter of a mile from the ship was a well-marked skerry, covered by a couple dozen seals. Terns exploded the water surface and shrieked in the sky. A single oil boom to one side of the ship showed water clear of oil but dense with jellyfish—clear saucers with purple rings, quivering against ragged red manes, all tight together like frog spawn. Having experienced the wilderness of the Shetland Islands, I felt a little uneasy here with so much industry. A plume of flame shot into the air above a silver stack. But perhaps this is the scar that highlights the beauty of the face? And of course it feeds the economy!

Back in Lerwick, I perched on the stone wall near the old harbor and talked with my friends. They could speak of nothing but the good weather. We labored up the flagstone steps between the ancient stone houses, up steep streets to the tiny museum where we had left our cars. The sun baked us yet more. The radio had announced that it had been the best weather and the highest temperatures since 1947! An old lady wearing a long dark gabardine coat tottered up to us on her sticks. She stared at the kayaks on the roof of the car. "Are those your boats?" she asked in that soft Shetland accent. "Yes!" we replied. Her eyes looked misty as she recalled how she and her sister used to row a small boat up and down the coast in her younger days. Her eyes focused back onto us. "Have you been here long?"

Fred replied, one arm around Katy, "Three weeks now! We carried all we needed and camped where we found ourselves."

"Oh! That must have been fun!" she said. "But isn't it a pity about the weather! It's been such awful weather this summer!" She gave us each a direct glance. "But it looks as though you've enjoyed yourself anyway!" She tottered away up the sidewalk with a final glance at the kayaks.

"The best weather since 1947," muttered Fred quietly, "how dreadful!"

25

ACROSS FRANCE BY CANAL

It was Tim's idea. We had each accrued a month of leave in lieu of working weekends through the year but had to take it before April. It was winter. How to use a month in winter? "How about spending some time on the beach in the Med? Sunshine, wine?" Tim had my attention.

"Yes, I found this book on the French canals. You can get all the way from Calais to the Mediterranean through the canals! We could zip down there, spend a few days on the beach then paddle back. It's only seven hundred kilometers. It starts near Belgium, goes up the Marne River valley, then down the Saône and Rhône to the sea." I was sucked in.

We borrowed a kayak—a red double semi-racing model that we lovingly referred to as the *Baguette Rouge*—and booked our vacation time. Then one evening Tim casually let slip, "Nigel, you know I said it was seven hundred kilometers? Well, it's actually seven hundred miles." While I silently digested this new information, he threw in "Each way . . . but it'll be canal paddling, and we'll be in a double, so we should be able to make good time."

Then one cold, dark, stormy evening Tim came breezing in with "Hi Nige!" He stopped just inside the door, shaking off the rain. He looked anxious, and I asked if everything was okay. He replied with a question: "Do you fancy a pint?"

"Okay!" I'm that easily persuaded. "But how is the planning going?" He looked shifty. Evading the question, he offered, "I'll drive! Get your coat!"

We ran through the rain to his car and he took off fast down the winding lane. Music tumbled from the cassette player while the heater blasted air at the windshield. I began again, "So . . . how is it going?" Tim sucked in his breath, peering past the rapidly sweeping wipers into the darkness. Sparks of rain flew like moths past the headlights. "I'll tell you at the pub!" Then he added brightly, "Tell you what, I'll buy the first round!"

The pub was half empty, but a log fire was blazing and the landlord cheerful. We found a table and clacked our glasses of creamy Guinness together. "Cheers!" Then with that magic foamy first sip, when the burnt malty hoppy bittersweet flavor in the frothy head filled me with contentment . . . right at that moment, when the most natural thing to do was to sigh in appreciation, Tim blurted out: "Two hundred and twenty locks!"

My exhaling was quicker than expected and my glass was still close to my lips. Foam flew. As I choked and spluttered, he added the coup de grâce: "Each way."

We camped on the canal banks under the rain sheet of a tent. I recall the reason: "Let's save weight and leave the inner tent behind. After all, there shouldn't be any biting bugs in March." Of course there would be no biting bugs in March—because it's too cold. We crawled out into hoar-frosted grass to find our plastic water bottle had frozen solid, banishing any hope of a steaming cup of coffee before we

Some nights there was little dry ground on which to camp.

launched. I looked out across the canal in disappointment and realized it too had frozen overnight. We crashed our way through thin ice until the first barge passed in the opposite direction. That evening we agreed to always fill a pan with water in the evening that we could thaw out on the stove in the morning.

The Marne to Saône canal stepped up, lock after lock, through hills and farmed valley. Each lock was a stone-walled chamber with a pair of huge hinged wooden walls at each end—"gates" that folded flat against the stonework when open, and closed together to block the entrance. Gates were either left open or closed, never partly open.

We approached each lock from the downhill side. If the gates were closed, we would pull in to the bank and Tim would clamber out. It was his excuse for a stretch, and a chance to practice his French on the lockkeeper. Dividing the work with the lockkeeper, he would handle-wind the sluices open to drain the lock on one side and swing the gate open, while the lockkeeper operated the other side. As the great jaws parted, I would sneak the kayak between so that the gates could be closed without the effort of fully opening them.

I would then be shut into the chamber with the gates and sluices closed behind me. At the best of times locks are dank, drippy, oily places with molds and slime on the walls. They seem to be the place where fish go when they die; there they float in pale limbo, prepared for heavenward flight, at least as far as the water surface, by inflating like blimps. Now the sluices were opened to let water in from upstream, and it burbled up from underneath in a seething boil or rushed over the top, depending on the individual lock. As the water rose, so did I—by paddling to keep my position against the current that pushed me toward the gates behind or by clinging to the fixed ladder that offered a last resort for escape. As I rose, my changing viewpoint revealed the lock cottage and then the dogs or geese the lockkeeper allowed to run free, and which invariably waited fiercely for my head to come within range. Finally I could see over the top. With the water stilled and the gates ahead opened, Tim could hop in and we would be ready to go again, now at a slightly higher altitude. This whole process of lifting our kayak vertically eight or ten feet used a whole lock-full of water. At some times of year the lockkeepers might balk at that expense, but it was March, the rainy season if France has one. It did that year.

Rain fell freely almost every day. The River Marne filled, and then it spilled and flooded the valley. Farms and fences protruded from the sheet of rushing water. Sometimes only the bank of the canal stood clear, with water on either side. We struggled to find a patch of grass big enough for the tent on the canal bank at night between the puddles and lay fearful that an early-morning barge would send the water washing over us as we slept. But everything was wet already.

But rain aside, we watched a golden eagle chase a hare and saw red kites circling over the fields. We accepted freshly gathered eggs from lockkeepers' wives and bought warm crispy-crusted bread from delivery vans. Occasionally we'd buy a cheese or a bottle of wine when we went in search of fresh water. Our little stove burned gasoline, which we purchased from gas stations.

In the upper reaches of the Marne, the canal dives beneath a few hills through long tunnels. Built in Napoleon's day, the tunnels have towpaths on either side for the horses to tow the barges. But there are some modern improvements. At each entrance was a traffic signal, a light that mysteriously changed color some time after we had signaled our presence. We convinced ourselves there must be a camera. Surely there wouldn't be just a timer allowing a set time for a barge to motor through before the lights changed again to let a vessel enter from the other end?

The light turned green and we left the driving rain for a cool and drafty but relatively dry place! A line of lights spaced at intervals along the wall stretched off into the distance. We could not see the other end of the tunnel! What would we do if we ran into a barge coming in the other direction? The towpath wasn't built at an easy height to get out and lift up the kayak. Besides, there were the sounds of unseen movements in the dark above us. We passed under one of the lights and realized the sounds came from large rats. With tunnels stretching up to more than four kilometers at a stretch, we had plenty of time to shelter from the rain—and plenty of time to spot rats!

The final tunnel, which reputedly runs underneath the source of the River Marne, comes out at the top of the Saône Valley. It had taken us three weeks to get this far, just half the distance across France. We had some catching up to do if we were going to reach the Mediterranean before the end of the month.

But the rain that had caused our discomfort now became our friend! The River Saône was in spate condition, rushing us south. We were swept past Lyon under a glowering sky, the water seething and surging beneath the bridges. Then we were thrown out into the wide expanse of the River Rhône, which stretched out beyond its banks like a sea. Islands of trees poked up like mangroves from the water. We passed the top of a diving board, with steps rising from the murk and, somewhere underneath, a swimming pool, in a flooded campground.

Here on the Rhône there were big barrages across the river, water thundering down between huge concrete stanchions. Beside were locks to bypass the falls, but not for us! The river was closed to commercial traffic, and although we did spot a sailing yacht way down in the bottom of one empty lock, we suspected it had sheltered there waiting for spring to arrive. Bollène lock on the Rhône has a fall of about eighty-five feet, making it the biggest lock in France. Locks that carry ships the size of coasters don't open for kayaks, but there were portage ramps and paths for canoes and kayaks. We had brought with us a pair of wheels from a baby carriage mounted onto a cradle for just this purpose, but once downstream of the barrages, the

The Saône and Rhône were running strongly.

crashing waves and churning whitewater from the flooded river made it challenging to launch safely.

Now that we were on our home run, we compared noses. Should that read "notes"? No, this was a nasal competition of sorts. Both of us had one pair of wool socks we wore on our feet when on land and another pair for paddling. At night they typically resided somewhere in the tent. Since all of them had been damp or wet for more than three weeks now, the odor was palpable. Exactly where we hid them became a topic of discussion, for clearly they should never be carelessly discarded near the head of the tent. Eventually it was inevitable that we must have a competition to see which pair could boast the most pungent smell of ammonia. By now we wondered if we had trench foot, but as neither of us knew anything much about that condition, we hoped for the best and steered clear of trenches, just in case.

Within a day's run of Port-Saint-Louis, we set up the tent on rough grass and watched the river speed past as the falling sun set the evening sky ablaze. At such a rare fine moment, it felt good to sit outside a little longer. It was then we heard the snuffling sound. It was so intermittent that whenever one of us turned to listen, there was silence. But as we chatted I became convinced there was something in the grass. Maybe it was just some animal grazing, but I was getting nervous. After about half an hour we grabbed our flashlights and boldly went to investigate. What we found was a man on his hands and knees in the tall grass, a small flashlight in his hand. Under the glare of our lamps he looked pretty harmless. I think we had him scared! When we demanded to know what he was doing, he turned without a word and held up a clear plastic bag. He was collecting snails!

We reached Port-Saint-Louis next day, leaving precious little time to spare to return to England for work. Tim pulled out his map to locate the railway station, but we soon discovered there was no passenger service from Port-Saint-Louis. Our alternatives were to return upstream as far as Arles or paddle the coast to Marseille. We had time for neither. By now Tim must have been clutching at straws . . . maybe hairs. "Ah!" he said, less than convincingly. "I think the buses have roof racks. We can strap the kayak to the roof of a bus to Marseille. . . ." We checked the bus timetable. Sure enough, there was a bus leaving early the next morning for Marseille. But roof racks? I thought that was stretching optimism!

It took longer than usual to get organized in the morning. Instead of packing the kayak, everything must now fit into the collapsible bags we had carried with us. They were tough white nylon laundry bags that when packed resembled giant snowballs and were about as easy to carry. That still left sundry awkward items such as paddles that obviously would not fit—and socks that would probably burn a hole through anything they touched. Finally we trundled the kayak to the bus stop. We had missed the bus. It would be a long wait for the next one, but after the effort of getting everything there, neither of us felt inclined to take it anywhere else. Instead we amused ourselves trying to thumb a ride from passing trucks. As though anyone would be likely to pick up a couple of vagabonds with bulging laundry bags and a twenty-foot-long kayak.

But we did get a ride, ironically from a girl driving a Citroen 2CV in the opposite direction. She looked, slowed, did a double take, swerved a bit on the road, and then sped away. But she returned ten minutes later and asked what we were doing. She was a kayaker. Her roof rack bars, barely the thickness of my finger, sat about two feet apart on the flimsy roof of her car. We tied the long *Baguette Rouge* onto it, piled all our gear inside the car, and squeezed in. Immediately I was aware of Tim's socks. Or perhaps it was mine. No matter, Colette swung open the window and we were on our way across the Camargue.

Colette dropped us at the foot of the steps outside the railway terminal in Marseille and drove away laughing. We attempted to buy a ticket to England with our kayak as accompanied baggage, to no avail. The kayak was too long! Undeterred, or perhaps more accurately almost desperate, we tried one ticket officer after another until finally one sold us a ticket. But now we had only enough money left for one of us to return by train. The other would have to hitchhike. To soften the ordeal, we agreed the train passenger would take the entire luggage. Then we flipped a coin.

26

FAEROE ISLANDS REVEAL A DARK SECRET

Vacationing in the Faeroe Islands, I was spending an afternoon kayaking alone along the coast, enjoying weather and conditions untypically gentle compared to what I'd grown to expect here. The Atlantic swell rolled around the base of the cliffs, hissing back down from the encrustations of barnacles and seaweeds and leaving the air chill and fresh with the scent of salty sea cut by an acrid hint of seabird guano. A mighty rock stack stood across the sound. Dwarfed as it was by the towering cliff behind it, it would be easy to imagine it to be much shorter than its six hundred feet. Even the mouths of the caves in that cliff were hundreds of feet tall.

The sea stack at the end of the headland and the cave running through.

Teased by a smaller open cavern entrance on my own side of the sound, I dared myself to enter—cautiously, for I still mistrusted the casual swell pattern and I was, after all, alone. Entering was like

Kayaking through a rainbow in the Faeroe Islands. Behind the spray is a cave entrance.

probing into a living body; the pink skin of the lower walls blemished by the slippery brown domes of closed sea anemones and scabbed by shellfish. The rush of water rising and gushing down this gut slapped and hissed then crashed and exploded ever deeper into the darkness. It was chilly in here, and my breath misted in front of my face. With each turn of the tunnel the light grew dimmer, the incoming waves more unsettling, and the noise seemed louder until I knew it was time for me to retreat. I was finally convinced by my natural cowardice that I shouldn't be there; I should not be there alone.

Back in the brightness again, I delighted in tracing the closest route beside the rock that could manage without my kayak touching, lifted up and around and then sinking back down with the water beside the hissing faces. But following this route I was soon tempted to probe into more caves. Finally I reached the end of the headland and found a huge wall of a stack separated from the cliff by a boulder-strewn channel. Looking up I could see that both stack and cliff leaned in the same direction. I wobbled off balance for a moment. There was no sky visible directly above me, only rock where the stack leaned over me. The sky was there to one side above the cliff. Across this gap, so high up it was difficult to confirm what I thought I could see, ran a thread of rope or wire rigged by local farmers who every year ferried sheep from the headland to summer grazing on the upper slopes of the stack. A couple of sheep at a time are hauled in a box from a farmer on the precarious cliff edge to another who had already made the journey across the gap in that same box. My eyes returned to something closer to horizontal, and my balance was restored.

I planned to turn back from here, but the day seemed so benign! Maybe I should at least continue far enough to see the view on the other side of the headland. I took the outer route around the stack, with an opening horizon of Atlantic Ocean until a new view appeared of a bay and, beyond it, steep green slopes rising to a crisp-cut edge from which cliffs dropped vertically more than two thousand feet to the water below. I took in the view. There was no tidal stream and almost no wind! What a day!

Curious now about the bay, I estimated I still had enough time for a quick stroll and a lunch break, so I paddled in. Landing on the back of a wave onto a rock shelf, I hopped out as soon as my kayak settled. A small dry-stone walled enclosure near the shore on the flatter land, almost certainly a sheep pen, was the only building in sight. From that center the slopes climbed steeply in all directions toward crags and ridges. Clouds of terns rained down at me when I strayed too close to their colony beside a stream that tumbled down the hill in cascade after waterfall. Dropping to the ground I lounged among arctic-alpine flowers to eat lunch and to soak up the thin sunlight. I could have sat for hours; I could have sat for days. But I was quick. I knew I had to get back. On the water I dawdled to the big stack, only to find water already gushing through the gap between the stack and the headland toward me. It was like a whitewater river! I felt stupid. I knew the tides were ferocious around the Faeroe Islands. I knew they could turn and strengthen quickly. Paddling alone I had somehow ignored all my usual rules! But I'd only been in the bay a short time . . . the tide couldn't be that powerful yet. It would be a fun challenge to work through the channel against the current.

I pushed from eddy to eddy, boulder to boulder, until the racing water was too shallow and the alternative routes too narrow to get any farther. This was not going to work! Whenever a wave rolled through, it threw me off course and I was swept out of control across the current. I'd have to go around the outside of the stack. I was soon there, cruising quickly up the eddy. There was an acute angle of powerful eddyline that churned and spun in vortices running from the cliff ahead. I sprinted toward the top end of this wedge and confidently spun the kayak toward the cliff the moment I hit the eddy-line. But despite my accuracy I was in an instant carried twenty feet sideways from the rock. Still sprinting full bore I began to drift backward. Moments later, still sprinting at my maximum directly into the current, I was fifty feet downstream and losing. I regained the eddy and tried again.

After several gut-busting attempts, it was clear I'd have to wait until the tide slackened. I was simply not strong enough to push around that corner. I returned to the channel behind the stack and found the current running faster than before. I was concerned. Still, there was simply nothing to do about it. Retreating toward the bay and passing a cave, my kayak spun from the cliff. There was a really fast current here! And it was coming right out of the cave! Curious I probed into the entrance and found it split into two, with water rushing from both sides. I pushed up the weaker flow and found that actually this current was a side-chute of the stronger flow, split off around a column of rock. There seemed to be only one main channel after all. It was tricky maneuvering to keep my bow directly into the stream. The slightest change in angle and the current forced my kayak to cross the narrow tunnel into the wall. Each time a wave lifted me, the kayak wanted to turn. The last thing I wanted was to be pushed under an overhang and capsized, or jammed between the walls with the tide pushing from the side. My kayak spun toward one side and I jammed in a quick bow rudder to avoid a collision, caught the upper blade on the roof, and felt a rush of adrenalin.

I held my position for a while in a wide part of the cave, getting used to the wave pattern, allowing time for my eyes to adjust to the gloom, and plucking up courage. The cave evidently ran right through the headland, but would it be possible to take a kayak through? I had no idea. I felt scared. I could imagine finding the exit too small and having to retreat in the dark along a narrow passage in reverse with the current pushing against me. Perhaps it would be best to wait for the tide to slacken. But I was just too curious, and this was too much of a challenge. I sprinted up against the current a short way. The passage grew narrow and the current was fierce, but I could see light ahead. That spurred me on, and I continued to sprint. I was barely making progress. If my willpower wavered, I knew I'd not make it.

Inch by painful inch I forced forward, so close to my limit and yet making such slow progress I doubted my ability to keep going for long enough. But it would be harder to retreat in reverse all the way back through that tunnel! Gradually the tunnel opened wider and I began making faster progress. Now it was like being at the top of a waterfall racing upstream—all the danger behind, yet no possibility to let up. I could smell the warmth of the air outside and hear the cries of seabirds. I didn't ease off until I was well clear of the exit. My heart was pounding and I buzzed with adrenalin! I'd never encountered a tide race in a cave before, and it had never occurred to me that such a thing might exist! I'd failed to paddle around the headland but managed to paddle through it. I went on my way with a head full of fearful imaginings of what could happen on a day with bigger swell, simply poking into a cave for fun and getting sucked in by the tide.

27

ICELAND REVISITED (PORTAGE)

With just a few free days before the ferry sailed, and my friends already flying home, I was looking forward to a short trip by myself. I left my vehicle where we had all been camping beside the fjord and packed my tent in my kayak again. After three weeks paddling I knew I still had plenty of food. It was quicker to repack everything into the kayak than to sort through it and leave behind what I didn't need. The extra weight meant little on the water. I slid afloat and cruised eastward from the fjord.

This place triggered special memories. Years ago I had paddled out of this fjord full of ambition and self-doubt at the start of a longer trip; that summer I hoped to paddle around Iceland, the whole island. It had never been done before, and I knew better than to expect success. With me was Geoff Hunter. We paddled out past these same mountains, although then they stood coated deep in snow. When we returned they had looked more like today. We were elated, yet subdued by the realization that the timeless nomadic existence we had grown to love, with its special sense of direction and purpose, had now ended. We must now look forward to a fresh adventure instead of the continuation of this one.

The last few days of that trip had been too hurried. Geoff, I think, knew better than I did that we could afford to relax and take our time, drawing out the last few days, savoring the solitude of that coast for as long as possible. Me, I was eager to finish, eager to know I had achieved what I'd hoped to. I was naïve. The pleasure is in the process, not in the final result.

So now I would take that time. I planned to paddle north for one day and then spend two days, maybe three, exploring what we had so quickly passed on the last day of our earlier journey.

I paddled across the mouth of the next fjord, surprised how familiar the scene appeared, as though etched on my memory all those years ago. I suppose the total package of being on the water, in the weather, looking at the surroundings, moving at the slow pace of a kayak, makes it easy to remember things. The view changes but slowly: There's plenty of time to soak it all in. Now I took time to look into each bay, stopped at each beach, bounced in the reflected waves at the base of columnar basalt cliffs. I poked my bow into a small cave where the frenetic wave action was complicated by rebounds from the multifaceted surface.

One particular headland had me recollecting. Offshore there were many shoals. Rocks hid just beneath the surface. Some jutted up like stubby stacks, but others, flat-topped lumps of rock, appeared and vanished again beneath the swell like whales. Today the sea was gentle, and although the waves sometimes broke across submerged

Remains of a sod building offer little shelter from the wind.

rocks, I could anticipate where by looking well ahead and picking my route so that a "boomer" wouldn't surprise me. When I was there with Geoff, we were in fog. Waves crashed out of nowhere around us. Our senses were heightened as we tried to figure out where the rocks were so we wouldn't get drenched, or run aground. We were already far from land, but the rocks there extend a long way offshore. We made it unscathed, but it would have been a wild place on a rough day.

Beyond the headland I reached a long beach hemming a flat-bottomed valley, broad and low. Surrounding this valley were mountain ridges. I was tempted ashore for lunch. There were no buildings I could see in the valley.

There's something about remote beaches that makes me relax. I wandered along the shoreline looking at the pebbles and sand, and the things the sea had littered there. Terns and gulls rose into the air as I approached a stream that ran out from the middle of the bay. I splashed through the clear water and climbed up the far side onto a marshy, grassy area above the beach. A bleached antler from a reindeer rested in the grass. Reindeer were introduced into Iceland from Norway in the eighteenth century. The first two herds did not survive the winters, but a third herd, released in 1850, was successful; a few still roam wild. The land stepped up inland as a series of beaches, each holding back pools of water that was silting into marsh. Wildflowers studded the grasses. Whimbrels lifted and flew ahead of me, their fluting calls mingling with the higher pitched cries of redshanks and the frenzied scream of terns. By now I was in no hurry to paddle farther. I thought maybe I'd leave later, but when I didn't I began looking for the best place to camp.

I pitched my tent beside the ruins of a building right beside the hill on the southern end of the bay. The building had been constructed from rounded stones packed together with earth, with sod wall above. The roof had collapsed. Gradually it would grow back into the ground to leave a grassy mound, but right now there were timbers visible beneath the fallen turf roof. Old ruins usually mark the places where the conditions for a building are best—where it's not too wet and where there is natural shelter.

An endless special twilight marks the Icelandic night in late summer. I built a driftwood fire and sat and listened to it crackle. Waves broke gently on the beach. I was content. This relaxation was what I sought, and I was soon in my tent asleep.

Sometime during the night the tent began to slam and squash in a strong wind. I crawled out and piled boulders all around the valance to hold it more securely and then tried to return to sleep, but the gusts hit ever more violently. Then I heard my kayak move. When I heard it roll away, I left the tent in a hurry and ran to catch it. I dragged it into a hollow and loaded it with boulders to weight it down. Then once again I tried to sleep.

By morning the sea was rough. Surf rolled in, and powerful gusts of wind slammed across the water from the headland. Offshore the headland to the south, the sea was wild with spray. To the north the sea was streaked with tumbling whitecaps. The next landing to the north is at the end of a fjord noted for squalls that funnel between its steep sides. There was nowhere sensible to paddle. North: no easy landing. South: against the gale around a headland studded with offshore shoals and rocks and with the wind accelerating around the headland. Today was a good day to stay on dry land. That's Iceland.

But next day the wind was still as strong or stronger. The sun shone, but it was no day to paddle. I began to get anxious. If the weather remained bad for one more day, I'd be stuck here, unable to catch the weekly ferry. It was essential I caught this one.

I had two options. I could hold my breath and wait till tomorrow in the hope the weather would improve. If the weather remained bad, I'd be stuck in Iceland for another week unless I abandoned my gear and hiked out. The alternative was to hike out today with my kayak. I looked at the map. At the back of this valley a footpath was marked leading over a pass toward the nearest jeep track. A "jeep track" is a designated four-wheel-drive-vehicle route, normally requiring a vehicle with high ground clearance. Some way down the track was a village and a road. From there I might be able to hitchhike back to Seyðisfjörður to fetch my vehicle, maybe.

I fashioned myself a yoke from a piece of driftwood and began my trek to the back of the valley, dragging my laden kayak across the marsh like a sled. As I splashed through the muddy water, the wind created fleeing waves through the grasses and blew a brown spray from my feet. When I was far enough inland for the ground to be dry, the grass became thin and scattered in clumps on bare earth and stones. I dodged from grassy patch to mossy patch, trying to avoid dragging the kayak across anything too abrasive. I winced every time I heard the whining scrape of a sharp edge against the fiberglass.

The valley floor gained height in a series of steps, each a steep slope of maybe twenty feet to the next flattish plateau. At each of the steep rises I unloaded the kayak and hauled it up empty, reloading it at the top. Eventually there was no more grass. Now I had to carry. Now I regretted not having taken the time to lighten my load in Seyðisfjörður when my vehicle had been so close. I divided my gear between two big bags and carried them one at a time a little way up the path, stopping when the exertion and discomfort of carrying a heavy bag over one shoulder became too much for me. Then I returned and hoisted the kayak onto my back and carried that. The wind now tormented me, spinning the kayak from my shoulder or sending me stumbling. The narrow path followed along the side of a steep stream valley. Beneath me the water tumbled over falls and twisted around boulders. Above me were mountain ridges. I paused to soak in the scene and then continued with the grunt work. Three times up and twice down each section of path, while the hours of the day plodded by. I reminded myself of my earlier assertion that the pleasure is in the process, not in the final result. I took a break to look at wildflowers.

Eventually the gradient eased, and soon after that I reached the track. It had taken me twelve hours to struggle to this point, and I was exhausted. I pitched my tent, cooked a meal, and straightway fell asleep.

Next morning at four o'clock I trudged the track with tired legs as far as the nearest village. The village comprised a few houses only, but at least there was a road to walk on from here. I walked for another hour. Not a single vehicle had passed in either direction. I sank onto the roadside grass and stared at the sky. My heels burned with blisters, and my legs ached. From my resting place on the grass, the sky looked good. I studied it for a long time.

The very first car to come along gave me a ride to a busier road. From there I had little difficulty getting another ride and then a final one that got me as far as Seyðisfjörður. As soon as I reached my vehicle, I drove back for my gear, finally easing carefully along the jeep track to where my tent and kayak waited. I threw my gear in the back, tied my kayak to the roof rack, turned around at the first suitable spot, and for the second time that day began toward Seyðisfjörður. It was night before I arrived, just hours before the ferry arrived.

The ferry left Seyðisfjörður past those familiar mountains. Guillemots skittered across the calm water. The wind had vanished. If I'd waited, could I have paddled back, taking just half a day? Possibly, but sea kayaking does involve an element of risk. When the risk seems too great, it's better to make an early decision in favor of safety, although my choice this time saw me carrying my kayak for longer than it carried me.

28

WHEN SHANGHAI POLICE HAVE THE LAST WORD

I hadn't gone to China to paddle, but I was on kayaking business. At the official opening of the "Point 65" kayak factory, a deafening barrage of firecrackers were lit to ensure the factory's good luck. "Just a couple of hours of fireworks should be appropriate," I overheard someone shout against the din. The sky disintegrated with ear-splitting explosions, while puffs of gray smoke swam as stars before the eyes from a blow to the head. Debris floated down like confetti.

We Europeans retreated to the relative peace of a nearby street cafe. At a table perched alarmingly close to the edge of a street full of crazy drivers, I tackled a bowl of spicy noodles that made my nose run. The shop fronts overflowed with colorful plastic containers. Street vendors pushed past our table wheeling carts heavy with fruit and vegetables. I was overstimulated by the color, scents, movement, and noise!

Returning to the factory we piled a dozen or so kayaks onto the flat bed of a faded blue truck, lashed them down, and headed for the Huangpu River. The Huangpu is the last main tributary to join the Yangtze River before it reaches the East China Sea near Shanghai. Here it appears gray under the drifting green rafts of water hyacinth. While we launched our kayaks, an open boat slowly crossed from a nearby island. A man in navy blue pants and sweater and a big straw hat sculled it toward us with a single long oar over the stern. Closer, he abandoned the oar in favor of a stout bamboo pole, pushing against the riverbed to maneuver.

Paul sprinted upstream to test a prototype kayak. I watched him grow small in the distance. Then my jaw dropped. Just ahead of him a barrier rose across the river. As I watched it lifted farther. Then I realized it was not a barrier but a giant rectangular net, about the size of a small city block, lifted by cables from four towers, two on our shore and two on the island. Finally the whole net hung in the air like a mesh bag. It was giant "industrial size" fishing net along the lines of the dip-nets that operate along the tidal reaches of rivers in France and elsewhere but large enough to capture our whole fleet of kayaks in just one corner!

When we set off to explore, we crept between the net and the shore. We could see fish flapping in the net near to us, but the net was so big we would have been pressed to identify anything smaller than a kayak at the far side.

Clear of the island, our view of the main river opened up. A line of moored barges stretched so far into the distance they faded into the haze. Each supported a girderlike spire—a loading crane. Myriad smaller barges motored between the barges and the shore, while larger vessels kept to the deeper main channel in the center of the river. Most of the barges appeared to be painted in red, blue, or green. We paddled closer to see better what was going on.

Preparing to launch on the Huangpu River.

Up close was noisy with clanking machinery and running engines, the crash and rushing sound of grab-loads of orange sand poured into the smaller delivery barges, and the shouts and laughs of the workers. There was the summer-shower-on-dry-earth smell of wet sand mingled with the blue haze of fumes and dust. Now I could better see what was going on. The barges anchored along the river were floating platforms for the cranes. Large barges full of sand tied up alongside on the outside, while a succession of smaller barges paused against the shoreside to be loaded. When the water was all but spilling over the sides of the heavy load, each smaller barge would pull away toward shore to vanish into one of the many small canal entrances we could see. The vacant berth at the platform would be filled immediately by the next empty barge, ready for loading.

As if to accentuate the scale of the operation, there was a steady stream of large barges clanking both up and downstream. The floating platforms stretched for miles in both directions!

So where does all the sand go? The Shanghai area population has grown by six million people in just ten years. The sand is used for

A fishing net rises from the Huangpu River.

building projects, and the most economic way to transport it is by water. We turned to explore one of the side canals, a small one with an entrance nearby.

The huge metal sluices were raised open, four stories high, on the flood-control gates, so we paddled straight through to discover an older and smaller sluice at a side turning. Once we'd poked under this one, the canal began to feel more like a ditch, and it smelled a little ripe too. A row of houses was set back from the waterfront trees, and along the bank ran ducks and geese, dogs and chickens, and children. Before each house was a small fenced garden with rows of green vegetables. Thatched pens on the bank stood ready to protect the ducks and geese overnight. Squashes climbed the chicken-wire fences, and what was evidently a pigsty, judging from the smell and the squeals, stood with walls made of bricks of orange and of cinder gray, carefully stacked without mortar, under a roof of clay tiles.

A man and woman with bright orange waterproof sleeves pulled over their forearms were loading an open boat with green vegetables. These plants resembled leeks but stood five feet tall. Like several identical boats in this little canal, this one appeared to be made of cast concrete. I resisted an impulse to call out "Your boat has a leek!" and instead waved a greeting as I moved past.

Plowing through dense rafts of water hyacinths, we dodged beneath a bridge prefabricated from concrete sections and burst out onto a wider section of waterway just as the sun, sinking into the distant haze, threw orange ripples across the water. It was time we found a road large enough for our truck to find us.

With drab two-story houses on either side of the channel, an access road wide enough for a car, and a similar width road crossing a bridge, we scrambled up a bank and dodged the cyclists to park our kayaks alongside a derelict building. I had no idea where I was, but our Chinese companions must have known more or less. After what sounded like a heated cell-phone conversation in Chinese, we settled down to wait. Half an hour later our truck squeezed as far as the nearest corner and we lifted up the kayaks one at a time. It was almost dark. Time to head back to the hotel for a shower!

But "almost dark" was the timing for the start of our second trip on the Huangpu! This was a trip Richard had wanted to attempt for some time. The Huangpu River runs through the city of Shanghai, splitting it into two, east and west. Pudong on the east side was designated a new open economic development zone, and where in the early 1990s there had been countryside and farmland, there is now a population of 1.5 million people. This is now China's financial and commercial hub. The spectacular and growing skyline of tall buildings includes the famous and distinctive Oriental Pearl Tower, the Shanghai World Financial Center—at 1,614 feet tall the third-tallest building in the world and boasting the highest observation deck in the world—and the 1,380-foot-tall Jin Mao building. Such a building plan requires a lot of building materials, evidenced by the sand supply chain we had seen earlier.

On the west side of the river lies the Bund. This was once a major international financial hub of Eastern Asia, but the international banks and trading houses moved out in the 1950s, only gradually returning in the late 1970s and 1980s. The nighttime skyline is spectacular, and a new tourist promenade has opened the riverbank to tourists to view Pudong across the water.

Richard, from Sweden, frequently asked if it was possible to kayak the Bund. "You cannot do it" was the usual reply. "But why not?" he would persist. "Is it illegal?" But China is not Sweden. The Chinese don't consider it in terms of "Is it illegal?" but rather in terms of "It's common sense that you must not do that."

So Richard decided it would be best if we didn't encourage our Chinese friends to come, in case they got into trouble. The truck carrying the kayaks rolled into the city while we scouted the riverbank. The banks have been built up to prevent flooding in the city, but there were three places where we thought we might gain access to the water. The first places were fenced and had guarded gates. We could not see whether we could get to the water, and the guards waved us away with clear gestures of confident authority. But at the third we could see the water from the road and see floating pontoons with several pleasure boats moored alongside. There were some people partying on board one of them. Richard, striding up to the gate, confidently waved the guard to come. He pointed to the people on the boat and gestured that we needed to go to the boat. The guard looked at us and toward the distant boat, thought for a moment, then pulled open the gate and let us through. On the dock we called and waved to the people on the boat until they came to see what we wanted. A little jocular conversation in international sign language was all we needed for the benefit of the watching guard.

The pontoon appeared reasonable for launching kayaks, although the current surged past rapidly. One section of dock was out of sight of the guardroom, so we decided we should launch there. We strode back to the gate, confidently thanked the guard, and headed down the road.

After a phone call and a short wait, the truck arrived, pulling up out of sight of the water. We unloaded and then carried the kayaks by hand to the gate, pointing once more to the boat. Richard made a gesture imitating lifting a glass to his lips and gave a thumbs-up sign. The guard opened the gate wide enough for us to carry everything through. Reaching the pontoon we wasted no time. Stripped down to the shorts and T-shirts we wore under our street clothes, we fed the kayaks down to the water, climbed in, and sneaked away, keeping as close to shore as possible to stay out of sight. We hoped the guard would assume we were on the boat partying.

It was dusk, and the buildings around us were lighting up for the evening. Towers of bright lights, flashing to give the illusion of falling water, splashed out with colorful signs. Brightly lit ferries and tour boats crossed paths with commercial barges and ships, while house-size TV screens on barges displayed advertisements. It was like New York's Times Square on steroids. As we drifted with the current, tourist boats beside us cast off without warning and turned toward us, oblivious to our presence. Out in mid-river we could see the dark shapes of barges heading downstream, one after the other. The river was teeming with traffic.

We kept dodging yet tried to keep within sight of one another. The noise of boats and land traffic was often too loud to keep within earshot even when we were close. Wakes rebounding from the river walls and docks splashed us with gray water. Five sets of eyes in five kayaks kept alert to the next boat to motor away from the dock, and five sets of eyes gawped at the giant advertising screens and the changing colors of the lights on the tourist boats and floating restaurants.

Then I saw the police boat at the side of the river. We'd been spotted. A man waved frantically for me to come to him. I waved back and then looked away until I was quickly swept beyond his sight. But the mood of our adventure had changed. Sooner or later we would have to turn around, for we knew of no other place where we could get on or off the water, and in the dark there was little hope of our being spontaneously creative. When we had passed most of the Bund, we turned around. The next part would not be so easy. The current was strong, and we made slow progress against it. As we crept along the shore, the police spotted us again. This time there was no escaping. Blue lights flashed, sirens wailed, and a voice boomed out toward us from a loudhailer. Amidst the calls, whistles, and hoots from spectators on the surrounding boats, we were hemmed into a corner by two police boats.

They wanted us to get on board, and we had no real choice. It was not the easiest thing to do, and it took quite a time. Would we end up in a Chinese jail, we wondered? Luckily, not this time. The police were amicable, although they spoke no English and we spoke no Chinese. They stopped at a ferry landing, passed the kayaks up to us in a hurry because a ferry was approaching, and then urged us away with waves and what I imagine were words of encouragement. Carrying the kayaks we emerged abruptly onto a city street. Suddenly I felt out of place under the lights of night dressed in shorts and T-shirt with an eighteen-foot-long kayak. Buses and taxis honked, cycles and cars dodged and weaved past us. We made it to the safety of a sidewalk and called for the truck. We were ready to go home. The wonderful nighttime spectacle of the bright lights as seen from a kayak on the Huangpu River was a one-off experience to long remember. Next time maybe we should try Stockholm!

FLOTSAM AND JETSAM

Of wrecks and wreckage: Here are the broken, the abandoned, the beached, and the sunk. Here too the harbingers of wreckage: seiches, storms, rogue waves, and lightning.

29

HELENA STAR

You could portray Seattle within a "ring of bright water," to borrow the title of one of Gavin Maxwell's better known books. The waters are the Duwamish River to the south, Puget Sound to the west, Lake Washington to the east, and finally to the north the 1918 ship canal, linking Lake Washington, Portage Bay, Lake Union, and Salmon Bay, via the Chittenden locks, to Puget Sound. The northern part of the ring welcomes ships from Puget Sound into Lake Washington, but to do so it steals the drainage from Lake Washington that once fattened the Duwamish.

Taken in combination these waterways create a fascinating urban kayaking area, with container docks at the mouth of the Duwamish, ferry docks and piers in Elliott Bay beneath the city, grain docks and commercial docks at Smith Cove, and dry docks, fishing terminals, seaplane ports, rowing clubs, and marinas and boatyards through the lakes of the ship canal. Quite large commercial ships access the lakes via the canal, so although some kayakers like to use the locks to rise from salt to fresh water, I prefer to launch on one side or the other and stay there. I've been through plenty of locks. One of my favorite outings close to home is to launch by Ballard Bridge on the "canal" and to check out the ships and boats in the Salmon Bay area.

I'm not alone in my fascination for these ships; Matt Broze—who with his brother Cam designed and sold their own line of rough-water performance sea kayaks, Mariner Kayaks, from their kayak store beside Lake Union—knows these waters and the resident ships well. It was Matt who recently added color to my research of a ship called *Helena Star*. *Helena Star* has been moored near the Chittenden locks for longer than I've been paddling there and first caught my eye because of its patina—that mix of worn paintwork and corroding metal that develops from the moment a ship is introduced to water. Looking up at the white-painted name, *Helena Star,* I noticed the welded plates underneath declaring the name *Fraternité* painted over with the gray-green hull paint. Having two names to research made it easier to find out the history.

Helena Star was built in Westerbroek in the Netherlands in 1947. It measures 51.36 meters long with a beam of 8.45 meters, but it has been here in Seattle for a long time and will likely never sail again. Why not? Matt, always a storehouse of eccentric stories, of which he is becoming one, added something of a personal touch to that story, so I'll begin by introducing him.

Matt grew up in Seattle in the early 1970s, learned to ski at age three, and became part of a new wave of snow skiers who focused on "hot-dogging," or "freestyle" skiing. He learned quite a lot of ski tricks before *Skiing Magazine* and Chevrolet first sponsored contests for tricks, moguls, and aerial tricks on skis in 1972. Traveling around

Helena Star *with her tree. The ship has been moored here for more than twenty years.*

the Rocky Mountains and living out of his VW bus in ski area parking lots, Matt heard about the upcoming Hot Dog contest in Sun Valley, modified his route, and took fourth place in the tricks event. Finding nothing written about freestyle skiing, he proceeded to write *Freestyle Skiing*, self-publishing it in 1972 before being approached by a publisher in 1978. The New Arco Press cover shows Matt in a custom-fit neoprene ski suit, his arms a blaze of multicolored floral designs, given to him by the manufacturer and serving Matt on the slopes for thirty years until it was finally cut from him after he was injured by his own stray ski on a slope too steep and icy for the ski's safety brake to hold. Matt says the suit was getting a little breezy around the crotch anyway.

Matt now skis in a one-piece suit he bought for fifteen dollars at a thrift store. His skis mostly cost even less than that. Now retired, and with his long flowing beard and long hair turned nearly white, he still skis much like he has since the 1970s. Many times in the moguls, seemingly out of control, often with one ski in the air pointing in a different direction than the one on the snow, he grabs the attention from others on the slopes, who become transfixed, waiting for a monster wipeout. However, Matt nearly always stays on his feet until the slope eases up and then flows into a graceful series of snaked carved turns with maybe a spin or two with one ski over his head for those watching. As a concession to his advancing years, he has managed to fit hockey hip and shoulder pads (from a thrift store) under an XL ski suit.

Sail maker Mike Lund performed a dance routine with his girlfriend, Patricia Karnik, that scored well in those early freestyle skiing contests. Mike was in his mid-thirties, a decade or two older than most of the other contestants, who were in their mid-teens to mid-twenties. He was one of the earliest competitors to do a Moebius flip in competition; that's a full backflip with full twist. While learning it Mike would crash time after time, but he would just get back up and try it again. The younger competitors wondered just how much of these crashes his "old" body could take.

Mike did well in all three freestyle disciplines and was respected by most of the competitors. During competitor meetings about the rules and the direction their sport would take, he was often called upon to make decisions, because both sides respected him but couldn't agree among themselves. His age, experience, and fairness in mediating disputes made him sort of a father figure to the group. I never met Mike, but while kayak-surfing alone in California, I was joined by another kayaker, sporting a braided beard and a big smile. Although we became great friends, it was several years before I discovered his girlfriend, now wife, was Mike Lund's daughter.

Getting back to the ship, *Helena Star* has a tree. It's not the kind that looks like a mast; it's bushier than that, and it grows straight up from the hold. When I first spotted it from my kayak, I thought it was a small bush growing on the deck. Seattle has great growing conditions for this sort of thing, and a lot of older wooden boats soon grow plants if they are not maintained. I kept an eye on this bush, and after a couple of years it became obvious it was a tree, and yes, it was growing from the bottom of the hold.

On April 15, 1978, the *Yocona,* a 213-foot US Coast Guard cutter, left Astoria, Oregon, on a general law enforcement patrol off the Washington coast. Spotting a small plane flying suspiciously low toward the north across the water, the *Yokona* followed and next day encountered the *Helena Star* about fifty miles offshore headed toward the Strait of Juan de Fuca—the gap that runs between Vancouver Island, Canada, and the United States and which connects to Puget Sound.

As *Helena Star* was not displaying a flag, the Coast Guard cutter made radio contact and was told the ship was of English registration, bound for Victoria on Vancouver Island. Sending the information back to base for verification, the cutter resumed patrolling but resumed interest when the *Helena Star* turned west and sailed through the night without displaying lights. Next day the report came back from Seattle that the *Helena Star* was not registered in Britain and that the Port of Victoria was not expecting her. Given her suspicious behavior, including night sailing without lights, the Coast Guard was directed to board the vessel to find out what was going on. About midday on April 17 there was an armed boarding about 150 miles offshore.

Checking the paperwork, it appeared that the ship's registration process had been started but not completed and had since lapsed. Other papers made it unclear whether the name should be *Helena Star, Monica Star 1,* or *Fraternité,* and there was no cargo manifest.

In order to more clearly identify the ship, the Coast Guard asked to see the main beam number—something like the chassis number on a car. But the captain denied there was one and was unwilling to open the cargo hold. When the boarding officers did gain access, they discovered bales of marijuana, seized the ship, and arrested the officers and crew. Stacked on board was thirty-seven tons of marijuana from Colombia worth about seventy-four million dollars.

Rapidly following up all the leads, the authorities linked the *Helena Star* with skier Mike Lund's sixty-one-foot sailboat, the *Joli*, once a top racing sailboat but now with its interior removed to make it a freight hauler. The *Joli* was severely scraped riding up and down hull against hull during a cargo transfer, which is probably why Lund had purchased the tug and barge headed toward *Helena Star* at the time of seizure. The plan had been to transfer the cargo at sea and move it to Lund's house.

Lund had bought the *Joli* in California from a Seattle businessman, offering him $285,000, with a $55,000 down payment, and paid his deposit by opening his briefcase and handing over $55,000 in used twenty-dollar bills! He sailed the Pacific coast back to Sequim, where he lived. The tug and barge had also been purchased by Lund with hard cash. He paid $80,000 for the barge and bought the tug for $122,500 after barely looking at it. By the time agents seized the *Joli*, Lund had vanished. His girlfriend had dropped him off somewhere south of Seattle and never saw him again.

The *Helena Star*, impounded in Seattle since 1978, has been slowly rusting away. Close to it is another ship that appears in even worse condition. You can see it when you look down through the clear water, although parts of it protrude. I haven't been able to find out anything about that one, but it's as though the boats impounded here are doomed to finally sink into the mud. Which made me wonder if the *Helena Star* smugglers are still "rusting" in jail? Sentences in those days were not as harsh as they are now, and most smugglers got away with fines and up to a couple of years in jail rather than the thirty years they might expect nowadays. But where was Lund? What happened to him?

Having headed south, Lund continued life under a new name, married, had children, and separated from his wife. Then, routinely fingerprinted during a child support payment issue twenty-three years later in 2001, his fingerprints matched those of the missing man! Lund was finally brought to trial, convicted, and given a jail term for his part in the 1978 smuggling operation. His sentence would have been a lot longer, but given that he appeared to have led a blameless life with no other convictions while on the run, his sentence was reduced to a year or so.

Following the disappearance of Lund in 1978, Matt continued freestyle skiing without the group's "father figure." He opened his kayak store, designed kayaks, and cruised on the lakes and ship canal whenever he had time for a break or wanted to check out a new kayak. Now that he's retired he skis more, paddles whenever he wishes, and hangs out till late at night at our house parties, where we tease stories out of him. And yes, it was a tree sprouting from the hold, not a giant marijuana plant!

Postscript: On March 7, 2011, the Western Towboat Company towed *Helena Star* from Ballard to the Hylebos Waterway in Tacoma, presumably to be scrapped. She was still waiting there in December 2011.

30

IN THE WAKE OF THE *BRAER*

In 1993 the tanker *Braer* didn't make its destination. Its entire cargo of oil, more oil than the infamous *Exxon Valdez* was carrying, spilled into the sea close to some of Britain's most convoluted coastline. It was big news for several weeks—then we heard nothing.

The Spill

January 4, 1993, was cold, wet, and windy. The rain blasted the small rectangular panes above my desk as I clasped my hands around a cup of coffee and reviewed a page of writing. It's good to be inside on blustery Welsh winter days. The radio chattered quietly behind me: I often work best with a little background noise around me. Suddenly I was listening attentively. An oil tanker was adrift off the southern coast of Shetland. Storm-force winds were carrying her toward land. The crew was trying to restart her engines.

To the mariner "storm-force winds" means something specific: wind speed fifty-two to sixty knots, a knot being one nautical mile per hour, or 1.15 statute miles per hour. So in statute miles, the measure we use on land, storm-force wind blows at sixty to seventy miles per hour. Such winds create sea conditions described by the Beaufort scale of wind force as "Very high waves (probable height 29 to 36 feet) with long overhanging crests. The resulting foam in great patches is blown in dense white streaks along the direction of the wind. On the whole the surface of the sea takes a white appearance. Tumbling of the sea becomes heavy and shock-like. Visibility affected."

I felt tense. My eyes turned to a map of Shetland on the wall. A few months earlier, in the summer of 1992, I had been lucky enough to paddle there with a group of sea kayakers during Shetland's best spell of weather since 1947. We had explored every cleft, cave, and tunnel all the way up the western cliffs, and I had grown to love the clear waters and the populations of seals, otters, and nesting seabirds. We had explored the rosy red cliffs, carved by the sea into stacks and arches, with myriad channels to cruise through. We had taken our time, gazing down into water of such clarity that it made me catch my breath and balance lest I topple and fall to the white sand thirty or forty feet below me. If I shadowed the glare on the surface, I could see starfish, sea urchins, and shoals of fish. Puffins and guillemots flew beneath the kayaks, streaming tiny silver bubbles.

The *Braer* had been attempting to pass between Mainland Shetland and the island of Fair Isle in storm-force winds. Somehow seawater had contaminated the fuel in the tanks, disabling the engines and leaving the tanker adrift in tumultuous seas near the south coast of Shetland. The crew was attempting to separate fuel from seawater, but it would take several hours to clear enough fuel for the engines to be restarted. Within that time the wind would almost certainly carry the tanker ashore on Shetland, but there was a slight possibility the tanker might be carried clear by the strong tidal streams. I listened and waited. The coast guard stood by, but sea conditions were violent.

The radio reported the drift of the tanker toward land. There was speculation as to how the heavy seas might have forced water into the fuel tanks through air vents that had not been fully secured. Then, when it seemed inevitable that the disabled tanker would be wrecked against the cliffs, coast guard helicopters moved in and hoisted the crew to safety. No casualties. Under the circumstances, in what was by now a severe storm blowing, with violent seas running and restricted visibility, it was a remarkable feat. But the abandoned tanker was still carrying a full cargo of light oil from Norway.

Fitful Head on the southwestern corner of Shetland has long been the nesting place for thousands of puffins, guillemots, and fulmars. In summer frantic wing beats keep the tubby auks aloft while fulmars scythe smoothly past, banking around my kayak and fixing me with a quiet stare. They sweep confidently close, wing tips almost brushing the water, and I stare back into their calm eyes, set under patches of dark-shaded plumage like eye shadow. On wings stiff as balsa boards, they turn and soar then bank around once more.

The cliffs, almost a thousand feet high, resound with the cackles of fulmars and the constant gargling of hundreds of guillemots lining the ledges. Seals wail on the rocks below, arching their backs at every wash of cold water as the tide rises. Shags and auks speed through the clear water after sprats and sand eels, while heavy Atlantic gannets fold their wings close to their bodies and plummet from sixty feet above the water to capture larger fish. Terns hover and dart lightly down to snatch sand eels from the shoals close to the surface. It is a place that seethes with life throughout the breeding season.

When the *Braer* was finally thrown ashore, it was onto the rocks just west of Garths Ness, a quarter mile from Fitful Head. Oil gushed into the churning sea, spouting from the punctured hull like a chocolate fountain. Quendale Bay, once a pale blade of sand, was rapidly enveloped in a morass of red-brown oil. The oil had been whipped into a mousse by the severe wind and chaotic waves. Fortunately at that time of year (January) most of the seabirds are out at sea, but there was immediate concern for the many salmon farms along the west coast. In nearby villages heavy fumes in the air made breathing unpleasant. Windows of houses became splattered with oil. There were fears for the well-being of livestock on nearby farms, where the grass turned black and grazing sheep turned reddish brown.

Back in Wales I paced the kitchen, bitter with anger. I felt bereaved, and I am not even a Shetlander. In the Shetland Isles it is not possible to be more than three miles from the sea anywhere, so Shetlanders live intimately with the sea.

In the days that followed the wreck, I looked at the notes I had written on my map while cruising the Shetlands. I had marked some of the more spectacular caves. Reading the notes I made about one particular cave brought back the experience to me. There had been a low, narrow entrance into a dark, cool chamber, where a glimmer of distant light and a breath of air on my face had lured me onward as I probed gently for a point of contact with the surrounding rock, hoping to avoid submerged rocks. Sparks of bioluminescence swirled from my paddle blades, and a pool of glowing green light from a submerged entrance silhouetted the kayak from beneath. Although the breeze against my face hinted of a possible exit, I wasn't certain it would be big enough for a kayak. Around a corner I spotted a slit of light, not bright enough to reveal the obstacles ahead. Creeping closer I saw the slit expand to a rocky doorway. My beard damp and clammy, my skin shivery, I emerged with a smile into warm dry air, sunshine, the scent of sea pinks, and the musty odor of fulmar petrels. After the cave, with its "water in the ears" muffled sounds and gurgles, I was surrounded by crisp sounds of crying oystercatchers, the slap of water against rock, and the whirr of wing beats. The sound of voices and paddles in the water told me my friends were approaching the exit.

At St. Ninian's Isle on the map, where I had previously written, "Beautiful tombola—sweep of white sand joins historic island to Mainland," I now added the note: "Oil reached here 7th Jan."

I remembered Burra Isle on the west coast where, while watching young ravens exploring from their nest, I had stirred up the flat discs of golden mica sand in the shallows beneath my kayak until they drifted, fluttering as they fell, dancing and shimmering in the sun. When the oil advanced along this shore, the Shetlanders tried bulldozing barriers and spreading booms between the smaller islands in an attempt to hold it back, but there was a limit to their effectiveness in winds that blew at more than eighty miles per hour for day after day after day. But it was something they could do: something better than sitting back and watching their coast become soiled.

The Braer *ran aground on the south coast of Mainland Shetland.*

There was an attempt to spray the main slick with dispersants during a brief lull in the weather, but the winds quickly rose again. The *Daily Post* on January 7 reported seals and seabirds caked in oil, grass on the hillsides taking on a brownish hue, sheep four miles from the wreck turning brown. The hurricane-force winds on January 6 moderated, but the forecast was for deteriorating weather with gale-force winds. By Friday January 8, the *Guardian* newspaper reported emergency plans to evacuate up to three thousand people from the area closest to the disaster because of fear of airborne oil pollution; a fine oil mist might coat people's lungs. Those with skin disorders or lung or kidney complains were advised to avoid exposure. By this time a fourteen-mile-long slick was spreading along the east coast toward the capital of the islands, Lerwick.

On February 4 the *Times* reported that an estimated two million salmon, raised at sixteen west coast fish farms, were believed to be contaminated. Fifteen hundred seabirds had died, with two hundred and thirty more oiled birds, three otters, and thirty seals also being treated.

Return to Shetland

Three months after the disaster, I returned to Shetland to instruct local kayaking groups. Uncertain what I would find, I paddled the west coast from Burra Isle to Fitful Head, past the wreck of the *Braer*, and round Sumburgh Head to the east coast. The cliffs were alive with seabirds. Seals basked up on the rocks within a couple of hundred yards of the wreck, and the wreck itself appeared only lightly oiled. Of an entire cargo of oil released from the wreck, there was surprisingly little to be seen. On the beach I ran my hands through the sand and found only sand. I crept into caves and gullies and rubbed my hands against the walls. I kneeled low in the grass to try to find oily traces. Again I found none. On the west coast of Burra, several beaches displayed signs warning of oil contamination, and here the rocks were splattered with oil. But what happened to the rest of it? Had the weather in the weeks following the wreck dispersed it? I distrusted my eyes.

When I returned again in 1994, I spoke with some of the residents of the Burra Isles about the oil spill. One woman told me how she had stood on the cliffs and watched the *Braer* run ashore. Two days later she smelled the oil from her house. "For a while everyone was issued masks. The water washing over the Grind" (that's the rocky tombola joining the southern part of West Burra to the northern end) was "just like coffee, dark brown coffee," the woman said. "A few months later when we were having some work done on the sea defenses on the Grind, they were putting in cages of rocks. The men were digging down, and they found the oil several feet below the surface. It must have filtered down, leaving the sand on the top fairly clean. But it's not gone away. It's still down there."

She told me that in wet weather much of the ground seems a lot wetter than it has ever been before, even where the ruins of houses stand. "The old folk always built where it was dry," she said. "They'd never choose a wet place to build a house." Now there were burns (small streams) running across the ruins in rainy weather. She believed a film of oil lay beneath the surface and prevented normal drainage.

The woman added that the grass had been burnt black by the oil and fumes. But when it started growing again, it came up a really vivid green, almost unnatural in color. That, she thought, was probably due to the oil breaking down and releasing nutrients. The flowers on the cliffs, she observed, had been unusually numerous since the spill.

On the island of Noss there is a bird reserve with a nesting colony of about six thousand pairs of gannets and a bewildering number of other nesting seabirds. When I questioned the warden, Simon, about the effects of the spill, he told me Shetland appeared to have come off very lightly so far as he could tell because the spill was in winter when most of the seabirds were elsewhere. The weather had been exceptionally stormy following the wreck, and the oil had been whipped into froth and dispersed by the wind and violent seas. Fortunately it had been light oil. If it had been heavy crude, the rocks would probably still be coated.

I asked whether the long-term effects of the hydrocarbons on the food chain were known. Simon said no, but if there were poisons in the food chain, there had been no noticeable effect on the birds as yet.

For other Shetlanders the spill was a mixed blessing. The traditional tarred felt roofs were damaged by the airborne oil, and grants became available for replacements. Compensation was also available for other damage, often on a new-for-old basis. Salmon farmers inside the affected area sought compensation for the salmon they were barred from selling. But despite the compensation many Shetlanders remain watchful, suspicious, waiting for some unseen consequence to strike.

As a paddling area Shetland remains superb, notable for its clarity of water, the cleanliness of its rock, and for its thriving populations of seabirds and otters. It is also notable for something else: At Sullom Voe, positioned roughly in the middle of Shetland, is Europe's largest oil and liquefied gas terminal, handling production from over a dozen nearby oil fields. Of course there are industrial safeguards against oil pollution from incoming tankers, but there are no safeguards for tankers, such as the Liberian-flagged *Braer*, simply passing by Shetland.

My kayak was built using petroleum-based products. I use a car to get my kayak to the water. I buy the cheapest fuel rather than question how one company might have been able to cut its costs. Would cutting down on my fuel consumption help cut the amount of oil that is shipped by sea? The wreck of the *Braer* really touched me. I cannot forget how helpless I felt. It was as if an old friend was about to die and I could only stand aside and watch, knowing in part I was to blame.

31

DRIFTWOOD

Back in the 1970s the British winter beaches were littered with wooden fish boxes washed ashore by storms. These sturdy boxes usually had the company of ownership stenciled along the side, though I doubt many found their way home from the beach. I expect most either slowly disintegrated into the machair or were collected for winter firewood. A kayaking butcher I met in Shetland used them to create small sheltered places in which to grow plants in a less-stunted way on his windswept land. I used fish boxes whenever I beached and needed a dry seat or a flat surface for my stove. I seldom went needy when kayak camping, but gradually the wooden crates vanished, to be replaced by plastic ones, which didn't ever compensate for the most useful function of broken boxes: firewood.

Driftwood fires played an essential part on many of my kayaking trips. Even busy English holiday beaches provided me enough small sticks of driftwood for a fire to cook on. Even nowadays in the age of plastic, it's possible to scour the cobbles of England's Brighton Beach and find sufficient fuel to raise a fire hot enough to explode the flints. Having enjoyed so many fires, when I lit a fire I'd seldom mention such a mundane pastime afterwards any more than I would describe making breakfast. Nevertheless, a fire was usually a magical addition to my overall experience on multiday trips, even if it made my eyes sting and my clothing stink of smoke. It's only more recently that I decided to forego a fire to minimize my impact. Yet I still explore the beach to gather sticks!

It seems impossible to travel by sea kayak without encountering driftwood, but driftwood is nothing new and seems to be in inexhaustible supply. It has been an important commodity throughout the ages.

Back in the 1970s and 1980s I became fascinated by the Faeroe Islands with their precipitous cliffs, extensive caves, and massive sea stacks. I loved paddling there. The islands are home to some prime seabird colonies, with examples of almost all the Northeast Atlantic seabird species. There are also tumbling and humbling tide races. Villages maintain the traditional turf-roofed houses that can withstand the hurricane-force winter storms, and wooden fishing boats stylistically evoke Viking long ships. On the west coast of Streymoy at a place called Kirkjubøur is an eleventh-century bishop's palace built from large logs. But there are few trees in the Faeroes, and those are only small ones.

The bishop's palace was built of driftwood logs and is still in great condition because of the scarcity of fungi. Through the centuries the palace has been under the guardianship of the Patursson family. Landing there I met one member of the family, Trondur Patursson. He had been a crewmember on Tim Severin's mid-1970s expedition by Irish curragh to retrace the route of the legendary St. Brendan's voyage from Ireland to Newfoundland and also on Severin's later "Sinbad" expedition. After those trips Trondur decided to build himself a traditional log house in the style of the bishop's palace, with an adjoining art studio. But where did he get all the wood, I wondered?

Exploring a driftwood log at La Push, Washington.

Trundur told me that by that time he had already gathered all the wood he needed. For years he had been collecting logs that had been thrown up by the sea onto a nearby driftwood beach. He had collected enough not only to build the house he desired but also to furnish it. Some of the interior paneling was cut from logs that had been burrowed through by teredo worms, and the finger-diameter holes added a curiously textured decoration!

The teredo worm, which is in fact a mollusk, begins life as a tiny free-swimming larva in salt water. It attaches itself to a wooden surface and then begins to excavate a hole. Over its one- to three-year lifespan it burrows into the wood using its sharp half-inch-long bivalve shell, digesting the cellulose with the help of bacteria in its gut. *Teredo navalis* grows up to two feet long, boring a hole up to six feet long into the wood and lining it with a calcareous coating.

Developing such a dense infestation of worms capable of creating the tracery evident in some of Trondur's timber must have taken several years. So where had the logs drifted from? Perhaps from South America via the Gulf Stream. Who knows how long the logs had traveled? Many of the logs thrown up on the north coast of Iceland are thought to have completely circled the Arctic, and the teredo worm is inactive in Arctic waters. Driftwood used by east coast Greenlanders for building kayak frames must surely have drifted on the south-flowing current from the Arctic Ocean. If driftwood is thrown ashore in such quantity in places where trees never grow, what are the beaches like where trees do grow?

Kayaking in the Queen Charlotte Islands in British Columbia, Canada, a group of us camped on a narrow wooded isthmus where the breeze blew gently between the trees from the ocean on one side, while we had a view of the water on the other. When the tide rose in the night, floating all the driftwood logs from the beach, the breeze blew them all together. The swell then rocked the logs, bumping them against one another with a deep booming and clunking sound to lull us to sleep. Many of these logs were probably escapees from the clear-cut logging that visually blights almost all of Canada's west coast with a patchwork of stripped land and straight-edged blocks of new growth. Rafts of logs are towed along the coast, the simplest way to move them around. But some inevitably break free. Trimmed of branches and with the ends rubbed smooth by contact against other logs, escapees gather like blunt torpedoes along the high tide line of west coast beaches.

In Washington State the mountains on the Olympic Peninsula rise to almost eight thousand feet. The rivers from these mountains are fueled by some of the heaviest rainfall in the United States—an average of almost twelve feet of rain per year. When the rivers flood through the temperate rain forest, the current undercuts the banks and fells trees, which are carried downstream into the Pacific Ocean. The winter Pacific surf beats the shore with a power that defies imagination. If the beaches were devoid of rock outcrops, the surf would be less menacing, but here and there the jagged teeth of bedrock jut from the sand. As though this were not enough, the logs roll and tumble in the surf, creating an additional hazard within the surf line. When logs finally strand on the beach, they get pushed ever higher with each tide, so the top of the beaches are littered deep with logs piled one onto another. Rough-water landings at the highest tides are challenging and dangerous, if not outright foolhardy. When the logs are lifted and tumbled by the water, they can snap kayaks and people like twigs!

Visiting La Push on the Olympic Peninsula this year, I checked out what must be the biggest driftwood log I've ever seen! This hollow log had such a cavernous entrance between the roots that I could crawl twenty feet inside and still sit upright with my head unbowed. Up above, children and adults walked the long trunk to the root-ball and clung to roots as if to railings to watch the surging waves below. It was such a contrast to my normal idea of driftwood. It made me wonder how much volume of wood an average sea kayaker might burn in a lifetime of camping on the beach. It made me wonder how many cooking fires one such log could provide if it was cut up into small sticks. And it made me think back to all those timeless moments I've spent staring into the embers on hidden beaches around the world, withdrawing into my thoughts until I could imagine myself as easily in the Stone Age as in the present day. Even though I seldom light fires nowadays, the slightest scent of wood smoke or glimmer of embers on an evening beach conjures up myriad memories of driftwood fires I've had on beaches all over the world. Driftwood links together all the places I've ever paddled.

32

WHISKY ON THE ROCKS

This incident made an impact on me but a greater one on my kayak. The kayak model was a "Whisky 16," and the impact was with rocks; hence "Whisky on the rocks."

My friend Jen Kleck lives in California where she owns a kayak store. Every spring she runs a sea kayaking symposium. California borders Mexico, which has some wonderful coastline. The section of coast Jen first introduced me to is not far south of the border— a place where a spectacular blowhole attracts tourists to stand at a paved viewpoint halfway up the cliff. As each swell pushes into the gully below, it builds in height as the gully funnels its huge energy into a great watery fist that punches so hard into the cave at the end that the compressed air sprays a plume of water and foam high into the air with a sound like a geyser. It is mesmerizing to watch the plume and to feel the explosion of energy vibrate the cliff. So much so that tourists often forget this is no fairground stunt. Some waves are bigger than others, so the spray rises higher and spreads wider. Occasionally there are screams of excitement and anguish when the crowd gets caught beneath a deluge of cold salt water.

I've watched waves all my life. The seawall at Rottingdean close to my childhood home catches the full impact of winter storm waves. At high tide they beat against the wall and burst skyward into the wind, which whips spray, seaweed, and pebbles up and over the top of the hundred-foot-high chalk cliffs behind. By watching the wave patterns and judging when a set of bigger waves had passed and a lull, or period of less-violent activity, might follow, it was possible to run from one dry viewpoint to the next. When we mistimed it we got drenched.

Dodging waves is an art, but waves are based on science. Wave patterns are produced on the ocean by wind blowing across the surface, and the winds are produced by weather systems. A weather system way out in the Pacific can send waves hundreds or even thousands of miles to reach the shore in Mexico. Another weather system elsewhere in the Pacific might send waves that arrive at the same place in Mexico at the same time as the waves from the first system. If the waves are "in phase" when they reach shore—that is, if the crest of the wave from one wave system aligns with the crest from the other source—then the waves combine, producing a much larger wave. Typically this will happen for a succession of waves before the waves start slipping out of phase. We call this sequence of larger waves a "set."

If the waves are perfectly "out of phase," then the crest of the wave from one source will fill the valley, or "trough," between waves from the other source. Then the sea will appear much calmer. This period of relative quiet is called a "lull."

When negotiating the passages between the rocks, it is important to watch the wave patterns.

With just two wave patterns, sets and lulls follow one another in a fairly predictable pattern. It gets more complicated when waves arrive from multiple sources and from multiple directions.

At another après-symposium visit to La Bufadora, I found myself escaping with my wife, Kristin, to dodge between the stacks and through the arches along the coast toward the headland. The same timing required for dodging the spray on land applies to safely negotiating the gaps between the rocks on the ocean. I appraise the gap, estimate how long it'll take for me to approach, paddle through, and find another safe haven and determine whether I need a small wave or not. Some gaps can be paddled on a big wave, but for others the big waves would lead to disaster. So watching the waves and being able to anticipate what is going to come next is essential. We worked our way all the way to the headland and after some waiting and watching, negotiated a longer and more risky channel between rock ledges and the headland. Once safely through, Kristin wanted to run it again. It had been technical and exciting, so we paddled around the outside

My kayak comes to rest on the top of the rocks.

and returned to the entrance. Then everything changed. Huge waves piled in, and for a time the ledges were completely enveloped by each wave. The channel churned heavily with white foaming water that boiled and rebounded in every direction, sending powerful currents through the gaps between the rocks. When the surging calmed sufficiently, we timed a second exciting run through the channel and flew out the other end into the face of the next arriving set.

Somehow the significance of this violent period at the headland was lost on me. It had taken us three-quarters of an hour or so to reach the headland. The progression of lull followed by set—smaller waves building to larger ones—continued in a typical pattern, and I was confident in my judgment of when to move and when to wait.

Finally, after about forty-five minutes, we arrived back at the bay where we had launched. There was a big crowd of kayakers waiting to land, so I waited. While I waited I looked at a horseshoe of rocks sticking up in the middle of the bay, its open end facing out to sea. I'd been in there before and knew that if I waited while a wave piled up into the enclosure, I could time my exit through a small gap near the far end, dropping over what for a short time would become a waterfall. The biggest waves poured through that same notch too, but then the turbulence was too great and too many rocks were exposed on the other side. I needed to wait for a wave smaller than the peak size of the waves in the sets. In the meantime I felt happy to bounce around in the churning water of the enclosure, where I could watch for the right moment. I moved into the space during what appeared to be the biggest waves of a set and attempted to "hover"—hold my kayak in one place while all around me the water foamed white with turbulence and the currents swirled and surged. As each wave piled up against the rock wall at the far end, it rebounded and made a fun play area. I was enjoying myself, and the waves had begun to diminish, when the unthinkable happened.

A wave twice the size of the ones I'd been watching all afternoon steepened beyond the enclosure. I could see it would trash me if I stayed where I was, so I sprinted for the exit. The wave broke before it hit me, carrying me backward with it. I managed to break free just in time to avoid hitting the rocks. But the next wave was already rearing up to a huge face. I sprinted in an attempt to get over it before it collapsed. My gut was heavy with uncertainty. Sure enough, as I plowed up the face, it broke around me, carrying me end over end backward.

I didn't feel good. Water dragged at my body as I was carried along upside down. I knew I would be taken onto the rocks. I expected to get hurt, badly. I twisted into position to try to roll upright, but suddenly there was an impact. I felt myself twisted in my seat. I grabbed the sides of my kayak and straightened myself again and then rolled. As I surfaced, the water seemed to pour away from me. The wave dropped me right on the top of the rock. I looked around. The swell was draining to expose a deep chasm in front of me, with nothing but rock ahead. I looked behind. Another large wave face was building and steepening. If I stayed sitting here, I would be washed onto the rocks below. I climbed out and grabbed the end of my kayak.

Moments later the next wave pounded into and over the rock in a welter of whitewater, throwing me off my feet across the rock. I clung on, dropping my paddle but retaining my kayak. Once that wave was gone, the next looked smaller. In fact the wave pattern settled down to "normal" again after that, with the biggest waves not nearing the top of the rock on which I crouched.

When the water had sufficiently calmed, a friend retrieved my paddle. I lowered my kayak to the water and scrambled in. Sinking fast, I sprinted for shore. Helping hands grabbed my kayak as I rode up the steep cobble beach on the back of a wave. I was safely ashore, and at that point I thought I was unhurt. However, I could see my kayak had suffered. Water was streaming from the holes. The nose-first impact with the cliff had folded the deck across, splitting the side seams, which undoubtedly cushioned the impact that could otherwise have hurt my ankles. I had also broken one of my foot braces, which had left me twisted in my seat after the impact. Landing on the jagged rock had also punctured the hull.

That night in the local restaurant, my musician friends, Phil and Russell, accompanied the resident band on a few wild numbers, singing "Smoke on the water . . . fire in the sky," changing the words subtly to "Smoke on the water . . . whisky on the rocks."

So what was happening that day that I had missed? There was a predictable pattern of lulls and sets hitting shore that I saw and could work with. But overlaying that was something more—a sequence of much bigger waves arriving every hour or so. By next morning the anesthetic of the cold water, adrenalin, and tequila had worn off. I could feel the pain in my bruised hip now and could not sit comfortably. I stayed on shore with my broken boat watching the waves, and I saw the swell pattern continue. As the day progressed and paddlers returned, so did more broken boats. Then my wife, Kristin, returned with her fingers in a splint. She had been surprised by a rogue wave and thrown onto a cobble beach, dislocating one of her fingers, which she had since tugged gently from its grotesque angle and reset straight.

So although not every encounter has a happy ending, we escaped this one without serious injury and, as always, continued to learn about the complexity of the ocean.

33

SEICHE

Pictured Rocks National Lakeshore on Lake Superior boasts pristine mineral-colored sandstone cliffs that have worn into caves and arches, towers and precipitous walls. I kayaked across clear and surprisingly warm water beneath those cliffs with Doug Van Doren prior to a weekend sea kayaking symposium at Grand Marais, a sleepy town in a protected harbor at the east end of the cliffs.

Grand Marais was the scene of a lumber boom in the late 1800s. With a safe harbor and a railway service, there were two thousand people living there before the timber ran out. The bust came around 1910, when both sawmill and railroad closed. The place became almost a ghost town. Its population now numbers only three hundred.

As we paddled, Doug described to me the fury of storm-whipped seas here—tumbling waves that bowled kayakers over like skittles. Today his descriptions seemed like the fruits of his dreams. Behind his voice all I could hear was the hollow echo of gull calls rebounding from the sandstone walls. The water was calm and reflective. There was a quiet hiss from a fine cascade of water falling from the cliff into the lake. Above us, streaks of copper green and rusty red-brown daubed the cliff faces where minerals oozed from between the strata. With only an occasional boat wake to disturb the surface, we poked into caves and threaded archways with impunity. How could it ever be different here?

Then, with the sun at its zenith, we strolled barefoot along a deserted white-sand beach in search of agates and skimmed stones out across the placid lake. The rings of ripples slowly spread until they crossed in a gentle dance. I could scarcely believe the hot, calm, sunny weather! But while this perfect weather was to continue into the first days of the symposium, hot summer weather can build storms.

The first storm began early Sunday morning before daylight. A flash of light blazed through my closed eyelids as I slept in my motel room, leaving me wide awake to feel the juddering crash that immediately followed. The noise reverberated through the building and trailed away into dark silence. I fell immediately back into sleep. When I next awoke it was daylight, and very quiet. I glanced at my watch and then sat upright. I was late! I must have slept through my alarm! I turned to accuse the clock, but it had stopped. I hopped out of bed and flipped the bathroom switch. No light! No electricity. I hurriedly brewed myself an espresso on my camping stove and left my room. It was wildly windy outside! A large freshly fallen tree lay across the drive. I skirted it and headed for the street. Branches and leaves littered the road and sidewalk with green debris. The trees on either side were bowing and shaking with a surflike roar under a glowering sky.

When I reached the large building we were using for lectures and vendor exhibits, it was scarcely quieter inside. The wind hammered the walls and windows and roared through doorways as people wandered aimlessly. It seems everyone had left the campground for safety.

Serene conditions led up to the night of the storm.

With the electric stoves out of action, the kitchen crew was busy in the half-light brewing coffee on gas burners. The event organizers were discussing the weather report and suggesting options for the day. Then someone burst into the room in a howl of wind. "There's been a seiche!"

We rushed down to the shore to see. By the time I got there, water was draining from the parking lot, running down in rivers past the picnic tables. "All the water drained out into the bay!" someone explained. "All the boats and the dock out there were high and dry! The level must have dropped at least three feet. Then it all came back in again and must have lifted to a good three feet above what it usually is. It floated all the kayaks that people had left along the top the beach. We've been trying to catch them. Some of them blew out onto the lake!"

A small fishing boat hurried out onto the lake to round up kayaks, and as the water level gradually subsided, I joined the others emptying and retrieving. Above our heads lightning fizzed and crackled, and the crash of thunder drowned the roar of the wind in the trees.

It took the rest of the morning before the last paddler had located his kayak and strapped it to his car. The symposium vendors had the worst job. Not only had their demo kayaks been scattered, and in many cases swamped, but they also had to deal with what remained of their tents and shelters. In the campground tree branches had ripped through tents and landed on cars. And there was still no electricity except for what was sizzling in the sky.

Most of us are familiar with tsunamis, or at least as far as understanding what causes them, and what the effect can be. A seiche is a little different. It's more like water slopping backward and forward in a bucket. At its simplest it's like a seesaw—there is a quiet line across the middle where the level remains constant. As the one side rises, the other side falls. But in the context of a large lake, the patterns can become more complex.

A seiche is typically caused by air pressure and wind. The strong downbursts of wind and changes in air pressure when a storm front moves rapidly across a lake can push the water into a slope, piling it up toward the far side of the lake. This has the effect of draining one side of the lake and flooding the opposite side. But then water returns, draining the far shore and flooding the shore that had first drained. This rebounding effect is the same as water slopping from end to end of a bathtub, and it continues for some time, gradually weakening until it flattens out.

Seiches can be disastrous. One serious squall on Lake Michigan in 1954 generated sixty-mile-per-hour winds and created a seiche that traveled at about thirty miles per hour across the lake. The seiche first reached the coast around the Michigan-Indiana border, and the rebound hit Chicago as a wave that reached a maximum height of ten feet; quite a surprise for anyone out on the lake paddling that day. Of the many anglers swept from the piers, eight were drowned.

The seiche at our kayaking event was thankfully more of a novelty than a danger, but it made me think about placid lake paddling. All the kayaks were rounded up in the end. The symposium finished early. We drove away through afternoon thunderstorms in saunalike Midwest heat and humidity, while the residents of Grand Marais cleared away the debris of fallen trees and branches and waited for their electricity to be restored.

Doug Van Doren enjoys Pictured Rocks National Lakeshore, Lake Superior, on a calm day.

34

NORMA AND GLADYS

In August 1978 Tim Franklin and I flew from England to Gander, Newfoundland, with our kayaks. We had been planning this trip for a few months and arrived excited to explore the coast, with everything it offered. Now after a few weeks we had reached Catalina, in Trinity Bay, on our route toward St. John's.

A forest fire raged inland, creating a bright orange glow and a pall of smoke in the distance when we arrived at Catalina. We found a place to camp a short hike from town, our tent partly sheltered from the brisk southwest wind at the edge of a marsh. It was a precarious position, for if the wind dropped we would be eaten alive by flies. But then it would be time for us to be away, pointing across the twenty-mile-wide Trinity Bay. In the meantime we explored on foot and read our books and chatted to visitors who hiked out to see the kayaks.

While we waited we watched the "water-bombers" fly down onto the bay to scoop up seawater to drop on the forest fire. We followed the news of American balloonists who had almost reached the Irish coast on a transatlantic attempt. After a few days of waiting, we learned the forest fire was finally under control but not yet fully extinguished. By now we were anxious to be moving and wondered when conditions would finally be favorable. Then a passerby told us of an old wooden sailing schooner that had arrived in Catalina that morning, August 16. At one time it had fished the Grand Banks. It would be fun to see it.

Walking into town we quickly spotted the *Norma and Gladys*. It was long and slender with a dark, shallow hull, and from the rigging of its two masts waved strings of bright-colored triangular buntings.

We chatted to one of the crew, who told us the Newfoundland government had bought the ship, a fishing vessel, in 1973 to be converted into a floating museum. She now carried messages to promote fisheries management and a conservation display favoring a two-hundred-mile coastal limit such as the one Iceland had recently fought for and won during the so-called "Cod Wars" against Britain. She made appearances at Newfoundland events but had also sailed the globe with her messages.

Discovering the boat was planning to sail across Trinity Bay next day, we pointed out that we also planned to head in that direction, if the weather only eased a little. "But perhaps you could give us a ride?" I asked hopefully. "You'd better ask the captain!" was the reply. So we found the captain and asked him. He suggested we phoned his boss in St. John's, a Mr. Wilson.

"Hmm, I don't see why not." Mr. Wilson said. "What time does she leave? Better get the captain to give me a call and I'll okay it with him, give him the official okay, all right?"

In the evening half-light we drew quietly alongside the *Norma and Gladys* in our kayaks. There was no way we could climb over the side and haul up our kayaks, so we found a place on the wharf and carried the kayaks from there. We parked them in front of the wheel, across the deck. The crewmember on watch showed us aft to change and then to the galley, where he made us coffee and opened a can of baby clams for us.

The cabin that served as galley and crew's quarters was in the bow, accessible through a hatch and down vertical steps. Varnished wooden bunks ran three high above the benches around the galley table. There must have been space for about sixteen bunks.

It was still quite early when the crew turned in for the night. We were shown our "shelves"; there was about two feet of space between each bunk and the one above, not counting the rough-hewn beams and elbows of wood that supported them. With the boat gently swaying and the comforting sounds of the ship creaking and groaning and the crew snoring, I was soon asleep.

We were woken at five in the morning by rousing shouts. I sat up abruptly, struck my head against a timber, and collapsed again. Rubbing my head I waited a moment longer while the sleepy and grunting crew tumbled out from their curtained bunks, dressed awkwardly in the tight space on the bench seats between the table and bunks, and clambered up to the deck.

Breakfast would wait until we had set sail, someone told me, passing me a mug of coffee. By 5:30 the engine was running and everyone was on deck. It was chilly and overcast. The air was damp and smelled of creosote. Daylight was only slowly emerging from the night. The mooring lines were cast off, and the schooner slowly turned. With the captain's gloved hand at the wheel, we maneuvered out past the channel markers onto open water.

A shout here, a reply there, a big diesel winch clanked into action, and up went the front main sails, slowly against the sky. Next the stern mainsail was lifted, the wooden rings sliding up the huge tree of a mast. But there was a hitch! One of the lines of buntings had blown across, and a flag caught in the pulley. Despite all the heaving and pulling, it remained stubbornly snagged, with the sail only partly raised. Eventually a heavy crewman with a dark beard climbed bearlike up the mast, but he changed his mind when faced with crawling along the spar to the pulley. So someone else scaled the mast to the top and cut free the line, allowing the sail to be lowered. The offending bunting was cut free, and the sail was raised again.

Meanwhile the *Norma and Gladys* had been holding her position, motoring into the wind. Now with both mainsails aloft, and the two jibs hauled up by hand, the ship was turned onto course across Trinity Bay. After weeks sitting in our kayaks, it felt exhilarating to stand on the gently moving deck, effortlessly surging across the water under a mass of canvas.

The engineer invited us down to see the twin engines and pair of diesel generators. His mouth inches from my ear, he shouted, "It's pretty noisy down here! But at least it's warm!" It was indeed a stark contrast to the chill morning breeze. Almost too hot! Sticking his finger on a dribble of liquid oozing from a fine pipe, he turned and shouted, "Got a slight leak here; I've gotta get a spanner!"

Conversation was difficult close to the booming engines, and I stepped with relief through the wood-paneled captain's cabin; past the chart table, Decca navigator, radar, and sonar; and up the steps to the deck.

Breakfast was ready in the galley—egg and bacon, toast and orange juice, and of course more coffee, with Carnation milk from a pierced can. At twenty-one years old, the cook was the youngest of the crew and was struggling to establish himself among his generally much older crewmates, but he was holding up.

It didn't seem to take long before the Avalon Peninsula was visible as a shadowy cliff in the distance. I took a turn at the wheel, feeling the boat twist on the long gentle swells, keeping the compass on about 162 degrees, aiming between the headland and Baccalieu Island.

Baccalieu Island

Norma and Gladys was nearly lost near Baccalieu Island in June 1981. Without power, she was deliberately run aground after impact with a buoy damaged the seal around the propeller shaft and flooded the engine room. She was successfully pumped dry and towed away for repairs.

Baccalieu Island is the largest seabird island in Newfoundland and supports possibly the greatest diversity of breeding seabirds in eastern North America. The island supports the largest known colony of Leach's petrel in the world—approximately 40 percent of the global population and about 70 percent of the western Atlantic population of this species. It is a nesting area for eleven breeding species, including Atlantic puffin (forty-five thousand pairs), northern gannet, fulmar, black guillemot, common and thick-billed murres, razorbills, herring gulls, great black-backed gulls, and kittiwakes, and has one of the largest winter populations of eider ducks in Newfoundland.

And then a plume of mist rose from the water ahead! A whale! The dark slope of the whale's back with a small fin rolled slowly forward and slid under. Off to the side of the boat, a huge tail fin lifted slowly out of the water until it paused almost upright then slid vertically down. Moments later another huge black tail lifted out! One whale had a flash of white on each side of its tail. I was excited to be surrounded by whales and in a better position to watch them than I would be in a kayak.

One of the older crewmen told me that when he used to sail out fishing, whales would come up just feet from the boat quite regularly. He said the engines bothered them a little, so then they didn't come close, but with no engines they were quite curious.

A harsh shower of rain interrupted us then, and I dived below, but soon there was the call, "Everybody on deck!" Two of the men were asleep, and they climbed out automatically as though sleepwalking. We were arriving at Bay Roberts.

The sails dropped quickly and were still being lashed down when the boat slipped gently against the wharf. No sooner were the mooring

Our kayaks on board, we sail on the Norma and Gladys; *Newfoundland, 1978.*

lines in place than the black sky drenched us with rain. Everyone ran for the hatches.

While the mayor of Bay Roberts visited the schooner, taking cheese and biscuits with the captain in his cabin, Tim and I were dragged out by a couple of the more-restless crew members. Gary in particular was in high spirits. Now we had reached a new port, he wanted to party and to find "wimmin!" The first port of call was the local club. We stepped into a stale atmosphere of cigarette smoke and beer to find a pool table, a couple of pinball machines, a broken juke-box, and three sullen customers. It was stark, quiet, and a dismal place to drink a round of beers. We took a taxi to the next place, which was similar to the first. We had still found no "wimmin" for Gary. The third bar, in a motel, was better. There was a woman about eighty years old with just a remnant of a tooth in her grin. Out of deference to her, I resisted an impulse to introduce her to Gary, who had finally acquired a glum look. In resignation he had taken to studying the bottles behind the bar.

Suddenly his face lit up. He had found something with which to amuse himself! He could find out how Englishmen reacted to Newfoundland "Screech"! Moments later we drank our first round of that paint-stripping, throat-searing liquor that masquerades as dark rum.

Thankfully there was a place nearby that served take-away chicken. We hitchhiked back to the boat and stumbled more than crept back on board. The galley was silent. There was not even the sound of a snore to welcome us back. Gary drew open the curtain to his bunk and rolled in. Then with a loud shriek he flew back out onto the table again as if stung! There was a low chuckle from behind me. As the curtains to the other bunks twitched aside and faces peered out, the chuckles grew and billowed into raucous laughter. Gary's crewmates had made him a "woman" out of overalls stuffed with clothes, a mop head, lifejacket, and Wellington boots. His evening quest had ended in success!

Next morning we lowered our kayaks over the side onto calm water, carefully climbed down into them, and took our leave of the crew. Pulling steadily away from *Norma and Gladys* into fog, we were soon out of sight. It would be the last we saw of her.

A Watery Grave for *Norma and Gladys*

The *Norma and Gladys* was built in 1945 in Trinity Bay at Monroe, just fifty miles from where we met her, and named by the first captain for his two daughters. In 1973 she was bought by the Newfoundland government, sailed the world, and received almost seventy-nine thousand visitors in nineteen European ports before returning home. Our encounter with her was in 1978. She was eventually sold at auction.

In October 1984 she was being taken from Grand Bank, on the south coast of Newfoundland, to St. John's for a winter refit. She had been laid up for three years without being taken out of the water. It seems the oakum caulking between the hull planks had soaked apart. They came adrift when the planks began to work open in rougher water, flooding her. The failure of the pumps hastened her demise. All crew were safely rescued.

Norma and Gladys was last sighted twenty-one miles west of Cape St. Mary's in Placentia Bay on October 28, 1984, and it is presumed she sank shortly afterward.

35

GLASS FISHING FLOATS

As a child I was fascinated by glass fishing floats. I'm not sure what exactly it was that inspired my curiosity, but I remember staring avidly through windows in Cornish fishing villages at green floats, each suspended and caged by dark, tarry webs of coarse netting, line that was knotted at its every crossing. There was something intriguing about them. In a similar way I was drawn to the strange bulging bull's-eye window panes in the latticed windows of old houses—that strange pattern of concentric ripples as from a pebble dropped into still water, yet frozen into glass with its sharp broken-edged center that would draw blood from my inquisitive fingers. Years passed before I discovered the secret of how crown window glass was blown then spun and cut into windowpanes.

And what about the manufacture of fishing floats? They have been blown, or sometimes blow-molded, since the 1840s or thereabouts and are still used as net floats in Japan.

Fishing floats don't always remain captive. Some escape to roam the oceans, washing ashore onto remote beaches in Iceland or pounded to beach glass against rocky shores. For years I dreamed of finding one intact for my own. I even contemplated buying one at a tourist shop, although that seemed like cheating. Besides, the ones in the tourist shop didn't look as though they had ever been used.

Then I paddled around Iceland and found dozens of them sitting on the dark sands of the south coast, some far from the reach of the waves. But I figured that to carry a cargo of glass balls in a kayak for a thousand miles would be foolish. Surely I'd find one close to the end of the trip. It would be seventeen years before I would spot another one!

With Spanish sea kayaker Federico Alvarez, I crossed from Rubha a Mhail, the northeast headland of the Hebridean island of Isla in Scotland, toward the Isle of Jura. Jura is perhaps the most rugged of the inner islands of western Scotland, yet the visual impression when you approach from this direction is one of arable land, with perhaps plowed fields along the clifftops and on higher slopes. But this is an illusion. The plowed fields are in fact boulder beaches from times when the sea level was considerably higher. These ancient beaches are made up of boulders large enough that in Jura's rugged weather, they have not yet become grown over, except by lichens. According to the *British Admiralty West Coast of Scotland Pilot,* the highest raised beach here is over 120 feet above the present sea level.

We stopped for a break on Jura north of Loch Tarbert and wandered across a jumble of boulders the size of footballs. There were several herds of red deer within sight, and I counted fifty in the largest group and twenty in the smallest. I could see a few ragged goats too. We sat down and watched, nibbling crackers and cheese.

I found this glass fishing float on Scotland's Jura Island.

Federico then stretched his back along a smooth sloping slab of rock, smiled, and sighed contentedly. I left him resting and hopped from boulder to boulder across the raised beach, exploring between the old-sea-level sea stacks to a cavern set behind them. Its wide mouth gaped and displayed a row of broken teeth above its lower lip: massive chunks of stone that had fallen from the cliff above to stud a bank of smaller fragments.

I climbed up onto the protective ridge, which was green with small plants, and stopped in amazement. The floor of the cave's huge interior was one smooth golden-brown carpet! A fringe of pale light-starved vegetation spread a few feet in from the entrance. Beyond that was dung, dung from deer and goats.

I walked down into the cave and onward, climbing gradually up a gentle incline toward the back where the cave branched. My footsteps were almost silent, muffled by the soft dung of centuries. Here and there gleamed white half-buried goat skulls, ribs, and leg bones. There were several carcasses still draped in their woolly coats on top of the dung, but there was almost no smell. The air was slightly acrid, but there was nothing strong smelling, nothing unpleasant. In fact I felt tempted to stretch out to sleep in the peace and quiet! When I reached the back wall of the cave, the highest ground, I turned to look back.

The floor glowed golden brown in the dim light from the entrance. The surface was completely covered in darker spheres of dung, while beneath lay a paler friable soil—who knows how deep? Goats hate getting wet. They scramble for shelter at a hint of rain. I imagine some of the herds of wild goats on Jura sheltering in here for quite long periods, warm and dry away from the harsh winds and rains of winter. After centuries of occupation, these coastal caves must hold bones and dung right down to the shells and sands of the early sea level.

When I climbed back out of the shelter, through the pale green fringe into the bright daylight and land of a more familiar color, I made my way back toward Federico, following the base of the old cliff line. I jumped goatlike from boulder to boulder, my feet gripping easily against the coarse dry lichens. I was watchful, for here and there between the stones lay shards of broken bottles, thrown up by storm seas and wild winds. Nails protruded from driftwood planks. The side of a clinker boat sported copper nails that stained the boards green around the protruding spikes. There were stone-ripped tree trunks and a section of the wing of a plane in aluminum honeycomb. Then from among the glowing globes of green, orange, and white plastic and Styrofoam fishing floats, I gently lifted an old green glass globe from its resting place between the boulders. How on earth had that been deposited here unharmed? I stared through it, seeing uneven thicknesses and bubbles captured like insects in amber. The last time I had seen one of these on a beach was in Iceland in 1977. Now finally I had found a float that I could maybe take home. It was nothing valuable, but it was something precious: a green glass float, blow-molded who knows where, with a story I may never learn and patina it will never lose—and a story of discovery I will never forget.

36

WHEN LIGHTNING STRIKES

We paddled in heat. My brimmed hat and sunglasses cut the glare, but the oppressive humidity of Florida in August caught my throat like steam from the stones of a Finnish sauna. Above the Atlantic, bubbling cauliflower clouds threw their wispy tendrils outward, blanketing the sky. The undersides were a dark slate gray rimmed with sun-glare silver—Florida's answer to the absence of mountains. "It's getting a bit close that one, Nigel," warned my friend Kevin, a helicopter pilot. "We follow a five-mile rule out on the airfield. Any closer and we get the hell out of there!"

I watched the cloud. A streak of white trembled for a moment against the oppressive gray, then another silver streak. "One hundred and one, one hundred and two . . ." I counted. After ten seconds there was the rumble of thunder. Now what was the rule? How fast does sound travel? I couldn't remember. We don't see that many thunderstorms in Britain.

"Let's get off the water!" Kevin said urgently. "It's headed this way." I called the others, and we retreated. Fast. Suddenly the sky glared brilliant for several staggering moments, and the roar exploded with it. We sprinted for the cover of the buildings, abandoning the kayaks on the sand. The storm was overhead! Rain sheeted down, granular spray bounding from the ground to knee height, water rushing across the parking lot and pouring from the flooded gutters. Florida summer, the smell of sun-hot asphalt doused. The sky sparked and fizzed and rumbled ceaselessly.

So had I left it a bit late to get off the water? Yes. Sound travels one mile every five seconds. Counting ten seconds between flash and thunder, the strike I'd seen was just two miles distant. There is a good chance that the cloud producing the lightning extends closer to you than its most recent strike. If you saw a strike only two miles away, the very next strike could be directly overhead.

Is there really a danger of being struck by lightning? Palm Beach Weather Department spokesman Paul Houle informed me that on average, ninety-three deaths and three hundred injuries are caused by lightning strikes every year in the United States. It has been reported that activity around water accounts for 40 percent of the deaths and that more canoeists die from lightning strikes than of any other paddling-related cause. Houle added that in one storm alone last summer, the weather department counted ten thousand individual strikes.

In July last year a Colorado paddler who'd recently moved to Florida was paddling near Sarasota when a storm approached. Perhaps unaware, like me, of the speed at which Florida storms develop, Daniel Lincoln Neifart lingered too long on the water. Carol Dyer of the Sarasota Police Department told me that three witnesses saw the lightning strike when Neifart was only a few yards from shore. He was thrown from the kayak by the blast. By the time onlookers reached the kayak, there was no sign of the paddler. It seems he sank. He was not wearing a float vest. His aluminum paddle showed burn marks. It was not until next day that the water cleared sufficiently for searchers to spot his body from the air, and divers recovered it from the bottom. The medical examiner, Linda Jones, confirmed for me that the cause of death was drowning. Had Neifart been wearing his float vest, he might have survived.

A second kayaking-related lightning death occurred in Maine last year. Here the group did get off the water and found shelter from the storm inside a World War II bunker. It might have seemed a reasonable decision, but mountain safety manuals advise never to shelter in a cave unless it has at least fifteen feet of headroom and at least three feet of space on every side. And never shelter under large boulders or beneath overhangs. Such a place with both roof and floor will act in the same way as a spark plug, with electrical current leaping the shortest gap. Unfortunately in this instance, the reinforced concrete bunker acted in the same way as a cave. There was a lightning strike. The current ran to earth through the bunker, sparking across the shortest gap between ceiling and floor, which was through the paddlers. The strike left one paddler dead and the others stunned.

I've had many anxious moments in thunderstorms when I've been uncertain what to do. Like on the Loxahatchee River in Florida, when the sky blackened above the green canopy then opened to let fly arrows of stinging rain and flashes of intense brilliance. The swamp reverberated with the rumbles and crashes of thunder as we hurried upstream. All around us the sheets of dark swamp water slipped by at increasing speed through the maze of trees and cypress knees. I was partially reassured, thinking I was protected by the trees. But next time we paddled the river, my friend Larry pointed out trees that had been split by lightning strikes.

In Stranraer, Scotland, lightning split two large stones at the base of the walls on either side of a waterlogged stretch of farm track. As the current ran through the surface water, it killed nineteen cows standing in it. So on that day in the swamp, was there anything we

A sudden thundershower in the Swedish archipelago throws a rainbow across the sky.

could have done to protect ourselves better? Beneath the trees, it was impossible to see the buildup of storm clouds, our normal early-warning sign. We should have heeded the weather forecast warning of thunder, but there is thunder most every afternoon in Florida during summer. So perhaps we should have paddled in the morning? Caught out as we were, our safest bet would have been to hurry to the nearest patch of dry land to sit out the storm. Waterlogged ground will not do. Electrical current seeks the easiest path to earth, spreading down cracks, gullies, and pools—paths similar to those taken by flowing water. Avoid such "low" routes, and seek a position partway up a slope if there is one. Dry or well-drained ground is best. Choose sand in preference to clay. Florida is flat. In other places we have more choice of location.

Why choose a position only partway up a slope? Lightning normally joins the cloud with the closest points on land, so ridges, peaks, and high spots are bad places to be. Woodland is generally okay, but you should avoid the tallest trees and sit between trees rather than up against a tree. In Britain, from nine hundred thunderstorms per year, there are only about one hundred strikes to trees. It seems a

Lightning blazes during a summer night storm in Florida.

reasonable risk, especially when you consider you're unlikely to suffer a direct hit in woodland. But you may be affected by ground currents, so sit or crouch on some insulating pad—even your float vest. Don't lean against anything. Keep your hands on your lap, and don't rest back on them, or ground currents from a nearby strike could pass up your arms and down through your body, through vital organs. Keep your knees up and your feet tucked close to you for the same reason. The important principle is to keep your contact points with the ground close together. You may get uncomfortably wet and cold, but you will reduce the risk of being struck.

If you begin to feel a buzzing, charged sensation as a storm approaches, don't hang around. If you do nothing else, drop into your protective position. Jersey, U.K., paddler Kevin Mansell described a close encounter. He had just landed with his party on the approach of a storm in France and was discussing the best way to retrieve his transport when he experienced a tingling sensation as his hair became electrically charged. Moments later there was a sudden flash and impact. He turned to discover that two teachers who had been standing less than fifteen feet away had fallen to the ground. One was dead. The other died later despite medical aid. Kevin sat out the rest of the storm in the shelter of a nearby building, feeling thankful to be alive. It is not overreacting to run for shelter or to drop immediately into a tucked position if you begin to feel static electricity. It might be your only warning.

At Great Torrington, Devon, England, is the following epitaph:

Here lies a man who was killed by lightning;
He died when his prospects seemed to be brightening.
He might have cut his flash in this world of trouble,
But the flash cut him, and he lies in the stubble.

37

ON THE TRAIL OF A B-17

In 2004 Kristin Nelson and I planned to kayak around northern Labrador. We were on our way to leave our car at the "end of the road"—at the airport of Happy Valley Goose Bay, Labrador, a place we could return to by coastal supply vessel after our trip. The gravel road ran through Labrador City, and that's where we met local outfitter Gary Shaw, who was excited about an upcoming project to try to raise a sunken plane from a Labrador lake. The plane, on a midwinter reconnaissance mission soon after World War II, had crash-landed on the remote and then-frozen Dyke Lake after running short on fuel. The crew was rescued, but the plane, floating downstream on the ice during breakup, finally sank. In 1998 searchers located the plane and set to work to complete and file all the necessary paperwork to allow them to attempt to recover it. That took some years, but now everything was ready. Gary, working on local logistics, was eagerly awaiting the arrival of the team from Seattle.

Kristin and I completed our own trip and some weeks later stopped again at Labrador City on our way back to Seattle. Gary excitedly led us to the railway yard to show us the fruits of his summer's labor. There spread the big metallic-gray sections of a B-17G "Flying Fortress." The long wings had been removed from the fuselage for transport and now rested on old tires on the ground. The gray US Air Force low-visibility insignia was still clearly stenciled on them. The four heavy engines, with their propeller blades bent, since the plane was landed on the ice with its wheels retracted in case they broke through the surface, stood aside, draped in yellow Caution tape.

Gary explained how the recovery operation had gone. First they had taken all their equipment by boat and established a base camp by the lake near the sunken plane. The team's divers attached air bags to the plane and inflated them, and gradually the huge shape of the plane drifted up to the surface. Having readjusted the air bags to float the plane level, they began to carefully tow it some sixty-eight miles downstream via the lakes of the Ashuanipi River to a road beside the Smallwood reservoir. It must have been quite a sight with its wingspan of more than ninety feet slowly negotiating the bends and narrows. Finally at Lobstick, close to the dam for the Churchill Falls Power Plant, they beached the plane and took it apart to transport overland to Labrador City.

I was surprised at the good condition of the fuselage and wings after all these years. Gary explained that was almost certainly due to the cold and very clean water it had rested in. There were a few holes corroded through some of the plates and a few little cakes of rust here and there, but overall everything was intact. I peered inside to where the crew would have sat or crouched and was stunned when George drew my attention to the fact that the tires were still filled with air and there were still new-looking bright yellow warning stickers in place on the fuel tanks. The fuselage had "790" stenciled on its side. Some of the pristine appearance was also due to the work of the recovery team cleaning off algal growth. That cleaning was not only for appearance; when dead, some algae produce acid that might etch into the aluminum.

The plane was now being prepared for its next long journey south to Georgia, USA, where it should eventually be restored to flying condition. Currently out of 12,700 B-17s produced, there are only forty-eight still in existence, with only ten flyable.

More than half of all B17s produced, including this one, were assembled in a huge factory on the banks of the Duwamish River in Seattle. The factory deserves recognition for its huge contribution to the war effort, but it cannot escape blame for its contribution to the pollution of the Duwamish River. Today the Duwamish is a Superfund site on the US Environmental Protection Agency National Priorities List. It was not always polluted.

When English explorer George Vancouver explored Puget Sound in 1792, less than a decade after the end of America's War of Independence, he was on a voyage of discovery. It was some thirty years later before people followed him looking for places to settle.

They chose a location close to where the Duwamish River enters Elliott Bay on the east side of Puget Sound—an area inhabited by the Duwamish Tribe, under Chief Seattle.

The native Duwamish, along with the Suquamish, also led by Chief Seattle, was one of very few successful tribes around the world that could be described as "sedentary hunter-gathers." The area had been inhabited for some ten thousand years. The site of the Duwamish village standing at the mouth of the river when Europeans came to settle had been occupied since the sixth century AD and was surrounded by climax forest, with trees between one thousand and two thousand years old, rising to nearly four hundred feet.

Fast-forward fewer than two hundred years to now, and here is Seattle with its almost one-thousand-foot-tall skyscrapers built in the 1980s and a surrounding population of a couple of million people. The mouth of the Duwamish—altered by the man-made Harbor Island at its mouth—is dwarfed by massive container cranes and cement works, and by ships and barges stacked high with shipping containers.

Gary Shaw leans against one of the propeller blades bent during the emergency landing of the B-17; Labrador City, Canada.

The water that once helped feed the population with clams and fish, and where otters and eagles once thrived, is now greasy and polluted with heavy metals. Even though notices are posted here in public places advising that the fish are toxic, that doesn't prevent seals from venturing upstream. There is nothing to stop people from kayaking here either. Though there's little temptation to swim, it is an interesting place to explore.

We launched from a small public park and paddled upstream with the tide as far as South Park Bridge. The two spans of this lifting bridge had been raised and left up. By remaining open, the bridge was closed to the people who used to cross it. The twenty thousand vehicles that used to cross the bridge daily now face a long detour until the bridge is replaced. But the nearly eighty-year-old bridge had been in dodgy condition since the Nisqually earthquake of 2001 and was finally considered too unsafe for further use.

On the west side of the river here, South Park grew up as accommodation for workers at the Boeing plant, especially when the United States entered World War II and needed war planes. On the east side of the river looms the huge boxlike factory. This facility, which began producing aircraft in 1936, was used during the war to manufacture the B-17 Flying Fortress. As such it was arguably one of the most important buildings associated with the Allied war effort in World War II. The high yellow factory walls, lined with rows of tall windows, suggest a multifloor building, but in fact most of the inside is one huge open space.

This vast factory steps out over the banks of the river on pilings, but like the bridge, it is idle. This year (2010) it was slated for demolition. Later, perhaps after a massive hazardous waste cleanup, it will be replaced by housing. The waterfront itself, however, will be restored or re-created to give a more natural appearance, perhaps contributing a small increment toward the Duwamish becoming a natural river again.

Although the factory has since completed its useful life, should it have been destroyed by an air raid from the west during World War II, the consequences would have been devastating to the war effort. With Seattle so close to the West Coast, it was considered a high risk. As a precaution the thirty-five-acre roof of the factory and its adjacent runways were camouflaged as city neighborhoods, with streets, houses, cars, and trees. Apparently there were even mockups of grazing cows! Black-and-white photographs from the time show the ground created from sheets of canvas spread across the entire roof of the factory, painted over with roads into city blocks. On it were built plywood houses and trees made of timber, chicken wire, and fiberglass; there was everything down to picket fences, street signs, and plywood cars.

The Japanese never did attack. Had they flown over, the factory would have appeared as part of the city, although underneath was a packed assembly line of warplanes, with workers swarming like ants. Now the hangar entrance is camouflaged from the water by a thicket of real brambles and purple buddleia.

There was not so much concerning a B-17 for us to see here from the water, but having chanced across that single plane, it felt good to see where it had come from before the factory was demolished. It was a short trip, though it had taken me some time to get around to making it. The day was sunny, and we had time to dawdle. When the tide turned we allowed it to carry us back toward the cement works, the barges piled high with containers bound for Alaska; past cranes and silos, blue and yellow tug boats, and cargo vessels; past a tall stack of crushed cars. A flotilla of Canada geese cruised swiftly by us between the giant concrete pillars of the man-made forest supporting the First Avenue South Bridge. Close to our pullout, the Seattle skyline loomed above the containers stacked on Harbor Island. Across the river girder cranes dangled their loads, while nearer to us gourds had been hung as nesting boxes from stakes in the river to attract purple martins.

It was interesting to daydream about the wrecked B-17 in Labrador and wonder at its condition after fifty-seven years at the bottom of a pristine Labrador lake, interesting to speculate how it would have fared had it rested at the bottom of the Duwamish River instead. We landed at the former village site of the Duwamish Tribe, now the Port of Seattle's Terminal 107, or T-107, Park. Carrying our kayaks we tiptoed through mud that once supported clams to feed the Duwamish Tribe, across land the Duwamish dwelled on to our car on a twenty-first-century asphalt parking lot.

38

WATERMILLS AND WHALE EARS

In 1980 I explored some of the western Faeroe Islands with a group of schoolteachers from East Sussex. The Faeroe, or "Sheep," Islands lie out in the Atlantic roughly halfway between Scotland and Iceland. We had come for the tidal rapids and, with big swells that summer, were not disappointed. The islands constrict the mid-Atlantic tides, accelerating the currents around the headlands and through the channels between the islands to rates of more than ten miles per hour. When added to the combination of turbulent stream and Atlantic swells, even the lightest breath of wind produced spectacular white-water conditions.

Passing beneath cliffs that soared more than two thousand feet above our heads, we marveled at the thousands of puffins and guillemots and the razorbills pouring to and from the nesting ledges. Gannets cruised by, plummeting into the sea around us. When we landed we hiked the cliff edges to peer down at the surging breakers, or when the mist shrouded the ocean, we gazed across the swirling mist toward jagged peaks that stood like rocks in a wild sea.

Two members of our party were land based. Frank, an ardent molinologist, was researching the sites of watermills around the islands with Bernie, who was there for the hiking opportunity. We met up frequently to learn about the mills. The mills found here were used for grinding barley, but unlike later mills, with their vertically aligned waterwheels and horizontal driveshafts, this older design employed no gears. The drive was direct. An upright tree trunk served as the driveshaft. Notches cut in the wood near the base of the drive-shaft held flat boards that radiated out to catch a jet of water from the millrace. When the water was released, jetting against the boards at one side, the shaft would spin. The grindstone fixed at its top end would spin against the fixed bed-stone, so grain poured in at the center emerged at the edges cut into flour.

Such mills were in use in Greece certainly as far back as 20 BC, and the idea spread across Europe and Scandinavia, probably first with the Romans, and then relayed farther afield by the Vikings. Sir Walter Scott estimated there were five hundred such mills in Shetland in 1814. In the Faeroe Islands it seems the mills replaced hand-querns sometime in the late eighteenth century. But gradually their use declined, first in the early nineteenth century with the introduction of the potato as an alternative food source to barley, and later with the import of flour from Denmark. Some mills were converted to produce electricity, until the islands were connected to a grid, and others were used for storage. Mostly what Frank was now finding were the remains of millraces, occasionally millstones and the ruins of buildings, and on one occasion a discarded driveshaft with broken teeth sunk into the turf. But he did find one restored mill.

Excitedly he led us from where we left our kayaks at Kvívík up the stream from the village. Finally we clustered around the small building. Its roof was a tangle of long grasses and wildflowers capping the birch bark that underlay the turf roof. Roughly constructed in stone and wood, the building sat like a box on two walls spanning a narrow gully a few yards from a rushing stream.

Happy to have an audience, Frank closed the sluice on the stream by sliding a board down into the waiting slots. Now he waited for water to build up behind the board before opening a sluice to the millrace.

Clear water gushed down the channel into a wooden chute that dropped from the millrace to the waterwheel beneath the building. Hitting the blades of the wheel, the water burst out as spray in all directions. The waterwheel was clearly stuck. Frank clambered awkwardly down into the spray and tugged at the wheel. It sprang into action and spun with a steady trundling sound.

I stared down at it mesmerized. Water was tumbling down the wooden chute, spinning the wheel and scattering onto the pebbles below, where it drained downhill to rejoin the stream. It was such a simple and wonderfully inspired invention to save the labor of a hand-quern. The breeze twisted at the grasses and the flowers around me. I could have sat and watched the spinning log all afternoon.

But keeping our appointment with the tides, we left Kvívík for Miðvágur, pointing our kayaks into a misty sea toward the place where the currents meet, creating pyramidal patterns out of the deep Atlantic swell. There we changed course on a compass line into fog toward the dark Vágar cliffs. We planned to meet Frank again in a couple of days at the tiny village of Bøur, where he hoped to show us evidence of another mill. From there perhaps the weather would offer us an opportunity to cross to Mykines, the most westerly island in the group and a legendary bastion for seabirds.

After two weeks of exploring, we returned to Tørshavn, our appetite for adrenalin sated for the moment. It was there that Drew caught wind of a whale kill. Some 230 pilot whales from a much larger group had just been herded by small boats into the channel between Streymoy and Eysteroy and finally to a beach near Hvalvík, a town whose very name means "Whale Bay." It was late in the day, but Drew was anxious to see, so we piled into our vehicle and I drove us there.

Nighttime view of 230 pilot whales on the beach of Streymoy, Faeroe Islands, in 1980.

The killing, thankfully, was over before we arrived. The whales had been hauled up onto the beach with ropes and now lay all around the bay looking in the half-light like a fleet of dark upturned curraghs. As we approached we could see the deep cut behind the head that severed the spinal cord to kill the whale. The water would have blazed red with blood. Each twenty- to thirty-foot-long whale had since been disemboweled. The several long cuts needed to open the belly revealed the thinness of the skin and the thick pinky-white layer of blubber immediately beneath it. These cuts, someone explained, were to prevent gases building up inside the body cavity. People with buckets were reaching inside the still-warm bodies to pull out the liver and kidneys, which by ancient law belong to anyone who cares to take them. Each whale now had a number carved into its skin for tallying, the numbers gleaming white from the underlying blubber.

There was little activity now, save for a few small boats zigzagging against the tidal stream in search of any whales that might have sunk after killing.

Dead pilot whales sink, which is the reason they must be so carefully herded to a beach before slaughter. Ironically the so-called "right whale" was named simply because it floated after death, so was the "right whale" to hunt. Whales that would sink would be the wrong ones to hunt. A few people clustered solemnly in small groups on the shore, kids running from whale to whale peering and poking. When our own group had seen enough, we returned quietly to Tørshavn.

Early next morning Drew hitched back to Hvalvík to see what had happened to the whales. He returned with the surprising news that there had been nothing to see. During the night all the whales had been butchered and the meat and blubber taken away. The entrails and bones had also been disposed of. The beach was once again clean. It seemed remarkable that so many whales could be dealt with in such a short time, but I suppose there is limited time before the meat spoils.

Meat is divided by ancient tradition among the person who first sighted the whales and raised the alarm, the participants in the hunt, and all the residents of the district in which the kill was made. Sometimes meat is given to surrounding districts, depending on the size of the kill. Meat is also offered to schools, hospitals, and other public organizations.

So what do residents do with all the meat and blubber? The blubber is generally refrigerated and eaten raw. Meat is nowadays frozen but was traditionally hung in strips under the eaves of the house to dry. Hard as a bone, these cudgels of dry meat made ideal provisions for coastal and offshore fishing trips. I tasted slices pared from a piece hanging from the eaves of the turf-roofed home of the Faeroese artist and expedition adventurer Trondur Patursson when I visited him at Kirkjubøur, sampling it, as he recommended, with a piece of raw blubber. It was easy to eat—rich and warming.

Revisiting the beach some years later, I spotted a curiously shaped white stone just an inch and a half long. Perhaps it was a shell? I picked it up. It was heavy for its size; too dense to be bone. It was polished smooth. Turning it in my fingers, I was struck by its odd shape. From one angle it appeared a little like a carving of a bald, shiny head with two eyeholes peering from the partial shelter of two oversized hands. A small hole on the other side seemed to spiral inward, with a pitted texture like an octopus tentacle. Was it carved? It didn't seem likely. Perhaps it was a fossil? I slipped it into my pocket to look at again later.

These pebble-hard whale ear bones were found on the island of Streymoy.

Farther along the beach I found another, almost identical to the first but a mirror image. Now I was curious to search for more. Soon I had collected a pocketful of pieces of two shapes, the second a distorted L-shape. They clacked together like stone. So what were they? Turns out they were whale ear bones. Whale ear bones are made of the densest bone of all. After a whale kill the heads of the whales together with the offal are usually discarded at sea. I was left wondering how these particular ear bones had washed up like pebbles on that sheltered beach, and how long they had remained there.

I also wanted to know how they work.

In humans sound waves in the air pass via the eardrum through little ear bones to move the liquid in our inner ear (cochlea) relative to the ear bone that contains it. The movement of this liquid stimulates nerve endings to send messages to our brain. The bone of our inner ear is denser than our other bones, and it is fused together with the skull.

Studies of cochlear bone density in human patients with Paget's disease, in which the bones lose mass, suggest that loss of bone density leads to loss of hearing, so the density of that bone is important. Other terrestrial mammals seem to have similar cochlear bone density to humans.

In marine mammals cochlear density is even greater. Does that mean whales have better hearing? Whales live in an environment that favors sound more than sight. There is limited visibility through water compared to air, yet sound waves travel much faster and farther through water than through air. Whales are much more dependent on hearing for communication, navigation, and locating food.

But how is the whale's hearing physically different from ours? First, the whale has no external ear. We gather and funnel sound into our ear canal with our external ear. Bats have evolved highly folded and complex external ears so that they can echolocate. It would be a disadvantage for a whale to have an external ear: It would cause drag and in doing so would create a lot of noise. Instead whales have evolved an internal sound-gathering and channeling system using fat deposits of a similar acoustic density to salt water. These deposits along the jaw of whales and dolphins resemble the shape of rabbit or bat ears and function in the same way as external ears, allowing many species also to use echolocation to find prey.

We can tell the direction a sound comes from in air because it reaches one ear before the other. But in water sound travels so fast it reaches both ears more or less simultaneously, making it impossible for us to locate its direction. Our heads are too narrow. Whales have developed wider heads, spreading their ears far enough apart to be able to tell where a sound comes from.

Our own cochlea is attached to the skull with bone, but if this were true for whales, a swimming whale would hear the sound of water rushing against its head by direct transfer of sound through the skull to the cochlea. It would be like us trying to listen in a gale. The whale cochlea is instead suspended from ligaments, isolating it from the skull in a mass of fat, so all the input of sound comes from the ears.

But what has this to do with bone density? The whale's hearing works a little like the Faeroe watermill. Imagine that I sit on the top stone inside the mill and squeeze my fingers into the gap between the millstones. Imagine water hits the blades of the waterwheel below. In terms of the whale, the equivalent is a sound arriving. The energy is transferred via the driveshaft to the upper grindstone, which moves when the waterwheel moves. If the lower grindstone is made of Styrofoam, it will move along with the upper one and I will feel nothing. If the lower stone is dense enough to remain fixed when the top stone moves, I will feel it immediately. In the whale the sound is funneled through the fat deposits and vibrates the liquid in the cochlea. The whale cochlea must be dense enough to remain fixed when the fat surrounding it, and the liquid inside it, vibrates; otherwise the nerve endings will not be stimulated.

So the more dense the bone, the less it will move with the arrival of sound waves through the fat. There must be a fine balance between hearing sensitivity and bone density. As I sit and tap the little ear bones together, they clack just like flints; but in truth I am holding the result of some remarkable evolution.

39

WHEN WHALES HAVE THE LAST WORD

In 1970 a dead sperm whale washed up on Oregon's beautiful coast, prompting complaints about the rotting stench from residents and holidaymakers. In 2004 in Tainan City, Taiwan, a seventeen-meter-long sperm whale weighing fifty tons was loaded onto a truck for transportation to a wildlife reserve after permission was refused for autopsy at the university. At Salt Spring Island, British Columbia, a dead whale washed up in 2008.

This kind of occurrence is not remarkable. After all, plenty of whales are hit by ships and wash ashore or are disoriented by naval sonar exercises and beach themselves. These three instances are notable, however, because the whales exploded.

The whale in Canada apparently blew up spontaneously and festooned the surrounding trees with rotting blubber, which hung around for a long time afterwards. The whale in Taiwan blew open a hole in its side and blasted its guts across a street. The whale in Oregon was even less controlled; it was blown up by local officials, who considered it too large to bury, in the hope that seagulls and crabs would eat what was left.

Maybe they used too much dynamite. Pieces of blubber rained down on bystanders a quarter of a mile away, and one large chunk flattened a parked car. Most of the pieces were probably still too large for seagulls. I imagine the gulls were engulfed in the blast or encased in flying blubber anyway. The remaining whale pieces were then buried in the sand and smelled like . . . well, they smelled. I remember taking an upwind view of a rotting whale carcass on a remote part of the south coast of Iceland some years ago, and the odor was unbelievably powerful! It would have been so much more intense downwind!

But the smell of a dead whale does diminish in time. We were kayaking along the east coast of Iceland in 1989 and stopped at a wonderful surf beach, Sandvik. Hiking along the ridge above the bay at about two thousand feet, we looked down the other side into the fjords to the north. There was a flattish promontory jutting out from one shore that looked inviting as a place to camp, so next day we headed there. The grass was deep and full of wildflowers, and scattered across it were iron cogs and rusting boilers we assumed must have washed up as a shipwreck. On the beach on the seaward side was the charred hull of a wooden boat that had evidently burned down to the waterline and washed ashore. We clambered over this and found a miniature meadow of butterfly orchids inside!

I thought little about all the debris on that point until last year. Then I returned to Iceland for the first sea kayaking symposium to be held on the east coast, at Neskaupstaður. We used the local museum close to the tiny beachfront clubhouse for meetings and presentations. Always curious to visit museums, I found myself among harpoons and other whaling memorabilia.

Apparently the first whaling in Iceland on more than an opportunistic scale was carried out by Basque whalers in the northwest fjords in the sixteenth century. Then in the 1860s two Americans established a shore base, which did not last long. In 1883 Iceland granted Norway permission to build whaling stations in Iceland, and eight were established in the western fjords. In 1902 these stations processed thirteen hundred whales caught by thirty ships—an average of three whales every week of the year for each of the stations.

When stocks became depleted five of the stations moved to the east. By 1913 there were too few whales left to keep any of them open. The Norwegians moved north into the Arctic, and in 1915 the Icelandic government banned whaling in order to protect the remaining stocks (possibly the first ever whaling ban).

The law remained in effect until 1928, when it was thought the stocks had recovered. Some whaling has continued, off and on, ever since. In 1977 I came across a whaling ship on the island of Flatey off the north coast of Iceland, with its harpoon gun mounted and ready at the bow. But it was the middle of the night when we arrived and nobody was around; the ship left early morning before we awoke, so I did not discover any information about it.

At the sea kayaking symposium, local kayaker Ari explained there had once been a shore-based whaling station just along the coast from Neskaupstaður in a neighboring fjord. I was interested to visit, so we made the detour on our way back from an overnight trip. There on the beach was the familiar burned hull and the scattered iron debris. So this had been the site of the whaling station.

I began to wonder what a land-based whaling station would have been like when it was operating. I can imagine the smell, even without the fires and the boilers used to render the blubber. And those were formidable. When a whale was hauled ashore, it would have been dragged up to the ramp Ari pointed out. Men with sharp spades would have cut into the thick layer of blubber, which would have been dragged away by chains as the men worked, peeling off the blubber like the skin of an orange.

The blubber would have been boiled to separate the fine oil so valued as machine oil and for burning in lamps. According to Icelandic sources dating from 1900, one sperm whale provided around ten tons of fat, three tons of carcass meal, and seven tons of bone meal. The remains of a carcass were simply dumped on the beach. In one place

The wreck of a wooden boat sits on the shore near the site of an old whaling station in eastern Iceland.

the locals complained the mess was hazardous to sheep that scavenged the shore for seaweed.

Sperm whales have been known to fight back when attacked by whalers. Whaleboats were frequently upended and smashed by whales, and in 1820 the whale ship *Essex* from Nantucket was rammed repeatedly by a sperm whale until it finally sank. It was close to the equator in the middle of the Pacific, and two of the survivors traveled forty-five hundred miles in one of the whaleboats before being picked up. Their story was the inspiration for Herman Melville's novel *Moby Dick*.

So wreckage from boats and from whales can find itself on shore. In 1977 kayaking along the sand coast of southern Iceland, Geoff Hunter and I were enclosed in our own limited-vision world of scudding low cloud, rolling surf, and an endless dark sand shore in which the boundaries between each were blurred with spray. We had noted little of interest for hours on end, just the usual driftwood logs and blobs of unidentifiable flotsam on the beach, when we spotted a vehicle speeding along the sand. We watched it for some time before coming to the conclusion that it was not speeding; it was everything else that seemed to be moving—the low cloud, the surf, and the spray.

It wasn't a vehicle either. It was a very regular square shape, so we concluded it was most likely a shipwreck shelter of the kind we had already seen on the coast, built and provisioned by fishing companies to help save lives in the event of a shipwreck. Wrecks along this coast have been fairly common, and often all hands survive the wreck, only to perish later on land through hypothermia because there was no shelter and nowhere to go. For us it seemed providential. In a featureless place we had finally spotted a feature!

We landed through the surf, dragged our kayaks away from the shore break, and then set off toward the hut, which was now obscured by the sloping sands. When we reached it, we found that not only was it smaller than we had expected but it wasn't even a shipwreck shelter. It was part of the skull of a sperm whale, fully twenty feet long and standing five feet tall! In an environment where there were no clues to scale, we had been deceived. We laughed at our mistake and then sat down to rest on the insulating bone where the oil-filled chamber on the huge bulbous head would once have been. It made a really comfortable seat.

APPENDIX

"Monkey Business in the Florida Keys," previously published in *Sea Kayaker* magazine, April 1999.

"1666 and the Sea Hare," previously published in *Ocean Paddler Magazine,* issue 23, December 2010.

"Tubenoses," previously published in *Sea Kayaker* magazine, June 1996.

"Bear, Be Gone!" previously published in *Sea Kayaker* magazine, June 2006.

"Manatees," previously published in *Ocean Paddler Magazine,* issue 15, August 2009.

"Gannets," previously published in *Ocean Paddler Magazine,* issue 18, February 2010.

"Seals and Selkies," previously published in *Sea Kayaker* magazine, December 1995.

"Alligators," previously published in *Ocean Paddler Magazine,* issue 20, June 2010.

"Newfoundland Squid," previously published in *Ocean Paddler Magazine,* issue 27, August 2011.

"Ungava Encounter." A version of this story was previously published in *Ocean Paddler Magazine,* issue 21, August 2010. The story is also told in Nigel Foster's "Stepping Stones of Ungava and Labrador," Outskirts Press, 2009.

"Farewell to Phyllis," previously published in *Sea Kayaker* magazine, April 1997.

"Escape from Holland," previously published in *Sea Kayaker* magazine, August 1996.

"Trees with Knees: Boatbuilders in Newfoundland," previously published in *Ocean Paddler Magazine,* issue 29, December 2011.

"Searching for Mermaids' Tears," previously published in *Sea Kayaker* magazine, April 1997.

"Kayaking below Sea Level," previously published in *Sea Kayaker* magazine, October 1997.

"Summertime in Sweden," previously published in *Sea Kayaker* magazine, February 1998.

"Queen Charlotte Islands," previously published in *WaterTribe* online magazine, 2000.

"Shetland by Sunlight," previously published in *Canoeist* magazine, February 1993; *Sea Kayaker* magazine, December 1996.

"Faeroe Islands Reveal a Dark Secret," previously published in *Ocean Paddler Magazine,* issue 22, October 2010.

"Iceland Revisited (Portage)," previously published in *WaterTribe* online magazine, 2000.

"*Helena Star,*" previously published in *Ocean Paddler Magazine,* issue 19, April 2010.

"In the Wake of the *Braer,*" previously published in *Sea Kayaker* magazine, April 1995.

"Driftwood," previously published in *Ocean Paddler Magazine,* issue 24, February 2011.

"Seiche," previously published in *Ocean Paddler Magazine,* issue 25, April 2011.

"When Lightning Strikes," previously published in *Sea Kayaker* magazine, August 1995.

"Watermills and Whale Ears." Part of this story was first published in *Canoeing* magazine, February 1981, as "They Said the Faeroes Were in Egypt."

"When Whales Have the Last Word," previously published in *Ocean Paddler Magazine,* issue 16, October 2009.

ACKNOWLEDGMENTS

My parents always encouraged me to keep a diary, however little I wrote in it. That helped me to write, and without that habit of recording, how could I keep the details straight? Thank you, Mum and Dad! My selection of stories in *Encounters,* coming from across the globe and spanning more than thirty-five years, draws detail from those journals.

I would like to thank the friends with whom I shared adventures. Also those who by welcoming me into their world, or teaching me from their expertise, have helped make these stories stand. Thanks to all those people who by proofreading or editing have improved my storytelling. That includes the editors of the various magazines whose sterling work I hope I have not completely undone by reshaping the stories again for this book, for many of the stories have been previously published in some form in magazines or journals.

Thanks to Globe Pequot Press, whose faith in me once again has allowed me to indulge a personal passion for storytelling.

Finally big thanks to my friend (and wife), Kristin Nelson, for all her support and encouragement.

INDEX

Italicized page references indicate photographs.

ABOUT THE AUTHOR

Nigel Foster's writing has been widely published in magazines. He is author of seven books and designer of more than ten kayaks plus paddles and accessories, and his instruction is in demand all over the world. He has become one of the best-known and respected sea kayakers, known for his gentle and patient approach.

In his spare time Nigel likes to canoe and to play guitar, but not at the same time. He lives in Seattle, Washington, with his wife, the ceramic artist and kayaker Kristin Nelson.